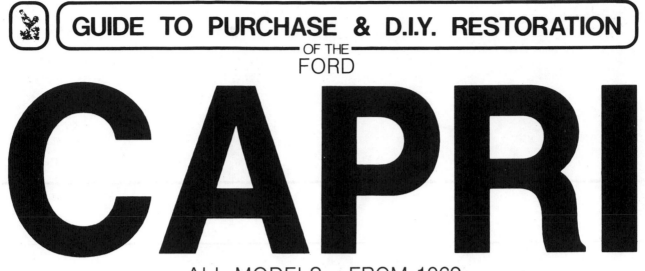

GUIDE TO PURCHASE & D.I.Y. RESTORATION

OF THE

FORD

CAPRI

ALL MODELS – FROM 1969

KIM HENSON

Foulis

Haynes

®

A FOULIS Motoring Book

First published 1989

Published by:
Haynes Publishing Group
Sparkford, Nr. Yeovil,
Somerset BA22 7JJ, England

Haynes Publications Inc.
861 Lawrence Drive, Newbury Park,
California 91320 USA

**British Library Cataloguing in
Publication Data**

Henson, Kim
   Capri (all models from 1969): guide to
purchase & DIY Restoration.
   1.   Cars. Maintenance & repair –
Amateurs' manuals
   I.   Title
   629.28'722

   ISBN 0-85429-644-1

**Library of Congress Catalog Card
No.**
89-84300

Editor: Robert Iles
Page Layout: Tim Rose
Printed in England by: J.H. Haynes & Co.
Ltd

Other Haynes Publishing Group titles of
interest to the enthusiast:
The Car Bodywork Repair Manual (F373)
Capri – Ford's European GT Car (F548)
*Ford Capri 1300 & 1600 (ohc) Owners
Workshop Manual (029)*
*Ford Capri 1600 (ohc) Owners Workshop
Manual (296)*
*Ford Capri 2000 & 3000 Owners
Workshop Manual (035)*
*Ford Capri II (& III) 1.3 (ohv) Owners
Workshop Manual (338)*
*Ford Capri II (& III) 1.6 & 2.0 Owners
Workshop Manual (283)*
*Ford Capri II (& III) 2.8 & 3.0 Owners
Workshop Manual (1309)*

All of the above should be available from
good bookshops. In case of difficulty
please write to the publisher.

Contents

Foreword by Chris Horton

It isn't hard to see why, at the time of the Capri's launch in 1969, Ford described it as 'the car you've always promised yourself'. Its sporty, fastback styling, its no-nonsense handling and roadholding and, in 3-litre form, its blistering performance, singled it out from the bland and anonymous saloons that, with a few notable exceptions, were the staple diet of the average family motorist in the late 1960s.

That the Capri should have become something of a classic is hardly surprising – it was a genuinely good, entertaining car, after all – but what is surprising, perhaps, is the dearth of authentic useful technical information on maintaining and restoring it that has hitherto been available.

That, however, is something Kim Henson has certainly put right with this book. Here, in one volume, is just about everything that anyone bent on long-term Capri restoration and ownership could possibly require – and all of it written by a man who passionately practises what he preaches. You don't keep a fleet of nine elderly classics on the road with just a passing interest in the subject or just a hazy grasp of its basic principles.

That said, this book is not a workshop manual. That and a good tool-kit are the basic requirements of any car restoration and maintenance. What it will do, though, is supplement the workshop manual by examining the fascinating production history of the Capri from its very beginnings in the mid-1960s to its demise in 1987, and then looking in some considerable detail at the possible pitfalls that await the would-be Capri owner.

There follows a detailed look at bodywork repairs and restoration for those for whom Kim's buying advice was too late, and the emphasis is very much on saving money – consistent, of course, with safety and high standards of finish.

Significantly, you won't find anything here about the Capri's mechanical components and its electrical system. Both are subjects that Kim covered comprehensively in his earlier work on the Escort and Cortina, and both are, of course, very thoroughly covered in Haynes' owners' workshop manuals. Instead, there is a chapter on under-bonnet restoration and presentation – absolutely vital for anyone intending to enter a concours d'elegance – and the sections on interior trim and modifications have been considerably extended.

Also taking advantage of the extra space are the appendices which, between them, offer a great deal of technical data, much of which, as far as is known, has never before appeared together in one volume. There are, for example, detailed specifications of all models (including USA-spec cars), a comprehensive list of production modifications, and, of perhaps the most use to the average owner, detailed information on how to determine the exact date of production and original specification of just about any Capri you care to mention.

All in all, it adds up to a very complete package that, I think, offers outstanding value for money whether you are a seasoned campaigner or an absolute beginner in this marvellously exciting business of restoring old cars. Doing it yourself may not be quite as easy as paying someone else to tackle the donkey-work for you, but you can take it from me that it's a lot more satisfying – and this book is surely the next best thing to an expert standing by your side!

Chris Horton
Editor, Restoring Classic Cars

Using this book

The layout of this book has been designed to be both attractive and easy to follow during practical work on your car. However, to obtain maximum benefit from the book, it is important to note the following points:

1) Apart from the introductory pages, this book is split into two parts: Chapters 1 to 6 deal with history, buying and practical procedures: appendices 1 to 7 provide supplementary information. Each chapter/appendix may be sub-divided into sections and even sub-sections. Section headings are in italic type between horizontal lines and sub-section headings are similar, but without horizontal lines.

2) Photograph captions are an integral part of the text (except those in Chapters 1 and 2) – therefore the photographs and their captions are arranged to "read" in exactly the same way as the normal text. In other words they run down each column and the columns run from left to right of the page.

Each photograph caption carries an alpha-numerical identity, relating it to a specific section. The letters before the caption number are simply the initial letters of key words in the relevant section heading, whilst the caption number shows the position of the particular photograph in the section's picture sequence. Thus photograph/caption "DR22" is the 22nd photograph in the section headed "Door Repairs".

3) Figures – illustrations which are not photographs – are numbered consecutively throughout the book. Figure captions do not form any part of the text. Therefore Figure 5 is simply the 5th figure in the book.

4) All references to the left or right of the vehicle are from the point of view of somebody standing behind the car looking forwards.

5) Because this book majors upon restoration, regular maintenance procedures and normal mechanical repairs of all the car's components, are beyond its scope. it is therefore strongly recommended that the appropriate Capri Owners Workshop Manual should be used as a companion volume.

6) We know it's a boring subject, especially when you really want to get on with the job – but your safety, through the use of correct workshop procedures, must ALWAYS be your foremost consideration. It is essential that you read, and UNDERSTAND, appendix 1 before undertaking any of the practical tasks detailed in this book.

7) Whilst great care is taken to ensure that the information in this book is as accurate as possible, the author, editor or publisher cannot accept any liability or loss, damage or injury caused by errors in, or omissions from, the information given.

Introduction and Acknowledgements

'The Car You Always Promised Yourself' is of course no longer produced. Yet to many people the Capri is still a very special motor car. Indeed it has truly become a classic in its own time. The appeal of relatively simple, straightforward design, hand in hand with sporting style and accommodation for four people and their luggage is obvious.

One of the reasons for the Capri's success and – since production ceased – its ever increasing popularity, is that it is a very practical car, yet has attractive styling in an age when the bland aerodynamic wedge shape has become the norm.

With mechanical components as used in other Ford models, ready availability of spare parts and ease of maintenance were – and still are – assets not enjoyed by many sporting coupés. The 'traditional', uncomplicated front engine/rear wheel drive layout still has a great deal to commend it, and certainly makes servicing and overhaul easy, compared with most of today's front wheel drive models.

Another great attraction of the Capri is that there is a wide range of models from which to choose, according to your particular needs. Therefore whether you prefer the docile 1300 or the fast and furious 2.8i, or one of the intermediate models, there is a Capri to suit you.

Since the car was acknowledged to be a classic even while it was still being produced, you can benefit from actually using the vehicle as daily transport, yet at the same time know that you have a car that is just that little bit different from the rest, and which will always be worth preserving.

Capris can be restored by anyone with enthusiasm, a reasonable tool kit and a little ingenuity. The signs are that enthusiasts will be reviving and caring for these cars for many years to come.

Do it yourself

The information contained in this book is aimed at helping Capri enthusiasts to buy and restore a car, using their own skills and efforts (where practical and sensible) to achieve a vehicle to be proud of, which will survive long into the future. In the course of writing the book, I have attempted to become involved with as much as possible of the practical work on several of the vehicles covered, in order to experience and relate the problems that can be encountered during restoration, and to describe how they can be overcome.

The book includes photographs based around the restoration of two vehicles – a Mark I 3000 owned by John Hill (Chairman of the Capri Owners' Club), who has carried out a complete structural restoration of the car, and a Mark II 2.0S owned by Chris Martin. This car has been the subject of a 'rolling rebuild' over a period of some ten months. After each working session, the car *had* to be fit for the road again, as Chris uses it as his daily transport! This gave us some 'interesting' moments at times, for example when the car temporarily lacked a driver's seat, due to it being in pieces!

In addition to these two 'project' cars, specific restoration procedures were shown being carried out on several other Capris, ranging from Mark Is to 2.8is.

Thank you

The production of a book like this is obviously not a job which I could have carried out alone, and my sincere thanks are due to a number of people and organisations, for their help.

For technical guidance on tools and components I should like to thank Mr. Pfister, of Sykes-Pickavant Ltd., Paul Toon,

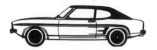

of S.I.P. (Industrial Products) Ltd., Mr. Medlicott and the staff of L.M.C. Panels, Simon Lee, of Janspeed, and Bob Dick, of Specialised Motor Components, Parkstone. Bob is a Ford enthusiast who kindly loaned components for photography, often at short notice and with the risk that he might lose a sale while a particular part was out on loan! There are several other organisations who have assisted in various ways: I hope that they will forgive me for not listing their names in full. The enthusiastic assistance of all has been very welcome.

I must also express my gratitude to the various owners' club officials and individual members, plus other Capri owners, who have so readily assisted with information, tips and so on. Some owners have even allowed their cars to be borrowed for photography, and to have work carried out on!

Special thanks in this respect go to John Hill, Chairman of the Capri Owners' Club. John has been very helpful with the supply of Capri information of all types, and with photographs. Notably, many of his photographs are incorporated in the 'Major' bodywork restoration section, where they relate to the restoration of John's own Mark I 3000, and in the 'Bodywork Kits' section of the 'Modifications' Chapter.

On behalf of the Owners' Club, John has also kindly allowed me to use information previously published in the magazine of the Capri Owners' Club, *Capri News* (later entitled *Capri Club International*).

To John and the Club, I am very grateful.

Another person who deserves thanks, for the supply of what was a fairly sad Mark II (now restored as far as possible to its former glory), and for his help with photography throughout the restoration, is Chris Martin. Chris managed to maintain his sense of humour (most of the time!) through many long hours of such activities as fabricating dozens of bodywork repair sections, rectifying bent and rusty wings, and the seemingly endless task of preparing surfaces for painting.

Among others who willingly loaned vehicles for photographs to be taken of them being dismantled, or rustproofed, or for the 'Buying' chapter, are David Acott, of Carcraft, West Moors (David found several Capris for me to attack), Ian Bachelor, Paula Harrison and Paul Woodhead.

For his assistance with the 'Respray' section of the bodywork chapter, I have to thank Ian Curly, and for his help with the 'Interior' chapter, Peter Exley.

Ford Motor Company were once again helpful in response to my requests for various information. In particular, for his assistance with information on long-forgotten trim codes, I am grateful to Mr. G.M. Townsend, and for unearthing some interesting shots of the Capri (including USA models) during its production life, for the 'History' chapter, I must thank Steve Clark, Supervisor of the Photographic Services Department.

The U.S.A. connection

Of course the Capri was sold overseas in large numbers, particularly to the United States, and my researches led to a number of American Capri enthusiasts to whom I am greatly indebted for their help in my quest for information. Among them are John Lloyd, of Mountville PA, Wayne Tofel, President of the Capri Club of Chicago, David Brownell, Editor of *Hemmings Motor News and Special Interest Autos*, Steve Singletary, of Colorado, Publisher and Historian of the Capri Car Club Ltd., and Paul S. Barrow, long-time President/Newsletter Editor of the California Capri Club. Paul kindly supplied me with a great deal of information about the U.S.A. specification cars, much of which is included in the 'History' chapter of the book.

My thanks to them all.

And finally

Many friends and relatives once again helped with the various stages of vehicle reconstruction and photography, and even in tracking down particular vehicles for specific photographic sessions. These include Paul Davis, Simon Frazier and my brother Clive, among others.

For their assistance in proof-reading, labelling photographs, and so on, my appreciation and thanks to my family, including my father-in-law, Peter, and, especially, my mother and father, who often worked for long hours, and late into the night, to help the project along.

For the strange smile and the look which says 'Daddy, why are you under that Capri again?', I must thank my little girl, Rachel, who, at the age of 18 months, has gained a healthy appreciation of what spanners and tinsnips are for. For a similar look, and for her support and help in every way during this project, I must thank Elaine, my wife.

Kim Henson,
Poole, Dorset.

1 Heritage

The background

A look at the Ford range of cars in the mid 1960s shows that the company catered well for the family market. The small car sector was taken care of by the Anglia (replaced by the Escort in the winter of 1967/68), the medium size family Ford was the ubiquitous Cortina, in its Mark I and II forms (and at that time fighting against BMC's 1100/1300 for the number one slot in the sales league), and the larger models were represented by the Zephyrs and Zodiacs, in Mark III and, from the mid 1960s, Mark IV form.

However, with the exception of the GT and Lotus Cortinas (and, later, the various fast Escorts), Fords were noted more for their practicality than for openly sporty looks and character. The Ford Capri changed all that . . .

Ford had used the name Capri for their fastback two door version of the Colin Neal designed, four door 'family' Classic, in 1961; the Classic was introduced in May, the Capri followed in September. Both models, with their unashamedly transatlantic, extrovert styling and quadruple headlights, were attractive looking motor cars. The Capri was the sporty model of

the two; with deliberate 'two plus two' bodywork, it was designed, according to a Ford advertising leaflet of 1963 "For dreamers and adventurers, as well as men on the go" . . . !

Both the Classic and Capri were, from their introduction, fitted with a 1340 cc version of the 'Kent' type overhead valve engine, which first saw the light of day in the 107E Prefect and 105E Anglia models of 1959 onwards. The 'Kent' engines (only known as such in later years) were 'oversquare' units, with the bore dimension exceeding the stroke, to give reduced piston speed, and hence bore wear, over previous designs. In addition, the oversquare engines could be made smaller and lighter, for a given capacity. From these beginnings, the Kent engines were built in vast quantities (in various sizes but based around a common bore size of 80.96 mm) for the Anglias, Cortinas, Escorts, Capris and, later, Fiestas, well into the 1980s.

The Classic and Capri received a 1498 cc, five bearing crankshaft version of the engine in August, 1962, and in February, 1963, a GT version of the Capri was introduced, using a 78 bhp version of the 1500 cc engine. The increase in power resulted from the engine being 'breathed on' by Cosworth, who had

established a reputation for successful tuning of the 997 cc Anglia motor. A high lift camshaft, twin-choke Weber carburettor, larger inlet valves, better pistons and copper-lead bearing shells, combined with a higher compression ratio, were the vital ingredients of this engine, which also powered the first (Mark I) GT Cortinas, from April, 1963.

Sadly, in many ways, the Classic and Capri models were phased out after a relatively short production run. The Classic was discontinued in October, 1963, to be replaced by the Corsair and the lighter, less complex Cortina. The more cost-efficient (from a manufacturing point of view) Cortina of course became a legend; the more luxurious Corsair was never sold in such large numbers, but is itself becoming rare today, and is an interesting vehicle in its own right.

The original Capri continued in production for some months, but was finally withdrawn in July, 1964.

The transatlantic influence

Although 1964 saw the demise of the original Capri, the year was

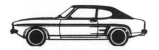

also to see the beginnings of a new model, also to be named Capri, which, like its forerunner, was to have deliberately sporty styling to set itself apart from the normal family cars of the time.

In the United States, Ford were experiencing spectacular sales success with their sporty Mustang model, and it was decided that a similar exercise by Ford in Europe would be a worthwhile proposition. For their 'Colt' project (the Capri name was not re-used until November, 1967), Ford aimed to build an attractive four-seater with dramatic styling, good handling, and quiet performance, while at the same time maximising the use of existing Ford components. The car had to offer a minimum accommodation for four people, plus ample room for their luggage, and it had to be economically priced.

In early 1965, the design studios started work, and various models were made to show how the new car might appear.

The development for the Capri was the responsibility of John Hitchman (who had also 'bred' such cars as the earlier 1500GT Capri, and the 1966 Corsair GT) and his team of British engineers. However, the views of the public across Europe were taken into account in the design of the car. Prospective car buyers were asked to comment about various aspects of the vehicle, then in fibre glass prototype form, and, without being told the make of car, its price or proposed date of introduction, were asked, at exhibitions in London, Cologne, Brussels and other European centres, to comment on its size, styling and accommodation. They were also asked what they would consider its optimum performance level to be. This research data was assembled and used extensively in formulating the Capri which eventually emerged.

By mid 1966, prototypes were running, using Cortina-based mechanical components, and on 14th July that year, a Ford management meeting, headed by Stan Gillen, gave approval for the project to become a production reality.

Ten original prototypes, under the supervision of development engineer Jim Moncrieff, were extensively tested in Britain and in Belgium, giving further valuable information to be incorporated into the production models.

By the second half of the 1960s, Ford were operating more on a 'European' than a national basis, and, at a meeting of Ford of Europe, in Paris, in June, 1967, the 'official' approval of the company was given, by Henry Ford II.

Development work continued apace, and, following adverse comments from prospective customers about the shape of the 'Mustang like' rear side windows, the rear bodywork treatment was altered, in October, 1967, to accommodate larger rear quarter lights.

One month later, the car assumed its 'Capri' title, and work continued on finalising the mechanical specifications.

Under the bonnet

Since as many existing Ford components as possible had to be used in the new model, it was logical that the engines should be taken from Ford models already in production. By November, 1967 the new Escort was being built at Halewood, and the 1298 cc version of the 'Kent' cross-flow engine, as used in this model, was chosen, in 52 bhp form, as the starting point for the British Capri range. The Capri 1300GT used a 64 bhp version of the same engine, the extra power coming from a more sporty camshaft, Weber carburation, and four branch exhaust manifolding. The 1599 cc Kent engine, as used in the then current Cortina

Mark II, provided the next step in engine sizes, producing 64 bhp, or, in 1600GT form, 82 bhp, from similar modifications as for the 1300GT unit. The two-litre V4 engine, as used in the Corsair and Transit van, and producing approximately 93 bhp, was to be the most powerful unit in the range, initially, although production of the V4 Capri did not in fact start until March, 1969. In contrast, the Capris to be built in Germany were to employ vee engines (as well as some parts of the running gear) from the Taunus range, starting with a 1300 cc unit, and with 1500, 1700 and 2000 cc motors completing their line-up. These engines had conventional combustion chambers, built into the cylinder heads, compared with the 'bowl in piston' design of the Kent engines. Power outputs from the German V4s and V6s ranged from 50 bhp, from the 1300, to 90 bhp, from the 2000 'R' version.

The British (Corsair) V4 engine was not based on the German units, but shared its design concept with the six-cylinder 'Essex' motors, used by Ford in Great Britain.

Drivetrain and running gear

Conventional transmission via a four-speed, all synchromesh gearbox and open propeller shaft to a live rear axle was employed on the new car, in the same manner as the Cortina and Escort. Automatic transmission was to be optional on the 1.6 and 2.0 litre models.

The steering set-up was derived from that of the Escort, with a rack and pinion system giving positive movement via short links, with few joints to wear.

Front suspension was of 'standard' Ford MacPherson strut design, with a front anti-roll bar

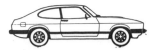

and lower 'track control' arm.

The rear suspension was by conventional semi-elliptic springs, with their limited travel controlled by staggered (one in front of the axle, one behind) telescopic shock absorbers, plus twin radius rods to further locate the axle.

The car was to run on 13 x 4½ in wheels – a very common fitting at the time – with GT versions having radial ply tyres.

Braking on all Capris was by front discs/rear drums, while the 1600GT and 2000 (only available in GT guise) models had, in addition, servo-assistance; this feature was optional on the less powerful cars. Capris destined for export markets were fitted with dual circuit brakes.

Inside story

The first Capri interiors were to feature vinyl seats, and loop pile carpets, 'colour-keyed' to the rest of the trim. The famous and very effective 'Aeroflow' ventilation system, first used on the Cortina Marks I and II, and incorporating 'eyeball' vents at each end of the facia, was also installed in the Capri.

The interior treatment of the Capri was, therefore, very much in line with that of the other members of the Ford 'family' of the time. In keeping with other Ford GT models of the late 1960s, the Capri 1600GT and 2000GT were fitted with a centre console, incorporating a clock, rev counter, oil pressure gauge and voltmeter; two-speed wipers were also standard.

The Capri is announced

Production started at Halewood, near Liverpool, in November, 1968, and the world debut of the car was at the Brussels Motor Show, on 24th January, 1969.

The car's introduction to the

U.K. public followed in February, with the advertising slogan "Capri – the car you always promised yourself". For many people, this was entirely true, for the Capri was the first of its kind – a car with true 'Grand Touring' styling at a price usually associated with more mundane saloons. Ford's clever marketing ploy was about to work wonders for them – the clothing of proven, straightforward mechanical components within an attractive body shell, giving the motoring public an eyecatching vehicle, at a reasonable price.

Therefore it mattered not to most prospective buyers that the cars were, to a certain extent, 'sheep in wolves' clothing' (with the exception of the GT models, and, rather later, the very potent three-litre Capri); they were attracted by the sheer style of the vehicle.

In fact, at the Press launch of the car in Cyprus, a few, very interesting and very quick Capris were presented, alongside the production models. They were fitted with the 16-valve, twin overhead camshaft Cosworth BDA ("Belt-driven, 'A' Series" – 'A' denoting 'Anglia', from where the motor originally came) 1600 cc engine, famous for its use in the Escort RS1600. However, this Capri never made it to volume production.

It is interesting, in view of the great success which four wheel drive cars have today in motor sport, that Ford chose to build a four wheel drive three-litre Capri prototype, to help the U.K. launch of the production cars, in early 1969. Roger Clark drove the car to victory in televised ('World of Sport') rallycross, further spreading public interest in the Capri.

Success

The Capri sold extremely well,

from the start; initial sales were in fact double those anticipated. This is perhaps not so surprising, in view of the prices asked for the cars. These started at £890 for the 1300, increasing to £936 for the 1600, £985 for the 1300GT, approximately £1,000 for the 1600GT, and, from March, 1969, just under £1,100 for the two-litre V4 GT.

To give a great range of permutations around the basic models, Ford introduced a range of 'Option Packs', which could be specified when ordering your Capri, and which could be mixed to give a wide range of extras. These started with the 'X' Pack, at just over £30, and which included reclining seats, two-tone horns, twin interior lights, dipping rear view mirror, handbrake warning light, reversing lights and so on. The 'L' pack added over-riders, bright wheel and bodywork trims, and a locking petrol cap, plus extra badges and 'dummy' air scoops, for £15! The combined 'XL' package cost just over £44, giving the benefits of both Option Packs.

In addition there was an 'R' Pack, costing £39, for GT cars, giving five-inch steel wheels with pressed mock spokes, a sports steering wheel, fog and spot lights, a map reading light, and various matt black areas around the car, to emphasise the sporting image. Of course, matt black was the sporty colour of the late 1960s/early 1970s, and the trend was reflected, in varying degrees, by the vehicle manufacturers.

The 'R' Pack was available with the 'X' and 'L' Packs, to give an 'XLR' variation; such cars are quite sought after today.

Brute power

Additional Capris, with considerable performance, appeared during 1969. For the German market, a 108 bhp, 2,300 cc V6 engined GT was

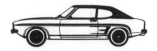

announced, in May, and, in the autumn, at the Frankfurt Motor show, a 125 bhp version of the same car. Performance was good, with a zero to sixty mph acceleration time of around 10 seconds, and a maximum speed of around 110 mph, for the 125 bhp model. The 2300GT had uprated suspension and wider wheels, to cope with the extra power.

In the U.K., the 3000GT Capri was announced, in September. This car used the 'Essex' V6 engine as fitted to the Zephyr and Zodiac Mark IV models, but considerably strengthened. It shared the same bore, stroke and basic design with the V4 (Corsair type) engine fitted to the 2000GT. The gearbox employed was the side-opening unit as also used in the Zephyr and Zodiac, with a casing designed for the Transit van, and a remote gearchange.

This, the most potent Capri so far – and the fastest production Ford to be produced in Britain at that time – had strengthened bodywork and suspension mountings, as well as stiffer front suspension and revised shock absorber and anti-roll bar specifications, at the rear. This helped to handle the extra weight and power – over 120 bhp of it – inherent in the V6 unit.

The three-litre Capri also boasted a 'power' bulge in the bonnet, a tubular three branch exhaust manifold linked up to a special high performance exhaust system, an alternator, wide sports wheels, and high speed radial tyres.

At the Geneva Motor Show, in March, 1970, a luxury version of the three-litre Capri – designated 'E', as with the upmarket Cortina 1600E of the same era – was announced, with the 'XLR GT' Pack as a standard fitting, this having all the features of the three option packs, with the exception of the sports paintwork scheme and the map reading light. The 3000E –

described by Ford at the time as the 'Ultimate' Capri – featured full instrumentation, opening rear side windows, a push-button radio, heated rear window, carpeting in the boot, lights in the engine bay and luggage compartment, and distinctive interior styling. A vinyl roof was the only extra available on this Capri! For this model you would have to pay £1,463.10.7, including Purchase Tax, giving you a very high speed, luxury touring car.

Character

So, what were the first Capris like to drive and to live with? Inside the cars, there was plenty of room for front seat occupants, while rear seat passengers found life a little less spacious, with leg and head room restricted by the fastback design. Nevertheless, the car was a true four seater, in all its forms. Interior presentation was very much in line with other Fords of the same time, with a large amount of plastic on display, and with similarities to the Cortinas and Escorts of the time.

The boot was surprisingly roomy for a car of its type, accommodating approximately 12 cubic feet of goods – or enough for the weekend luggage of four people. Heavy loads were – and still are – a little awkward to lift over the high rear sill, and the boot lid was fairly short from front to rear, restricting the size of luggage items which could be carried.

Performance from the 1300 Capri was not breathtaking, the engine having to work fairly hard to propel the Capri bodywork along, so that it would take around 20 seconds to reach 60 mph, with a maximum speed in the mid 80s per hour. On the other hand, fuel consumption was reasonable, with figures in the mid to upper thirties, per

gallon, being typical in varied use. The 1300GT would, in contrast, reach nearly 95 mph, with a nought to sixty mph time some three or four seconds quicker than for the standard model, while overall fuel consumption was similar.

The 1600 cc Kent engine, in standard form, would take the Capri to 60 mph in approximately 16 seconds, and on to 90 mph or so, while the GT version knocked a couple of seconds off the sprint to 60 (to around $13\frac{1}{2}$ seconds), and allowed a maximum speed of nearly 100 mph. Normal average fuel consumption would be in the region of 30 mpg.

The V4, two-litre GT gave a top speed of over 105 mph, passing 60 mph on the way in under 11 seconds, while the 3000GT/E models would top well over 110 mph (114 mph was claimed by Ford), and scramble to 60 mph in around 10 seconds. Fuel consumption, for the 2000GT, would normally work out to be in the mid to upper twenties, per gallon, while that for the big V6 cars would more usually be on the lower side of 25 mpg, with little more than 20 mpg being seen if the performance was used to the full.

RS 2600 debut

The Essex engined V6 was one fast Capri to appear at the Geneva Show in the spring of 1970; another was the German RS 2600, in 'pre production' form. This exciting car – production of which did not commence until September that year – was developed by Ford in Cologne, following racing experience at Nurburgring, and in the Tour de France and Tour de Corse. It featured a 2.6 litre (90 mm bore, 69 mm stroke) V6 engine, with mechanical fuel injection and a specially tuned exhaust system, to give 150 bhp. To handle the power, the car ran

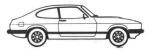

on modified suspension, with gas-filled shock absorbers, negative camber front suspension and single leaf rear springs, and 6 inch wide magnesium alloy wheels, shod with 195–70 HR 13 inch tyres. Standard fittings included large halogen headlights, and doors, bonnet and bootlid moulded from glass fibre material, for lightness.

The RS2600 – Ford's first production fuel injected car – proved to be a successful vehicle for racing, but equally it was a formidable road car, with enormous reserves of power, fed through a four-speed gearbox of Taunus origin. The car had a maximum speed of almost 125 mph, and scorched to 60 mph in under eight seconds – impressive figures now, but virtually unheard of in 1970. With 'no nonsense', sporty looks and interior, plus exhilarating performance, this rare model is very much sought after today.

Capri goes to U.S.A.

The year 1970 was a significant one for the Capri; by April, more than 275,000 had been built, and from the same month the car was imported to the United States; the 'Federal' Capri. The car's debut was at the New York Motor Show, where it was described as the 'European Sporty Car', and it was, at first, available with either the 1.6 litre cross-flow engine from the Cortina, or the two-litre overhead camshaft 'Pinto' engine. The car was built around British components, although, in later years, the pendulum swayed in favour of Ford of Germany. Indeed, by the time that imports into the U.S. of the Federal Capri ceased, in 1977, all the cars were coming from Germany. By this time, more than half a million Capris had found owners in the U.S.A., and there is still a loyal following there for the cars today.

There were a number of detail differences between the U.S.A. specification cars and their European counterparts, notably heavier bumpers and the fitting of four round headlights, within rectangular surrounds, as standard. The concept and appeal of the car, and its attractive body lines, remained the same on both sides of the Atlantic, however.

Developments

Throughout 1970, the Capri continued to make its mark in sporting events, notably the Safari Rally (although none of the Capris actually finished!) and in European Championship races; success on the track was to follow the Capri right through its long production run.

At the same time, fast road cars were very much in demand by the motoring public, and in September, 1970, Ford of Germany introduced a 125 bhp, 2.6 litre GT, replacing the 2300GT. The larger engine had the same power output, but better torque. With a nought to sixty mph time well below 10 seconds, and a top speed in excess of 110 mph, the car had obvious sporting appeal. Ford of Cologne also 'rationalised' their two-litre V6 Capri, discontinuing the 85 bhp version, leaving the 90 bhp, 2000GT model as the only two-litre survivor.

Already a number of specialist firms had taken to the Capri, in providing a wide variety of extras, from subtle bodywork modifications to full performance packages. For example, the Wembley Auto Transport Supply Company Ltd. could supply four headlamp conversions for between £41 and £52. If you owned a 3000GT and wanted still more power, the same firm could sell you a Weslake engine conversion – giving 170 bhp – which would set you back £155. This included two modified

cylinder heads, revised camshaft, uprated carburation and inlet manifolding, plus chrome valve covers and air cleaner lid. This gave you over 120 mph, and on the way would see you shoot past 60 mph in 7.8 seconds, and through the 'ton' barrier after 23$\frac{1}{2}$ seconds, from standstill.

1971 models

In September, 1970 (by which time approximately 400,000 Capris had been sold worldwide), Ford announced changes to the Capri range for the following model year. These were in line with improvements made within the Ford range generally, and were particularly notable in the uprating of the in-line Kent engines. The engines gained power as a result of modifications to the valve timing, porting and combustion chambers, plus revised carburettor jetting. These alterations gave an extra 5 bhp (representing 9.6 per cent) to the standard 1300 cc engine, bringing its total output to 57 bhp, and its claimed top speed to 89 mph. The 1300GT engine gained an extra 8 bhp (equivalent to 12$\frac{1}{2}$ per cent), to produce a total of 72 bhp, and a maximum speed, according to Ford figures, of 99 mph. The standard 1600 engine was boosted by 4 bhp (6$\frac{1}{4}$ per cent), to 68 bhp, with a new top speed of 96 mph, while 1600GTs also gained 4 bhp (or a fraction under 5 per cent), giving a total of 86 bhp, and a potential of 105 mph.

Further improvements announced at the same time (together with a general price increase!) included the fitting of a vacuum servo for the brakes on the 1300GT and standard 1600 Capris, and radial ply tyres on the 1600cc cars. The bodywork and trim colours were revised, and the choice of 'Custom' Packs was streamlined. Under this revision, the 'X' ('interior refinement') and

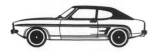

'R' ('sporty dress-up') packs disappeared, as separate entities, these only being available together, on GT models, under the 'XLR' banner. The choice otherwise, was between 'L' ('exterior dress-up') and 'XL' packs only.

Special models

During 1971, the Capri made further advances in the sporting arena, with wins in the European Championship (for example with the RS2600, at Salzburg), and with further successes in the European and South African series. Rallycross victories were also scored, and the special four wheel drive Capri gained glory by winning the televised Castrol Rallycross competition, in Britain.

In the meantime, the Capri remained as popular as ever, and, in the autumn of 1971, the first production Capri 'Special', based on the 2000GT and carrying the XLR designation, was announced. Only 1,200 of these specials were produced, all in 'Vista Orange' and all carrying a host of extras as standard fittings. These included a black vinyl roof, heated rear window, push-button radio, black cloth upholstery, louvred rear window, and a glass reinforced plastic matt black spoiler on the bootlid.

The Capri Specials were the subject of a nationwide contest at the time of their introduction, under which visitors to Ford main dealers were asked to name the Capri Special and, in not more than 20 words, to state which Capri they preferred. Jackie Stewart – then World Champion driver – was the competition's judge, and the first prize was a Capri Special.

Both the louvred rear window and the rear spoiler were developed by Ford Advanced Vehicle Operations, and were generally available for purchase by Capri owners, through Rallye

Sport Ford dealers, at a cost of £11.50 for the spoiler and £14.75 for the rear window louvres!

Capri goes topless – and the V6 goes faster!

The Earls Court Motor Show in 1971 revealed the 'Caprice' – the convertible Capri produced by Crayfords, of Kent. Very few of these cars survive – indeed I was very surprised to find one undergoing restoration in a lock-up garage not a mile from where I live – needless to say the owner could not be persuaded to part with it!

Significant changes to the Essex engined three-litre Capris were also made at this time, to give better all-round performance. This involving re-working of the cylinder heads (including the inlet ports and manifolding), revision of the camshaft design (giving higher lift and increased valve overlap) and re-jetting the Weber carburettor, to release an extra 10 bhp which had been waiting to get out. In addition, the gear ratios were revised, to make good use of the extra power, reducing the 'step' between second and third gears. The final drive ratio was altered too, to a slightly more long-legged 3.09:1 (from 3.22:1), giving 21.8 mph per 1,000 rpm, in top gear.

According to Ford figures, these changes put the top speed up from 114 to 122 mph, and brought the time taken to reach 60 mph from standstill down from 9.2 to 8 seconds, for manual versions. For automatics, they claimed an increase in maximum speed from 110 to 118 mph, and a reduction in time taken for the zero to sixty sprint of some two seconds, from 11.4 to 9.4 seconds.

It was further claimed that the improved efficiency of the revised engine led to reduced exhaust emissions, combined

with improved fuel consumption, typically from 24 to 24.8 miles per gallon when touring, for manual models. For automatics, the gains were proportionately higher, with touring consumption improving from 22 to 23 1/2 miles per gallon. These gains were helped by the fitting of a viscous drive fan to the automatics. This gave maximum efficiency and cooling at low speeds, with the drive fully 'locked', but, at engine speeds above 3,000 rpm the drive was designed to slip, resulting in a constant speed for the fan. This arrangement reduced mechanical power losses, and hence gave better fuel consumption.

Better cooling for the front brakes, combined with the fitting of a bigger servo unit, helped to contain the extra power now produced by the three-litre cars. At the same time, the rear suspension was softened, and minor styling alterations were effected.

The price asked for the 1972 model 3000GT was now £1,484, while the prestigious 3000E would cost another £182, at £1,666. This compared with £1,021 for the 1300, £1,094 for the standard 1600, £1,197 for the 1600GT, and £1,242 for the 2000GT. Interestingly, inertia reel seat belts, taken for granted today, would cost an extra £15 then.

RS2600 alterations

Changes were also made to the fastest of the German Capris – the RS2600 – in October, 1971. The suspension was softened and the ride height raised, while the updated car could be identified by the fitting of new alloy wheels, plus quarter bumpers at the front, with a full width bumper at the back (previously the RS2600 was bumper-less!). The braking was also improved, with the use of ventilated discs. The drivetrain was upgraded by

the employment of the Granada gearbox, as fitted to the British 3000 V6 cars.

Sporting achievements

The year of 1971 saw considerable track success for the Capri. The European Saloon Car Championship was clinched by Dieter Glemser, in the four hour race held at the Spanish Jarama circuit, on 3rd October. Ford's overall win was helped by victories in the Brno Grand Prix, the Nurburgring Touring Car Grand Prix, the 24 hour saloon car race at Spa, Belgium, and the 12 hour race at the Paul Ricard Circuit in the south of France; this was Europe's richest ever saloon car race at that time.

Capris continued to be raced during the following year, and in June, 1972, two of the three Capris entered in the Le Mans race in France finished 10th and 11th.

Range revised

During 1972 Ford continued to keep the Capri range in the public eye, and in June a limited run of 1600GT, 2000GT and 3000GT Specials, with extra trim and fittings, was introduced, all with 'power' bulge bonnets – originally only the three-litre cars had these fitted.

In addition to the power bulge, the Specials featured a choice of black or Emerald paint, and were fitted with many 'extras' as standard, including side repeater flashers, heated rear window, cloth trim, matt black facia and console, plus the opening rear windows as built into the 3000E.

Up to the end of May, 1972, Ford had sold nearly three quarters of a million Capris, in total, confirming the soundness

of the original design concept. However, it has been Ford policy in recent years, to carry out regular model revisions, even on their best selling cars, to keep them up to date, and to the fore in the minds of the public.

Therefore, in September, 1972, the complete Capri range was revised, with many important changes being made to the specification. These, according to Ford, totalled some 151, and were the result of press and public reaction to the original Capri.

For the 1973 model Capris, the basic body shell remained the same as for the original cars, but most other areas received attention from the Ford designers. At the same time, the range was 'streamlined' to include just L, XL, GT and the three-litre only GXL versions (albeit with a range of options available within these designations), plus a 'Rally' option on the GT, which included twin fog lamps, body side stripe, leather gear lever knob and sports road wheels.

Major changes were made to the suspension; the new 'Facelift' models received a full width, one piece rear radius arm/anti-roll bar, replacing the twin radius arm/link type rear axle set-up previously employed. In addition, five-inch wheels with radial ply tyres were fitted as standard to all Capris above 1300 cc. The ride was softer (all round) than on the earlier cars, but the rear suspension was designed to stiffen progressively, with redesigned rear axle bump control, and to give positive axle control, over rough surfaces, while also reducing axle tramp. The aim was to give better handling and an improved ride quality. In addition, Ford pointed out that the single anti-roll bar system transmitted less noise to the car than the rigid radius arm design.

Bodywork changes were easy to spot, with all models now having a 'power' bulge in the bonnet, and all Capris received

larger and more powerful rectangular headlamps (except 3000GXLs, which had four circular units) plus larger rear light clusters, now incorporating reversing lamps. A new style radiator grille matched the headlight surrounds, which were coloured according to the model designation; L and XL models had satin surrounds, GTs had black and GXLs featured grey! Further external distinguishing features included matt black panels below the doors, and the fitting of the indicator units within the front bumper bars.

The revisions continued inside the car, where new 'wrap around' seats, with better lateral and lumbar support, were now fitted, and there was an extra half an inch of legroom for rear seat passengers, due to the backs of the front seats being 'hollowed out'. New door trims and combined door pulls/armrests were fitted across the range, and the luxury GXL had elasticated map pockets fitted, adjacent to the footboard.
A single, more powerful central courtesy light was now used, in place of the twin units previously employed.

In the driving compartment, a two-spoke steering wheel, with an impact absorbing centre, was now fitted, and new (Granada and Consul-like) push button switches were installed, together with larger instrument dials. The heater controls were illuminated on XL, GT and GXL versions. The centre console (where fitted) incorporated a tray, central armrest and glovebox. There was now no parcel shelf at the front, but, instead, an illuminated, lockable dashboard glovebox.

There were changes under the bonnet too, for the 1600 cross-flow Kent engine disappeared from the Capri, to be replaced by the overhead camshaft 1600 cc (Pinto based) unit also used in the Cortina Mark III. Therefore the only cross-flow Capri was now the range-starting 1300, in L and XL

form; there was no longer a 1300GT version available.

There were two stages of tune for the overhead camshaft 1600 engine – in L and XL form it produced 72 bhp, while in GT guise, with twin-choke carburettor and other performance modifications, it achieved 88 bhp. In standard trim, the new 1600 was claimed to reach 95 mph, while Ford quoted 106 mph as the maximum speed for the GT version, with 0–60 being attainable in 11.4 seconds. Overall fuel consumption of around 30 mpg was attainable from the new models.

The V4 2000GT remained the next step up in the range, which was now topped by the 3000GT and 3000GXL models, the GXL replacing the 3000E, which had been phased out in July, 1972. The 3000GXL featured the same luxury fittings that had been available on the 3000E, and was a car of very high specification. This now included four circular, five-inch halogen headlights, twin foglights (also halogen), radio, heated rear window, opening rear side windows, and sculptured sports road wheels. The three-litre cars were all now fitted with a viscous coupled fan, running on a Teflon covered hub. The fan stabilised automatically at between 2,000 and 2,700 rpm, regardless of higher engine speed, saving noise and up to five per cent of engine power.

Another welcome feature of the 1973 model three-litre Capris was a lighter, more direct gearchange. This was made possible by the use of the top-opening gearbox of German Ford descent, allowing a single rail gearchange to be used. This was far slicker in operation than the previous, Zodiac, type.

Automatic transmission was optional on all 1973 Capris, except for the 1300 models.

In summing up the changes made to the Capris for 1973, Ron Platt, Director of Car Sales for Ford of Britain said, in a far-sighted statement in September, 1972 "The changes we have made to the 1973 Capri range represent an honest attempt to meet the points of criticism. The Capri has become a classic car. It was the first of the family sporting cars in Europe and it has been the most successful. We think that this very advanced engineering programme makes the entire range better value for money than ever."

The RS3100

The much acclaimed RS 2600 continued in production through the early 1970s, and indeed the millionth Capri to be built was one of these fast and desirable cars, rolling off the Cologne production line in August, 1973. However, for the 1974 racing season, the rules allowed four valves per cylinder to be used in a limited run of engines, and Ford turned to the British V6 power unit, with the help of Cosworth, who had great experience with racing engines (and with Ford – the Escort RS1600 motor, for example).

Work began on a racing version of the three-litre Essex engine in mid 1972, with twin, belt driven overhead camshafts fitted to each bank of cylinders, and aluminium cylinder heads, housing four valves for each cylinder. Racing versions appeared with 3.4 litres capacity but for road use the engines remained at 3.1 litres. The RS3100 was designed and developed at South Ockenden, the home of Ford Advanced Vehicle Operations (which, incidentally, closed in December, 1974). The road-going cars (around 250 in total), built at Halewood, from December, 1973, were sold through RS dealers, and were based on the Capri 3000GT, but with a front airdam and rear spoiler. Quadruple headlights, GXL style, highlighted the front, as did quarter bumpers. These, like the full width rear bumper, were matt black. The 'chassis' and running gear was mainly from the (revised) RS 2600, and the car had the suspension, vented disc brakes and so on of the smaller RS model. The RS 2600 was now discontinued, after more than 4,000 had been built.

With 148 bhp on tap from the 3,091 cc V6 engine, performance from the RS3100 was plentiful, so that 60 mph was attainable in around eight seconds, and a top speed approaching 125 mph was available – all for under £2,500.

V8 Capri?

It was possible to buy what many people consider to be *the* ultimate Capri – one with V8 power. Apart from the many private installations of V8 engines which have taken place over the years, there were professional conversions which could be carried out. For example, in late 1972, Jeff Uren Ltd., of Hanwell, London, introduced their Capri 'Stampede'. The company specialised in sporting Ford conversions, which included the 'Navajo' (Escort with two-litre Cortina engine), the 'Savage' (Cortina with three-litres under the bonnet), and another Capri, the 'Comanche', with 190 or 220 bhp available!

The Stampede featured five-litres of Ford Mustang V8, driving 14 inch wheels concealing Formula One vented discs at the front. These were probably required to work fairly hard, since a zero to 60 mph time of five seconds was claimed, with 100 mph appearing after a further seven seconds, and an ultimate speed of 160 mph!

With the petrol crisis of 1973 brewing (although as yet not

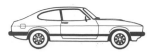

forecast) the Uren literature of the time did not elaborate on fuel consumption figures, but simply quoted 'Shoosh!' Similarly, prices were not detailed in pounds and pence, but simply as 'One quarter of a Muira, one fifth of a Daytona, or one third of a Pantera'!

Bullit Capri

There were, of course, a string of other modified Capris available, particularly during the 1970s, and, sadly, there is not sufficient space in a 'restoration' book to describe them all. However, one of the most well known is the Broadspeed Bullit Capri. This car, introduced in 1970, was based around the 1600GT or the V6 three-litre GT, but had modified cylinder heads, high lift cam, rejetted carburettor and induction system, and a more efficient exhaust. The suspension and brakes were uprated to cope with the considerable extra power, and a front airdam was fitted to help keep the car stable at speed. These modifications helped make a Capri which, in the case of the V6 version, would accelerate to 60 mph around three seconds more quickly than a standard three-litre GT, and which had a maximum speed in excess of 125 mph.

If even this wasn't fast enough, Broadspeed went on, in the early 1970s, to build their 'Turbo Bullit', which, as the name implies, was turbocharged. This was at a time when making use of the exhaust gases to drive a turbocharger in a petrol engine was a rarity. This makes the car even more interesting, and, even today, it is considered to be an extremely potent vehicle. With 218 bhp available, performance was, not surprisingly, shattering, with 60 mph appearing in a little over 6$\frac{1}{2}$ seconds from standstill, and 100 mph taking under 16 seconds to reach. The

top speed of over 140 mph underlines the car's potential, which could be 'switched off' at will by the owner, by means of a key within the car, which would revert the engine to normal aspiration when required.

To keep the car on the road, wide (6J) wheels – in light alloy – and tyres were fitted, and the steering and suspension was modified extensively. In addition, the front airdam, incorporating driving lamps, helped to improve stability at high speed. Four cylinder callipers and ventilated Formula One type front discs, plus a servo unit, helped to slow the car down.

Although the Capris on which the Bullit was based were comprehensively equipped anyway, Broadspeed offered a wide range of optional features for their customers who required them.

The exciting Turbo Bullit would cost just under £1,500, for the manual model, or £1,660 for an automatic. In terms of today's prices, around £10 for each mile per hour seems very reasonable!

Hatchback Capri II

Although the 'Facelift' had given the Capri a revised lease of life in late 1972, falling sales figures needed to be reversed, and Ford took a close look at their sports coupe with a view to modernising and improving it still further. The result was the Capri II model, introduced in February, 1974.

The new Capri retained the appeal and sporty image of the earlier car, but had crisper lines, and – an important point for a vehicle doubling for family transport – was now far more practical. For Ford had now fitted the Capri with a deep and wide opening tailgate, together with rear seats which folded forward, giving welcome extra versatility to the car, allowing the carriage

of loads of around three metres (nearly ten feet) long. While the new model was not so popular with the sporting enthusiasts, it certainly did the trick as far as sales were concerned, and helped prolong the production life of the car.

The new Capris were a little over two inches wider than the earlier models, and were slightly longer and heavier. They featured a much larger glass area at the back (both side and rear windows were bigger), giving a slightly less claustrophobic atmosphere for rear seat passengers, as well as making rear vision better for the driver.

Mechanically the cars were identical in concept, but updated in detail. For example, the brakes were improved by the adoption of larger discs at the front, with wider linings at the back, and power steering was now an option. Another subtle alteration was the softening of the suspension for the new model. The electrics, too, were uprated; in line with most manufacturers in the mid 1970s, Ford began fitting alternators as standard equipment, in place of dynamos, and the Capri II range were so equipped. In addition, the upmarket Capris featured voltmeters, under the title 'battery condition indicators'!

In an attempt to help reduce underbody corrosion, the hollow 'chassis' sections of the new model were filled with a rigid foam.

The range designations were revised for the new Capri, so that the range now started with the 1300L, still with the overhead valve, cross-flow Kent engine, then moved on to the overhead camshaft 1600 model, in L, XL and GT form. The V4 two-litre engine had disappeared, in favour of the two-litre 'Pinto' overhead camshaft unit, also used in the Cortina Mark III and the German Taunus. This 98 bhp engine gave the car a top speed of over 105 mph, and 60 mph was reached in well under 11 seconds, while

overall fuel consumption in the upper twenties, per gallon, could be expected. The two-litre was available in GT form, or the new Ghia specification. The Ghia models (in two-litre or range topping V6 three-litre guise) replaced the previous GXL versions, and were built in Cologne, with many standard 'extra' features which were introduced in conjunction with the Ghia firm (in Turin, Italy), which was by then a subsidiary company of Ford. In recent years, of course, any Ford with a Ghia badge has stood for a top of the range model. So it was in the case of the Capri, for the standard specification list included such luxuries as a vinyl roof, tinted glass, 5^1/$_2$J cast alloy wheels, slide and tilt sun roof, bodywork side mouldings, halogen headlights, rear screen wash/wipe system (this was optional on the lower specification Capris), a push-button radio, special front seats with head restraints, and new upholstery. Another plus point for the Ghia and GT Capris was that the rear seats were split so that they could be folded down to provide seating for two, three or four people, according to the loads required to be carried at any particular time. These, in any case, could be far larger than previously, since the luggage capacity of the Capri II was some three times the volume of the original car.

Automatic transmission was a popular option on Ghia models, and was also available on the other Capris in the range, except for the 1300s. The Ford designed and built C3 transmission system was used, this being built at Bordeaux, in south west France. It is interesting that, according to Ford figures, 12 per cent of the new Capri IIs were ordered with the automatic option, compared to just under 10 per cent of Cortinas, and more than 50 per cent of Consuls and Granadas.

Overseas

The German range of Capri II cars were different from their predecessors in the same way as the British models. However the line-up was rather different, as it always had been for the German versions, with variations in the engines fitted. Starting the range were two 55 bhp 1300 models, the L and XL, and, in addition, an interesting 1300GT version which was sold only in Europe. The 1600 cars, with the overhead camshaft engine, followed the British designations and had the same power outputs; L and XL (72 bhp) and GT (88 bhp). The next model in the German range was the 2300, in GT or Ghia trim, and fitted with the 108 bhp version of the Cologne V6 engine. For those who wanted more power, they could specify a three-litre Capri, in GT or Ghia form, with the British V6 engine under the bonnet.

In the meantime, in the United States, customers had been offered the 1974 Capris, built in Germany and imported for the Lincoln-Mercury Division of Ford, and with a number of features not seen on the European cars.

The American Capri 2000 was fitted with the overhead camshaft two-litre engine, with twin-choke Weber carburation, and the Capri V6 featured the 2.8 litre V6 engine, of German Ford origin, and with a Holley-Weber twin-choke carburettor. The Capris for the American market had originally been fitted only with the British 1600 cc cross-flow engine, but were later available with the 'Pinto' two-litre overhead camshaft unit, and, from 1972, with 2.6 litres of V6 power. From 1974, the U.S.A. Capri could be purchased with the 2.8 litre V6 engine.

The U.S.A. market Capris were externally identifiable by their quadruple, 5^3/$_4$ inch headlights set into squared

surrounds, and their large, protruding 'Hi-flex' energy absorbing bumpers (to meet the stringent U.S.A. safety standards), front and rear. The bumpers were designed to return to their original shape, following a mild impact, and consisted of a urethane outer skin with integrally moulded, vertical energy absorbing sections, outside of a full-width steel bar, rigidly mounted to the vehicle's 'chassis'. Safety featured high on the specification list, and among the many standard features considered to be very advanced (in Europe) at the time was, for example, the use of laminated glass for the windscreen, and the fitting of dual-circuit brakes with corrosion-resistant brake pipes, and so on.

Side marker lamps were set into the front and rear wings, and the overall styling was complemented by steel Rostyle wheels. Inside, the car was very well equipped, with such items as a heated rear screen as standard, and with full instrumentation, including tachometer, oil pressure gauge, battery charge meter, and temperature gauge. The Capri V6 had, in addition, a tripmeter, and wide (185/70 HR x 13) tyres, for better traction. The optional 'Decor Group', available in black, tan, or saddle, gave the customer a trimmed gear lever knob and steering wheel cover, reclining front seats, a suspended clock, adjustable map light, twin horns, and remote control door mounted mirror. Other options included a radio (FM or AM/FM), a manual sun roof, and a black vinyl roof. Both models had optional three speed 'Select-Shift' automatic transmission, in place of the four-speed manual gearbox.

To sum up the American view of the Capri, Ford, in their advertising literature of the time, talked of the Capri 2000 as 'The sexy European you can afford'!

Special, sporty versions of the Capri were available in the United States as well as in

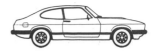

Europe, and the 2.8 litre V6 'RS' model, based on the Capri II body shell, and available through a 'hand picked' group of Lincoln-Mercury dealers, was a real extrovert driving machine. With large 'Capri RS' decals along each side, an 'Air Dam Racing Spoiler' at the front, bright metalwork, wide spoked wheels and louvred rear window just ahead of a sharply lipped tailgate spoiler, the car was not easily missed! It was described in the advertising literature as 'Designed and proven by Ford of Germany. Built for you with love, by the Sunroof people' . . .

Interestingly, there was no 1975 model for the American market, but in 1976 the U.S.A. Capris were fitted with Brazilian built 2.3 litre overhead camshaft or 2.8 litre V6 engines.

The Capri II develops

As 1974 passed, the Capri sales figures improved in response to the changes made for the introduction of the Capri II. Inevitably, in a time of high inflation, manufacturers felt obliged to update their prices to keep pace, and Ford were no exception. For example, in September, 1974, prices across the Ford range were increased by an average of 8.4 per cent. This meant that a 'typical' Capri such as the 1600XL would cost £1,592 instead of the 'old' price of £1,363.

Despite the price increases, the Capri continued to flourish, and, in March, 1975, a new version made its debut at the Geneva Motor Show. This was the Capri 'S', in Midnight Black, which was initially available only for sale in Europe, where the choice was between 1600 (overhead camshaft) engined or 2300 cc V6 versions. From June, 1975 the car was available in Britain, in 1.6, 2.0 and 3.0 litre form. The paintwork of the 'JPS'

Capris was based around the livery of the Formula 1 'John Player Special' Team Lotus cars of the time. It was complemented by gold panel linings, and gold alloy wheels (although various wheels were fitted to the Capri S during its lifetime). The door handles, exterior trims and window mouldings were also finished in black, and the black interior trim was offset by gold cloth inserts on the seats, which had head restraints. Tinted glass and a sports steering wheel were standard, as was a rear screen wash/wipe system, and halogen headlights.

Underneath, the S featured uprated (firmer) suspension, with gas-filled rear shock absorbers, and a thicker anti-roll bar, and a mechanical specification owing much to the GT models, which it replaced from October, 1975. By this time, the S models, built in Germany, had been put into volume production.

It is interesting to note that variations of the JPS Capris, known as the "Black Cat" Capri, were sold in the U.S.A., and fitted with 2.8 litre V6 engines.

An announcement from Ford Motor Co. Ltd. on 10th October, 1975, also saw changes to the other Capris in the range, introduced as part of Ford's 'VFM' (standing for 'Value For Money') campaign, which also meant alterations to the Escorts, Cortinas and Granadas. The idea was to make the cars more attractive (without making them significantly more expensive) to a buying public which were hit hard by inflation at the time.

To further encourage buyers, an unlimited mileage, 12 month warranty scheme was introduced on all new Fords.

In announcing the 'VFM' Programme, (Sir) Terence Beckett said that the scheme was designed to help motorists faced with inflation as well as with a pay ceiling, and to fight imports 'product for product and price for price'. He also stated that discussions with private motorists

and fleet owners had revealed that 85 per cent preferred to have an increase in the vehicle's specification, rather than a price cut.

Therefore the U.K. market saw the introduction of a 'base' model 1300 – the only Capri then produced with a non-folding rear seat. Ford claimed that it had more standard equipment than the previous L model, nevertheless it was a very basic motor car, with black bumpers and trimmings in place of chrome, plain wheels, fixed seat backrests, a rubber mat in the boot, and no door mirror. It did, however, feature carpets inside, cloth seats, hazard lights, heated rear window, and a servo/disc-equipped braking system. At £1,717, this base model Capri was £116 cheaper than the Capri 1300L. The 1300L, like the revised 1600L, now featured sports wheels, a dipping rear view mirror, a door mirror, reclining cloth covered seats, load area carpeting and coach lines.

Two new GL versions replaced the previous XL models, in 1.6 and 2.0 litre form, and, compared with the L cars, these had GT style cloth seats, halogen headlights, inertia reel seat belts, rear wash/wipe system, body side mouldings, sports wheels, a clock, a centre console, and load area lighting. In all, according to Ford, there was £182 worth of (net) extra value included in the GL specification, against that of the previous XL.

The new S models, which now officially replaced the GT versions, were available in a range of paintwork colours (not just black!), with contrasting coach lines. They still, however, featured epoxy coated bumpers, door handles and locks, and twin door mirrors, finished in black. At this time, many of the 'gold' trimmings and other peculiarities of the original JPS Capri disappeared, for example the interior trim colours were changed, the gold trimmings

were no longer found on the bonnet and wing tops, and the wheels were no longer gold in colour.

Ghia Capris across the range now had a remote control door mirror fitted as standard, and, in total, gained £126 worth of 'added value'. Meanwhile, three-litre Ghia and S models had power steering fitted as standard, at no extra cost – indeed this fitting could (optionally) be omitted from the car's specification, with a reduction in price! The 3000S had black door mirrors, contrasting colour seat panels, and a three-spoke steering wheel.

These changes saw the production Capris into 1976, while on the sporting side, the last 'Works' entry for the Mark I based RS3100 was at Kyalami, South Africa, in November, 1975, where, alas, the car retired.

Minor changes

The following two years saw relatively few major changes to the Capri's construction and specification, but a number of minor alterations were made.

In February, 1976, the Kent engines were revised, and Ford's Sonic Idle carburettor was introduced to 1300 and 1600 cc Capris. It was claimed by Ford to improve economy by up to 15 per cent, and this unit in fact gained a Design Award for Ford.

Ford's 'Bordeaux' automatic transmission was available on all except the 1300 cc Capris (as was tinted glass). In early 1976, if you chose a 3000 Ghia and preferred manual transmission, you could expect a £199 price reduction! On the other hand, if you wished to specify a sliding sun roof on any but the Ghia Capris (on which it was standard), you would have to find a hefty £115 extra.

By May, 1976, low compression versions of the 1.3

and 1.6 litre German Capri engines had been made available, producing 54 bhp and 68 bhp respectively, and the standard equipment levels on the German models had increased. At the same time, a new two-litre V6 German engine was introduced, developing 90 bhp. The following month saw the general introduction by Ford of their three stalk steering column controls, which some customers did (and still do!) find rather confusing compared with the earlier, perhaps more logical system.

Halewood and 'Federal' Capri production ceases

In October, 1976, Capri production at Halewood came to an end, after 337,491 cars had been built. From this point on, *all* Capris were to be built in West Germany, where the Ghia and S versions were already produced. One reason for this sad (for U.K. Capri enthusiasts) change was that Ford in Britain wanted to produce more Escorts at Halewood.

Across the Atlantic, sales of the Capri were gradually dropping, and Ford in the U.S.A. were anxious to promote their own 'home grown' Mustang, so, in August, 1977, production of the 'Federal' Capri ceased in Cologne. The Capri name was 'mopped up' by the Mercury Division of Ford, but Capri enthusiasts would not forget the 513,449 'Federal' Capris which had found homes in the U.S.A.

Capri III arrives

Life continued, of course, for the German built Capris, after Halewood Capri production was stopped, and in November, 1976,

minor changes were made to the S models, including the fitting of a front airdam and rear spoiler, to improve stability.

However, work had been going on 'behind the scenes' to make the Capri generally more aerodynamic, and to update the range to take it into the 1980s. This was set against a market in which sales of the Capri II were beginning to drop, and revisions were felt necessary to keep the car attractive in the eyes of the car buying public. In March, 1978, the Capri III was announced.

The designers had turned their attention to the body design so that the sporting hatchback appeal was maintained, while at the same time the car could slip through the air more easily, making it more efficient. Therefore the Capri III was to retain the useful hatchback facility (allowing some 22.6 cubic feet of luggage space), while being more aerodynamically efficient, yet still keeping its 'sporty' image.

Combining these varying requirements into one vehicle took some doing, yet Ford achieved their objectives and the public liked the new model.

Aerodynamic Capri

The Series III Capris were redesigned in many areas to improve their aerodynamic efficiency, starting with the front grille, which was now slatted, with 'aerofoil' sections. This started flush with the bonnet lid, which itself was 'lipped' over along its front edge, shrouding the four headlights. The 'bulge', which had for a long time been a feature of the Capri bonnet, was less obvious on the Series III models. The new Capri also featured a front airdam, and (on S models) a rear spoiler, to help keep them stable at speed. Another identifying feature of the

new bodywork treatment included the use of black, wrap-around bumpers, with built-in indicator units, at the front. Larger rear lamp clusters were fitted, incorporating foglights on the GL/Ghia cars, which also, like the new L versions, featured deep (and perhaps ugly) bodywork side mouldings. The S had a tailgate mounted spoiler and side stripes with the 'S' motif.

The interiors were modified too, with a range of new trim colours, and the use of a parcel shelf which lifted when the tailgate was opened, on GL, S, and Ghia models. The padded facia was a safety feature, while the sports steering wheel (leather trimmed in Ghias) was to enhance the sporting aspect of the car. The useful hatchback facility was retained, of course.

The engines were 'retuned', with carburettor modifications to give improved economy/emissions, and further mechanical refinements included the use of gas-filled shock absorbers on all but the basic 1300 cc model. Ford amended the servicing schedules so that a major service was now required every 12,000 miles, with an intermediate oil change, plus a 'plugs and points' examination at 6,000 miles 'Sealed for life' lubrication was extensively employed on the car – for example the rear axle and gearbox, and the steering and suspension joints were designed to be lubricated for 'life'.

The range line-up for British customers now started with the basic 1300 and 1300L, still with the overhead valve Kent engine, producing 57 bhp. The 1600L and GL versions, with the 72 bhp overhead camshaft engine, provided the next steps upward, with the 88 bhp 1.6S topping the 1.6 litre models. The 98 bhp, two-litre cars came in L, GL and S versions, while for three-litre customers there was a choice of S or Ghia equipment, with both models employing the 138 bhp

V6 running gear used in the previous Capri 3.0. The three-litre Ghia model had automatic transmission and power steering fitted as standard. All S and Ghia Capris featured a rev counter, trip meter, oil pressure gauge and ammeter, as well as a Ford push-button radio – this was optional on the lesser models. The Ghias emphasised comfort (extensive use of carpeting throughout the car, etc.), compared with the openly sporting character of the S versions.

In publicity material advertising the new range, Ford summed up the Capri III as follows – 'Space, performance and versatility – the Capri has the lot. And it'll probably cost you a lot less than you think'. In fact the new cars ranged in price from a little under £3,000 to just over £5,500, when introduced.

It is interesting to note the position of the Capri in terms of the sales league in Britain at this time. In 1977, when Ford held a share of the market standing at nearly 26 per cent, 42,816 Capris were sold, to give them seventh place. Above them were the Vauxhall Chevette, Austin Allegro, Mini, and, in the top three, the Morris Marina, with 66,088 sales, in second place, the Ford Escort, with 103,389 sold, and, way ahead in first place, the ubiquitous Cortina (Mark IV), with sales of 120,601. In 1978 the picture was similar, wth Ford holding a 28 per cent stake in the market. 23,611 Capris were sold, to give the Capri ninth position in the league. Above the Capri were the Chevette, Cavalier, Allegro, Fiesta and Mini, with the top three remaining as Marina, Escort and Cortina, but now with sales of 43,478, 70,127 and 102,600 respectively.

The Capri range offered for sale in Germany differed from the British line-up, with the addition of a 90 bhp, V6 two-litre model, and with the 108 bhp 2300S/Ghia Capris giving an interesting, intermediate

alternative to the two-litre and three-litre cars. The 1300 Capri was still available with the 73 bhp GT/Sport engine for Italian and French buyers, while in Sweden one could buy the 1600 Capri with a low compression engine, developing 63 bhp.

Further changes

Only a year passed before the Capri III was itself updated, with the most significant changes being under the bonnet, where viscous-coupled fans were now fitted on the 1300, 1600 and 2000 cc engines. This gave back power in varying degrees, but every little helps, of course! The 1300 was therefore now rated at 60 bhp, the 1.6 litre cars at 73 bhp and 91 bhp (S models), and the two-litre at 101 bhp. The German 2300 cc V6 engine was uprated from 108 to 114 bhp, a useful increase.

Other changes included the fitting of automatic chokes to 1.6 litre models, and lower profile tyres to the 2.0S Capri; all cars now had a brake fluid warning light.

The Capri continued to notch up sporting successes, with three-litre cars winning the Spa 24 hour race in 1978 (driven by Gordon Spice) and 1979 (Martin Brothers), and with the Zakspeed Turbo Capri (450 bhp from 1.4 litres!), driven by Hans Heyer, winning its class (and coming second overall) in the German Championship, in 1979.

Further changes were made to the road-going Capris in the same month, with rear fog-lights being fitted as standard to L cars, and with GL versions receiving head restraints, a passenger door mirror and remote control driver's door mirror, plus headlamp washers. The S cars also gained the driver's door mirror, and had the benefit of improved soundproofing to the bonnet and rear quarter panels.

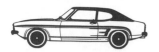

For the 1979 Capris, a stereo cassette player (with mono radio) featured for the first time as standard equipment, in the Ghia models. The Capri S gained the integral rear fog-lights previously fitted to the GL and Ghia cars.

The cumulative effect of all these modifications was to boost the sales of the Capri, which had been facing increasingly strong opposition (especially in West Germany) from other competent sporting models such as the Opel Manta and Volkswagen Scirocco. Although 'home' sales in Germany were still declining during 1979, the figures were better than they had been a few years earlier, with, in addition, cars continuing to be produced in large numbers for export markets. The loss of the United States market in 1977 had been compensated for by the cessation of production at Halewood, in the previous year, so that Capris built in Germany were still very much in demand. Indeed, sales in Britain rose from just under 32,000 in 1978 to over 49,000 in 1979, proving the wisdom of updating the model.

Extras

The late 1970s were a boom time for the fitting of optional extras to motor cars, and many useful (and some not so useful!) accessories were available for the Capri. For example in December 1978 a 'speed control unit' was available as an extra for Fords of two-litres and above, following the popularity of such cruise control devices in the United States, where one in three cars were fitted with them. The cruise control allowed a pre-selected road speed to be maintained (useful on motorways, and on main roads), until over-ridden by the driver. This device would cost around £100, fitted.

Another desirable accessory which was gaining popularity in the late 1970s was the stereo radio/cassette player, such as the Ford SRT 32, which could be purchased and fitted to any Capri which did not have its own 'in car entertainment' fitted as standard.

Sporty accessories and kits were also gaining ground at this time, and, for example, Ford's 'X' Packs, based around the 2994 cc V6 engined cars, and available between 1978 and 1980, allowed modifications to be made in stages. Two ''Series X'' Capris were made available to the motoring press at the International Test Day in 1979, fitted with a full range of the 'Series X' performance and body components, which were available through any of Ford's 75 Rallye Sport dealers.

As an illustration of the variety of components that were available, the modifications to the bodywork on the two test cars included the fitting of blended wide wheel arches, covering 7$\frac{1}{2}$ inch alloy wheels shod with Pirelli low profile tyres, a deep front airdam, and so on. The running gear was improved by the employment of ventilated front discs with larger calipers, uprated suspension and a limited slip differential, all the better to handle the 175 bhp produced by the modified V6 motor (compared with 138 bhp from the standard engine). The power improvements were due to the use of three Weber twin-choke carburettors, large valve cylinder heads and high compression pistons. These combined measures pushed the top speed up to over 130 mph, compared with 124 mph from the standard three-litre car. As Ford put it in a press release at the time 'The result is a highly individual sports coupé'.

Into the 'eighties

The 1980s saw the introduction of 'Special Editions' as a marketing ploy by many manufacturers, and Ford were no exception. Therefore in March, 1980, a limited edition 1600 Capri was made available – the GT4, based on the 1600L, but with special seats, in 'Beta Plus' fabric, and with a rev counter, oil pressure gauge and ammeter, plus silver sports wheels shod with 185/70 tyres.

In October, 1980, changes were made to the wheel specifications, so that 5$\frac{1}{2}$ inch wheels (with 185 tyres) were now optional on L models, and standard on GL cars, on which six-inch steel wheels with 185 tyres were available as an alternative. These were also optional on Ghia models, and standard on S versions.

Such subtle but useful changes helped to keep the public interested in the Capri. Therefore at the time of the 1980 Motor show, at the N.E.C. in Birmingham, Ford were describing the Capri as its 'class leader', with it taking nearly 17 per cent of its market segment, according to figures available for the first eight months of the year.

Further modifications to the S followed in January, 1981, when Recaro seats became a standard fitting, together with revised interior trim. At the same time the LS designation was introduced, the new car having the 1593 cc engine and replacing the 1.6S. The 1.6L and GL models continued to be available, along with two-litre GL and S models. A single venturi carburettor was fitted to the LS, giving 73 bhp from the 1.6 litre engine, compared with 88 bhp in the S. However, equipment was not lacking, and a centre console, a clock, sports wheels, a tailgate spoiler and S type suspension were all standard on the LS.

The other Capris in the range were also improved, with detachable rear parcel shelves becoming a standard fitting on all versions, and with additional extra features on some models.

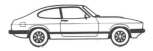

For example the Ghia two and three-litre cars now had metallic paintwork, rear seat belts and a stereo system fitted as standard.

The 2.8i arrives

The arrival of the 2.8 litre fuel-injected Capri, at the Geneva Motor show in March, 1981, was significant, for, once again, it gave a new lease of life to the range.

The 2.8i was the result of the efforts of Ford's Special Vehicle Engineering (S.V.E.) Department, set up in Britain the previous year. This was the up to date equivalent of the 'Advanced Vehicle Operations' (A.V.O.), established in the 1960s to build 'special' performance Fords. With its own production line at Aveley, A.V.O. had built cars such as the Escort RS1600 and Mexico. A.V.O. had also been involved with the Capri, providing the engineering for the famous RS3100.

It was therefore fitting that the first model to emerge from the newly formed S.V.E. department, in 1981, was the 2.8i Capri (they were also, of course, responsible for the Fiesta XR2). Using bodywork based on the Ghia three-litre, but powered by the 2.8 litre V6 Granada engine, equipped with Bosch K-Jetronic electronic fuel injection, the new Capri was a potent mix. It is interesting to note that the 2.8 litre V6 engine had, in less powerful, non fuel-injected form, already been used in Capris sold in the U.S.A. However, the new 2.8i was the first 'European'Capri to use this engine. With 160 bhp under the bonnet, it was also the most powerful production Capri, and the fastest (131 mph) European production Ford, to date. From standstill, 60 mph would be reached in under eight seconds. Wide (seven inch) alloy wheels with low profile tyres, ventilated front brake discs (as on the V6 Granadas), power steering, plus lowered and uprated suspension employing gas-filled shock absorbers and thicker anti-roll bars, helped to tame the beast!

Four-speed manual transmission was fitted (there being no automatic gearbox option on this model), the power being fed to the rear wheels via a 3.09:1 differential, as used in the three-litre Capris.

Initially available only in left-hand drive form, the 2.8i was introduced in right-hand drive form, to Britain, in July, 1981. A steel tilt and slide sun roof, stereo radio/cassette player, door mirrors and a rear spoiler were standard fittings, with Recaro sports seats and two tone metallic paintwork being optional.

The sporting appeal of the car caught the imagination of the public and, at £7,995, while not cheap, it was competitively priced.

Sadly for three-litre Capri enthusiasts, the 3.0S and 3.0 Ghia models were discontinued in favour of the new car, with the old V6 Essex engine giving way to the smaller, cleaner burning 2.8 litre unit.

Zakspeed Capri

Meanwhile in Germany, Ford RS dealers had been able to offer 200 turbocharged Capri 2.8 litre specials, in honour of the success of the Zakspeed cars in circuit racing. The road-going Zakspeed models, on sale from July 1981, had aggressive body styling, with wide wheel arches, plus an accentuated front airdam and rear spoiler. Under the bonnet, the 2.8 litre engine ran without fuel injection, but was fitted with a KKK turbocharger, to produce 188 bhp, and 205 lb.ft. of torque. This rare, exciting car, available only from July 1981 to September 1982, was capable of over 130 mph.

More special editions

The launch of the 2.8i overshadowed, to a certain extent, the announcement of the two other new Capris introduced in the same month. These were further special edition models, the Cameo and Calypso. The Cameo was based on the 'L' version of either the 1.3 or 1.6 litre Capri, but came without a rear parcel shelf, clock, radio or centre console. On the other hand, the inclusive prices – £3,995 for the 1.3 and £4,250 for the 1.6 – were attractive.

The more 'upmarket' Calypso was based on the 1.6LS, with two-tone paintwork, tinted glass, head restraints, tailgate wash/wipe system and full carpeting through the car, including the luggage compartment. The Calypso was, of course, more expensive, at £5,120, and there was an option pack available for another £200.

In September, 1981, further minor changes were made to the options available on the Capri range. Ford's 'Econolight' system (aimed at saving fuel by illuminating coloured lights under wide throttle conditions) became available on all except the 2.8i, and a new stereo radio/cassette player became an option on all Capris.

During the same month, Klaus Ludwig furthered the Capri's sporting reputation by winning the German Championship outright, in a Zakspeed Turbo car.

Another special edition Capri was introduced to the U.K. in May, 1982 – the Cabaret. Based on the 1.6L, but with the two-litre power unit as an option, the Cabaret had decorative body flashes, a sun roof, rear spoiler, 5½ inch GL type sports wheels, the fabric seats of the LS, and door trims of Ghia models, a centre console, and full instrumentation. The 1.6 Cabaret was priced at £5,106, while the

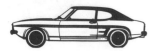

two-litre version cost £5,484, inclusive of taxes.

Aston Martin Tickford Capri

The Birmingham Motor Show of October, 1982 saw the showing, in prototype form, of a very special Capri – the Aston Martin Tickford model. This vehicle was a result of co-operation between Tickford – for engine design – and Ford, who provided the development funds and the basic machinery of the vehicle. Resplendent in white, complete with stylish bodywork modifications and with an opulent red leather interior, the car proved to be a major attraction. However, Ford later withdrew from the project and Tickford produced the car on their own.

The car was far from just a 'modified' Capri; it was a vehicle totally stripped and rebuilt by Tickford (which incidentally was later 'separated' from Aston Martin, to be run as an independent company) to exacting standards.

Based on the 2.8i, the 'Tickford' featured an intercooled Japanese IHI turbocharger, which pushed the power output up by a massive 28 per cent, to 205 bhp. This was enough to give the car a zero to 60 mph time of around 6$\frac{1}{2}$ seconds! Nor was torque lacking, with a substantial 260 lb.ft. available, at the comparatively low engine speed of 3,500 rpm (standard 2.8is produced 152 lb.ft at just over 4,000 rpm).

Other running gear changes compared with the standard car included the fitting of AFT digital electronic ignition, improved gearbox lubrication, the use of a limited slip differential, rear disc brakes, 'A' frame rear axle location, and so on.

The bodywork was strikingly different, with glass fibre reinforced panels which helped to reduce front-end lift considerably – very useful, in view of the car's top speed potential of around 140 mph!

The inside story was also vastly different from that of the standard car, with walnut/leather facia and leather trim; Wilton carpets and a full leather interior were optional. Electrically operated windows and an automatic burglar alarm system were included in the specification.

This luxury Capri cost just under £15,000 at the end of 1982, making it a pretty exclusive vehicle. The Tickford Capris will remain exclusive, as only around 100 examples were sold altogether.

Updates

1982 was another good year for the Capri. Helped by the range revisions in 1981, the car led sales for sporting coupés in Britain, taking 1$\frac{1}{4}$ per cent of the total car market. However, Ford regularly update their models, and in January 1983 the 2.8i received a five-speed 'overdrive' gearbox (giving better fuel economy and more relaxed cruising), followed a little later by the two-litre Capris.

In the same month, another special edition Capri was introduced – the Cabaret II. This was similar to the earlier Cabaret, and based on the L model, in 1.6 or 2.0 litre form. It featured Recaro reclining seats with head restraints, revised interior trim, a centre armrest, a stereo system with electric aerial, opening rear side windows, tinted glass, a locking fuel cap, a 'torch' key, and 185/70 tyres.

Prices were slightly higher than for the earlier model (of course!), at £5,250 for the 1.6, and £5,550 for the two-litre.

Range streamlined

As the production life of the Capri continued, the range was 'rationalised', and, in March 1983, the long standing L, GL and Ghia versions were discontinued. The streamlined range now consisted of the 1.6LS, the 2.0S and the 2.8i. The LS now boasted a sun roof, uprated suspension (as on 'S' models), tailgate wash/wipe system, remote control driver's door mirror, improved seats and new trim. However it was still fitted with the four-speed gearbox.

The S did now benefit from the Sierra type five-speed gearbox, and it too had a sun roof and new trim, similar to that in the 2.8i, incorporating Escort XR3i sports seats. It also had S.V.E. type suspension, and opening rear side windows.

The 2.8i continued unchanged, retaining its Granada originated five-speed 'Hummer' gearbox and 3.09:1 final drive ratio, as used in the earlier three-litre cars. Inclusive prices for the 2.8i were now £8,228 (with 'normal' metallic paintwork) or £8,306, with a two-tone finish.

From September, 1983, electronic stereo systems were fitted to all Capris, and Ford 'formally' put the Tickford Capri on sale.

Laser arrives

The Laser Capris were introduced, as special edition models, in June, 1984, and either 1.6 or 2.0 litre versions were available, costing £5,990 and £6,371, respectively. The new Capris were, according to Ford, designed to fill the gap between the existing LS and S models. They featured colour-coded frontal treatment (grilles,

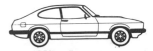

headlamp surrounds and mirrors), a remote control driver's door mirror, alloy wheels (four spoke variety) with 185/70 tyres, new cloth upholstery, a leather gear lever knob, comprehensive instrumentation, and a four-speaker stereo system, complete with electrically operated aerial.

The Lasers were significant models for, from October, 1984, when another 'range simplification' took place, they were to become the sole surviving production representatives of the Capri name, apart from a new 2.8 Injection Special . . .

Injection special

The new edition of the 2.8i boasted a number of luxury safety and performance extras, including leather interior trim panels, rear seat belts, a (Salisbury) limited slip differential (previously available to special order), and seven-inch RS spoked alloy wheels. For £9,500, the car was not cheap, but it did represent a lot of motor car for the money. Ford now offered a six year anti-corrosion warranty on the new 2.8i, and on the Laser models.

Changes were also made to the 'ultimate' Capri – the Tickford – in the autumn of 1984, with, for example, alterations to the ignition and cooling systems. These went hand in hand with a price increase, taking the cost of a Tickford to £15,999 (an increase of six per cent). Production of this Capri 'supercar' was then running at three cars per week.

The final years of production

Inevitably when a car has been in production for as many years as the Capri had been, by late 1984, there was continuous speculation regarding when production would be finished, once and for all. For even at that stage, the car, with its 'traditional' grand touring image, was regarded as somehow old fashioned, in the midst of all the new, aerodynamic (and often ugly), front wheel drive sports hatchbacks which were appearing at the time.

However, the car remained popular with the public, especially in the U.K., and production continued. All the same, left-hand drive versions were discontinued in November, 1984, the Europeans apparently preferring the more 'up to date' designs on offer. The Cologne Ford plant continued to build the right-hand drive Capris demanded by the more conservative British, although, in view of the relatively low volume of production, the inevitability of an end to the Capri was looming. Ford had, however, assured the future of the model for at least another year when, at the Birmingham Motor Show, in October, they had announced that production was to continue through 1985.

Still successful

Despite the spectre of an eventual end to production, the Capri was still returning excellent results in the world of motor sport. In June, 1985, a production 2.8i racing Capri finished first in the Snetterton 24-hour race, with another three Capris in the top five. It was also announced that the Capri had beaten all comers to win the BTRDA Rally Championship.

During 1986, sports success continued, largely in the hands of private entrants. Three 2.8is finished in the top four of the Snetterton 24-hour race, and a privately entered Capri came 32nd in the Lombard RAC Rally.

Revised Tickford

Early in 1986, the decision was taken by Ford to keep the Capri in production for another year. In recognition of Ford's decision to carry on building the car, Tickford revised their Capri. A major improvement was the fitting of a new integrated remote control central locking system, to protect this sophisticated vehicle, which now cost £17,220. Other revisions included a redesigned facia, the use of pearlescent paintwork and new badging.

Capri power

From June, 1986, the Ford-approved Turbo Technics Capri became available through Ford dealers. With the 2.8i as the base vehicle, Turbo Technics turned the car into a 200 bhp flyer.

They fitted the 2.8 litre engine with an intercooled Garrett turbocharger and associated manifolding. In addition, to handle the extra power, uprated suspension bushes and brake pads were also installed. The complete conversion cost was £1,604, and this made the car an extremely potent machine, with a top speed of around 143 mph available.

The last Capri

By December, 1986, though, the very last production Capri had been built, at the end of a run of !,038 special edition Capri '280' models, announced in the U.K. in March, 1987.

The Capri 280, costing £11,999, was, of course, a very special Capri, with a number of attractive features. These included 'Brooklands Green' metallic paintwork, Raven (Connolly)

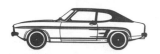

leather upholstery, with leather-trimmed steering wheel and gear lever knob, Recaro front seats, and 50 series low profile tyres on alloy wheels. The 280 had the same power unit, five speed gearbox and limited slip differential as the 'standard' 2.8i injection models.

For an extra £1,604, including VAT, customers could specify the Turbo Technics conversion, which of course pushed the top speed up to well over 140 miles per hour, and brought the acceleration time to 60 mph down to 6½ seconds!

Capri lives on

So ended the production story of this 'evergreen' coupé (as Ford described the Capri), with the car bearing the chassis number GG11896J having the honour of being the very last Capri to be built by Ford. After, 1,886,647 Capris, produced during eighteen years, the 'Car you always promised yourself' was no longer available.

However, the Capri's place in motoring history is assured. It is unusual for a relatively new car to assume 'classic' status even before production ends, but that is exactly what has happened in the case of the Capri. It is certain that enthusiasts will ensure that it lives on for many years to come.

H1. ▲ The 1968 Capri – in this case a 1600, with the overhead valve cross-flow 'Kent' engine – was an attractive looking motor car. Its flowing lines and sporty styling attracted buyers in large numbers.

H2.◄ Even at the rear, the lines blended well. The first Capris featured inset Escort-like lamp units, forming part of the rear panel.

H3.►The rear compartment looked inviting, and in fact the back seat was not uncomfortable. However, lack of head and leg room meant that rear seat passengers were rather cramped, and often felt claustrophobic!

H4.►The luggage compartment was quite accommodating for a sporty car, although the rather high rear sill and limited bootlid aperture depth made loading and unloading a little awkward.

H5.◄ The facia featured logically placed instruments and rocker type switchgear, with the 'eyeball' vents for the Aeroflow system situated at either end of the dashboard. This is a 1968 GT XLR Capri, with extra instrumentation and fittings.

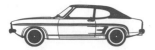

H6. ▲ This is a typical GT Capri, dating from 1969 and featuring attractive 'Rostyle' wheels. This vehicle shown is a V4 powered two-litre GT; the 1600 looked similar, apart from the badging.

H7. ◄ Spot the 'power bulge'! The three-litre Mark I Capris, like this 1969 example, featured bonnets with a subtle bulge, indicating that the car had V6 Essex power!

H8. ▼ The RS2600 is a rare and desirable Capri; this is a 1972 model. The front quarter bumpers (fitted from October 1971) and four spoke RS wheels show that the car is something special . . .

H9.► ...and this is confirmed by a look under the bonnet, which reveals a 2.6 litre, fuel-injected V6 engine, pushing out 150 bhp.

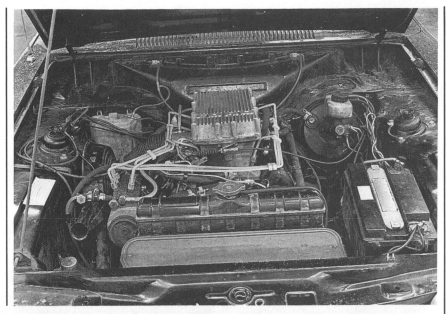

H10.▼ The autumn of 1972 saw the introduction of the 'Facelift' Capris. The same basic styling was applied, but with subtle updating; for example all Capris now had the 'power bulge' bonnet, a new grille, and front indicators set into the bumper. The suspension and running gear were also revised. The three-litre GXL versions, like this one, had four halogen headlights.

H11.◄ The overhead camshaft, Pinto based 1.6 litre engine replaced the 1600 cc Kent cross-flow engine, for the Facelift models. This fitted neatly into the Capri engine bay. This car is a 1973 model 1600XL, featuring the rectangular style headlights fitted to all but the three-litre 'Facelift' Capris.

29

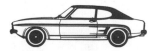

H12.►*The facias altered too, for 1973 versions, as shown by this 3000GXL. A two-spoke steering wheel replaced the earlier three-spoke variety, and the dashboard style was generally updated.*

H13. ▲*The 1974 model RS3100, produced at Halewood, was identifiable by the prominently lipped rear spoiler, plus a small airdam below the front panel. Four-spoke RS wheels were fitted to this powerful (148 bhp) model.*

H14.◄*This head-on view of the RS 3100 shows the airdam, and the front quarter bumpers, which gave away the fact that this was no ordinary Capri.*

H15. ►The smoother, sleeker Capri II (this is a two-litre GT example) arrived in February 1974. The new bodywork lost some of the detail curves of the Mark I cars, and gained square headlights, plus a new grille. Even more important, from a buyer's point of view, was that the new Capri featured . . .

H16. ► . . . a lifting tailgate, or hatchback. This, in conjunction with folding rear seats, made the Capri a much more versatile vehicle.

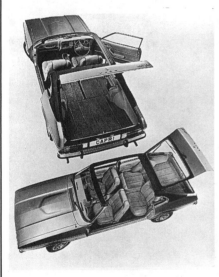

H17. ▲ These cut-away views of a Ghia version of the new Capri show some of the permutations of passenger/luggage carrying capacity available on Ghia/GT models. With a split folding rear seat backrest, there was a choice of having all the seats in use, or both rear seat backrest sections folded forward (giving a long, flat load platform), or just one backrest section folded, allowing the carriage of long items as well as one rear seat passenger.

H18. ►The accommodation within Ghia models was quite plush, as befits a top of the range model. The attractive seat coverings, 'wall to wall' carpeting and many standard fittings usually found only as extras blended well within Ford's 'luxury' Capri.

H19.►This shot of the load area in a 1974 XL shows that long and fairly wide items could be carried within the deceptively large bodywork of a Capri II. There were few sporting cars in the mid 1970s which could swallow so much luggage.

H20.►The 'Midnight' black Capri S, announced at the Geneva Motor Show in March, 1975, was the first of the 'S' models. It featured black paintwork with gold coachlining, and attractive alloy wheels.

H21.▼ March 1978 saw the introduction of the 'Capri III', with its aerodynamic grille and round headlights, plus black bumpers and trim. This Capri 'S' shows the new frontal treatment, and the stylish alloy wheels used on this model.

H22. ►The rear view of the new three-litre Capri S showed off the tailgate mounted spoiler, 'Lego brick' type rear lamp units, and wrap-around rear bumpers. Note the twin exhaust tailpipes, mounted on opposite sides of the car to relieve the gases from each cylinder bank of the lusty V6 engine.

H23. ◄The underbonnet layouts were similar to those of earlier Capris. This is a 1978 2.0 litre S, with its overhead camshaft Pinto engine sitting well back in the large engine bay. Access was very good for maintenance.

H24. ▼ Towards the late 1970s and early 1980s the Capri became available in several 'Special Editions', based around existing models but with various extra features to make them stand out from the crowd. This is the stylish 'Calypso' of 1981.

H25. ►The interior styling of the limited edition cars was normally very attractive; this is the Calypso.

H26. ▼ Of course for a real head-turner there was always the exclusive Aston Martin Tickford. Based around the 2.8i, the Tickford Capri was a totally rebuilt vehicle. Extensive bodywork modifications were part of the package. These included front and rear airdams and a rear spoiler, plus side skirts and revised grille.

H27.◄ The car was just as smooth from the rear, with full width 'rear lamp' panel giving the car a wider look. The flush-fitting wheel caps continued the image.

H28. ◄ *Luxury! The leather trim and polished walnut wood cappings summed up the interior of the Tickford cars. They were specifically aimed at those who liked the basic style of the Capri, but who also required extra in terms of power, fittings and equipment.*

H29. ◄ *Under the bonnet of the Tickford cars was the 2.8 litre V6 engine, to which were linked an IHI turbocharger, Bosch K-Jetronic fuel injection and a digital ignition system. Power was a hefty 205 bhp!*

H30. ▼ *Another 'Special Edition' Capri, the Laser, in 1.6 and 2.0 litre form, was announced in the summer of 1984. By the autumn of the same year, the Laser and 2.8i Capris were the only production models surviving!*

H31. ▲ To many people, the 2.8i Capri is the model that they would most like to own. When introduced at the Geneva Motor show in March, 1981, it was the fastest and most powerful European production Ford. By the time this 1985 model had been built, a five-speed gearbox and a limited slip differential had become standard fittings.

H32. ► The 1987 model Capri 280 was the final, final Capri. With its 2.8 litre, fuel-injected engine, the 280 retained the basic shape and sporting image which had made the Capri so popular from its introduction in 1968. Few cars – especially 'sports' models – enjoy a production life of some 18 years!

H33. ► The 280 featured sports front seats and leather trim, to finish an interior designed to complement the unique 'Brooklands Green' exterior paintwork. It was fitting that the last Capri should be a rather special vehicle.

Capris for the United States

I have included notes on the 'Federal' Capris, built for the United States market, in the main 'Heritage' chapter, putting the cars into context in the overall Capri story. However, it is interesting to look specifically at the development of the U.S.A. specification Capris, throughout their six years on sale.

What follows is a brief resumé of the history of these cars, based on notes kindly provided by Capri enthusiast Paul Barrow, of California. Paul was President and Newsletter Editor of the California Club for many years, during which time he built up a substantial library of Capri information, and he became extremely knowledgeable about the cars.

The Mercury Capri, 1971 to 1977

Ford Capris of 1971 model year were imported to the United States and sold through Lincoln-Mercury dealers. The first units arrived in late 1970, and in place of the "FORD" logo on the hood and trunk (bonnet and boot) lids, "CAPRI" was spelt out, in block letters across the hood, and in script at the right hand edge of the trunk.

All U.S.A. specification Capris on sale between 1971 and 1977 had four round headlights. Early cars used only the 1600 cc cross-flow engine, because it was already "legalised" for sale in the 'States, having been used before in the Cortina. This engine, allied to the standard four-speed gearbox, was installed in a German body, which of course was already 'set up' for left-hand drive.

In late 1971, the overhead camshaft, four-cylinder 2000 cc 'Pinto' engine was made available. During 1972, the 1600 cc power unit was dropped, and the 2600 cc V6 power unit became an option; extra instrumentation was installed in cars so equipped. Automatic transmission was also available.

Notable changes

During 1973, marked changes were made to the specifications, starting with the exterior bodywork. The front bumper was extended forward by about three inches, with a plastic spacer inserted between the bodywork and the bumper. The bumper also incorporated a pipe-like structure, inside it, for extra strength. Both front and rear bumpers had heftier bumperguards (over-riders) fitted. The new models were also identifiable from the front by the new 'eggcrate' style grille, compared with the horizontally barred type previously used.

The tail light units were enlarged, and incorporated back-up (reversing) lights.

Inside the cars, the dashboards were updated, with larger instruments, and a new steering wheel.

Other changes to occur during 1973 included the replacement of the 2000 cc engine with an in-line 2300 cc unit, and the deletion of rear axle locating links; an anti-sway (anti-roll) bar was added.

In 1974, both front and rear bumpers were replaced by plastic-covered, body coloured units, and the 2600 cc engine was enlarged to 2800 cc. Many of the V6 engine components were interchangeable, unlike those of the two in-line four-cylinder units.

Capri II

No imports were made for 1975,

but 'leftover' 1974 models continued to be sold. However, in 1976 Ford introduced the new Mercury Capri II, sporting a hatchback instead of a trunk (boot), and with much more glass area.

The 2300 cc and 2800 cc engines continued, although 'smog' equipment affected performance, due to far stricter laws. The dashboard and interior remained basically the same, with various consoles and trim levels, depending on the model.

The hatchback made the car more practical, with the rear seatback folding down to give extra luggage room; the Ghia models featured a split folding backrest.

The suspension remained as for 1973 models, while the large body-coloured bumpers were carried over from 1974 Capris. While the Capri II looked much sleeker, it was found that the original Capri actually had a better aerodynamic coefficient of drag.

Variety

While the early Capris were only available in two forms – with four-cylinder, in-line engine, or V6 power, with corresponding trim and instrumentation levels – the Capri II gave far more choice.

Models available included the 'standard' Capri II, Capri II Ghia (luxury version), the 'Shadow', the 'Black Cat', or 'S' model, the 'White Cat' or 'Ghost Cat', and the 'Rally Cat'.

The 'Shadow' featured rear window louvers (louvres)/shade and tape stripes. The 'Black Cat' or 'S' model was a special edition in black, with black trim and gold tape stripes, the black and gold theme continuing to the wheels and interior. The 'White Cat' or 'Ghost Cat' was white with black trim, gold tape stripes, plus black and gold wheels and interior. The 'Rally Cat' was a sport version,

with added rear spoiler and lots of tape stripes. Mechanically speaking, all these models were practically identical.

Modified Capri

An aftermarket, modified version of the Capri was available at the dealership, known as the 'Chastain Capri', and based on the white 'S' model. Roger Chastain, maker of the rear window louvers (louvres)/shade, came up with a body panel kit, consisting of riveted-on fender blisters (mudguard extensions), airdam and spoiler. Added to this was the window louver (louvre) kit, stripes, and wide, wire-look aluminium wheels, with fat, white-lettered tyres.

Originally, Ford's 'S' model and the Chastain Capris were to feature sporting suspension parts – i.e. stiffer springs, lowered one to two inches, thicker anti-sway (anti-roll) bars, and so on.

However, Ford/Lincoln/Mercury shied away from such modifications, due to feared liabilities and/or possible owner complaints of harsh handling.

The final U.S.A. models

1977 was the last year that the Capri was imported into the U.S.A. The Roman numeral 'II' was dropped from the hatch logo, and a run of Capris was imported using stalk controls for the wipers, sprouting from the steering column, in place of the push-button type switches normally found on U.S.A. model Capris.

Stalk switched Capris are rare in the United States, although both 1976 and 1977 model cars can be seen with either stalk-type or regular style switches.

Paul adds . . . ''Ford has cited the Dollar vs. Mark exchange rate as the reason for stopping the Capri, although Capriphiles know in their hearts it was because the Capri II outsold and outran the current Mustang II.

Capri Club owners found the attitude of non-owners, typically some of the press and Ford Mustang/Chevy Camaro admirers, was to compare the Capri with the Chevrolet Vega – not very complimentary. We, though, thought of our cars as competition for the likes of the BMW 2002. Looking back, this was probably a large part of wishful thinking, although many a Vega owner was left wide-eyed in our dust.''

USA1. ▼ *Capris received an enthusiastic response in the United States, too. The first cars imported were fitted with the 1600 cross-flow engine, as used in the Cortinas of the time, and already 'legalised' for use in the U.S.A. Note the four headlights, repeater lamps, and 'C-A-P-R-I' lettering across the hood (bonnet).*

USA2. ►*The engine bay of this early U.S.A. specification 1600 differs from that of U.K. models, with extra (emission control) pipework, and the brake servo unit mounted on the left hand side of the bulkhead. Cars for the United States had a dual braking system, with separate circuits for the front and rear brakes.*

USA3. ▲ *The Mercury Capri from late 1971 featured a two-litre overhead camshaft engine. The external treatment of these cars was similar to that of the cross-flow models.*

USA4. ◄ *The front view of the U.S.A. specification Capri was striking, with the four round headlamps set in 'squared' surrounds, and with grille-mounted turn indicators. This is an overhead cam, two-litre model.*

USA5. ▲ An alternative to the two-litre engine, from late 1971, was a 2600 cc V6 power unit, as fitted to this 1972 car. The engine size was increased to 2800 cc in 1974.

USA6. ► A typical engine compartment of a V6 engined, U.S.A. Capri. Although obviously taking up more space than the in-line fours, the V6 engines still allowed reasonable access for maintenance.

USA7. ◄ The Lincoln Mercury Capri II models also displayed subtle, but nevertheless noticeable, styling changes, compared with their European counterparts. This is a 2.8 model. Differences from the European cars included the use of reinforced bumpers and additional lights (including side repeaters). Power was from a V6 2800 cc carburettor engine.

2 Buying

Which vehicle

If you are looking for a secondhand vehicle of any sort, it is helpful to have a good idea in your mind of the kind of car you are looking for. The same, of course, applies when contemplating buying a Capri.

There are several important factors to take into account, and these usually include, to start with, the amount of money you have to spend on the vehicle, and the amount of time and effort you intend to apply to it, having bought it. For example, you could set out with the intention of buying a complete wreck of an early Capri, with the express thought of stripping and rebuilding the car to 'as new' condition. On the other hand, you may prefer to buy a later car in roadworthy condition, with the intention of carrying out just 'running repairs', and gradually improving it while using the car for everyday transport.

Then again there are those cars which are bought in anticipation of them being put into use fairly quickly, but which in the event turn out to be major rebuild projects.

So it is good to be aware of how much money, time, effort and skill you are likely to have to expend on your chosen vehicle, before you actually buy it.

However, even before you get to this stage, you will need to know roughly which model you are going to aim for – whether this is to be an 'original' Mark I Capri, for example, or a late 'Injection' model.

If you have already read the 'Heritage' chapter in this book, you should now have a reasonable idea of the character and performance potential of each Capri model, and you will probably know whether you want a car strictly for family use, or whether a fast road vehicle is your aim. Fortunately one of the advantages of choosing the Capri range as a starting point is that there are so many different models, with widely differing characteristics, to choose from.

While on this subject, it is also worth considering very seriously the insurance costs of your car, even if it is going to be some time before it is restored and actually used. For insurance groupings vary from relatively low (Group 2) for the smallest engined cars, to Group 7 for the 2.8i, for example. For turbocharged or otherwise 'breathed on' motors, the groupings could be higher still! If you are a young driver, or pay high premiums anyway, this will obviously be important.

It may in any case be worth taking out an 'agreed value'

collector's car policy on older or rare models. Such policies normally specify the car's value, agreed between yourself and the insurance company (often subject to the report of an independent valuer or engineer), and may carry low premiums in return for a limit on the mileage covered each year. While these policies are fine if you use the car, say, just at weekends, or only for high days, holidays and old vehicle rallies, they may not be of much use if you intend to use your car for daily transport, and cover, say, 10,000 miles a year. Your best bet is to talk to a member of the British Insurance Brokers' Association for expert specific advice, when you know which model you are looking for.

Wreck or unmarked example?

Presumably, if you are reading this book, you are interested in carrying out at least some restoration work on the car you eventually buy. However, it is often easy to be led into believing that a restoration project will soon be accomplished, and that a total wreck can be transformed into a gleaming concours winner in a matter of weeks. Such hopes can

soon be dashed by a few horrific discoveries made when you start work on the vehicle – guess how I know?

Make no mistake, restoring a car from 'the ground up' is hard work. It is also, almost inevitably, expensive, at times very frustrating (especially when you cannot obtain a vital part, for example), and extremely time-consuming. As a general rule, make an estimate of the time and money you reckon you will need to complete a major rebuild, and the figures obtained can almost certainly be at least doubled.

There will also be times when you really wish you had never started the project, and, sadly, many people do give up halfway through, and often after much of the hard work has already been done.

Other serious problems can arise when rebuilding a total wreck, simply through lack of skills or facilities. For instance, for any structural bodywork repairs, welding is essential, not just desirable. Unless you know someone who is willing to do the work for you, or you are able to weld yourself, you may end up with terrific bills for structural restoration – often sufficient to drain funds originally put aside to complete the mechanical jobs, for example.

I don't wish to put anyone off, but it is a good idea to be aware of the potential problems before you start; that way, it is easier to overcome them!

Therefore, it is wise to take into account – and be honest about – your own affinity for d-i-y work, when viewing your would-be project vehicle. It may be more sensible (and cheaper in the long run) to spend a little more on a car in better basic condition, and carefully restore the paintwork and mechanical parts, for instance, than to take on a 'jigsaw puzzle', back to basics restoration.

There are sufficient Capris being restored these days to come across 'half done' cars, often at bargain prices. In many cases the owner will part with the car at less than cost price, just to see it go to a good home, although this doesn't always apply, of course.

Such cars usually give plenty of scope for work, but, if the basic structure has already been tackled properly, they can save a lot of your money and time.

If you are not sure what you are looking for, it pays to take someone with you who at least understands cars, and preferably who is also particularly at home with Fords. In any event two heads are better than one for spotting dodgy areas, and for balancing your own view of the vehicle. This applies equally to buying a wreck, a restored vehicle, or an original example.

Of course ''All that glistens is not gold'' is a saying which is especially true when applied to secondhand cars. You may find a Ford that positively glows from a distance, and which may be advertised as ''fully restored'', or ''much bodywork carried out'', etc. Unfortunately not everyone is honest, and what appears to be shiny bodywork in excellent condition just could be harbouring large areas of quickly disguised rust and old body filler. It therefore pays to treat everything the vendor says as possibly doubtful, at least until you have satisfied yourself. The old trick of running a magnet over any 'suspect' areas of bodywork still applies today; a magnet will stick to steel, but never to filler! Tapping the surface can also tell you a lot about what lies beneath the paintwork – a dull thud is a possible indication of the presence of glass fibre and filler, compared with the more hollow ring of sound metal, but this isn't a conclusive test, unless you are absolutely sure what filler sounds like!

It is much more difficult to tell if a car is a hastily prepared 'rogue' vehicle when the paintwork is new – at this stage it will look very much like the superbly restored car you think you are looking at! Far better, if possible, to look at a car several months after its restoration, when, if it has been a job done properly, it will still look in first class condition. If, on the other hand, the bodywork rectification has been hastily carried out, without proper attention to rust killing, and with areas quickly filled, you will find evidence of this, with rusty bubbles emerging, and with filler cracking in places due to weathering. Filler applied on top of rust soon lifts off again.

Is it sound?

If you are confident that you can tackle any aspect of bodywork repair, you may not be concerned so much if the floor, 'chassis' sections and suspension mountings are in imminent danger of collapse.

If, on the other hand, you are looking for a sound vehicle as a basis for a less 'in depth' restoration, you really need to be sure that these areas on your Ford are in good condition, and the most important aspect of inspecting the vehicle is therefore its underside. Whatever the type of Capri you are looking at, try to view the whole of the underbody of the car by putting it on ramps, and with the aid of a strong light; take a torch with you.

Whatever you do, NEVER crawl under a car supported only by a jack – it may collapse. ALWAYS use axle stands or ramps.

The following sections should be helpful when viewing any Capri, with the text highlighting specific checks for each model, as appropriate. However it is wise to bear in mind that each individual car is different, with its condition normally owing a great deal to

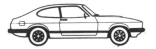

how well it has been cared for by previous owners. You may well, for example, find isolated areas of rust on a particular car, in places where you would not expect Capris, as a breed, to suffer! So it is vitally important that the *whole* of the vehicle is examined, and not just those areas specifically mentioned here.

Front suspension mountings

All Capris use MacPherson struts with integral front springs and shock absorber units. Their security in terms of attachment to the vehicle is vital for safety, for detachment from the mountings (not unheard of!) means no steering, no suspension and no brakes . . . !

So, when surveying any Capri, put the front suspension mountings high on your list of areas to examine closely.

Start by opening the bonnet, and look carefully at the tops of the inner wings. The upper mountings for the suspension legs are marked by the three securing bolts, spaced around the top of the strut. The surrounding metalwork should be absolutely sound, with no flaking, and without any rusty holes. Any weakness in this area can be very dangerous, especially if the reinforced suspension turret webs, below the wing tops, are also suspect, but more about these later.

On most cars more than a few years old, you will find that the original inner wing tops have rusted through from below, and have been reinforced by the addition of a plate attached to the top of the inner wing. This may look fine, but it is important that this plate should have been attached to the original metal by continuous welding, around the plate, and by no other method.

If the plate has simply been tack welded at intervals, or

brazed, or riveted, then further attention is necessary to do the job properly. It is also possible, although extremely difficult to check from a visual examination, that although the area has been repaired by welding a plate on top, the metal below could still be extremely rusty. The natural cavity between the new plate and the original metal is, of course, a breeding ground for rust, as are all such 'sandwiched' metal joints, and the surrounding metal can rust through again later. Therfore, look hard for evidence of rust eating through around the edges of the plate.

Many people mistakenly believe that simply welding a plate to the top of the inner wing cures all ills with regard to rusted MacPherson strut mountings. Unfortunately this is not the case. For when these cars were new, the weight of the vehicle, and the loads imposed by the suspension system, were spread along the inner wing structure by means of a stiff turret web, around and behind the suspension unit at each side of the vehicle.

As the cars age, moisture and salt accumulates around the tops and sides of these webs, eventually eating through the metal and dangerously weakening the structure, as, increasingly, the loads are taken by the upper mounting and inner wing area. This eventually bends or breaks under the strain, giving rise to the unusual spectacle of the suspension struts trying to escape upwards through the bonnet!

So, apart from checking that the upper mounting appears to be solid, from under the bonnet, look hard to establish that the inner wing plate is not distorting upwards, and then closely examine the under-wing area, around the suspension turret webs. Look particularly hard at the top, where, in bad cases, the inverted dish, into which the suspension leg fits, may be parting company from the web sides and the upper part of the

inner wing. Brush away accumulated mud for a better look, and suspect any car on which these areas appear to have been treated with a heavy, recent dose of underbody sealant – it could just be filling up rusty holes here!

Apart from obvious safety considerations, these areas are among the most vital to examine if you are buying the car with a view to immediate use. Rectification is quite tricky, and expensive if you are not doing the job yourself. It is also time-consuming, since to do the job properly, the front wings need to come off – this in turn can be expensive, since they are welded on and can often be destroyed in the process of removing them!

The good news is that if you are contemplating a major, 'off the road' rebuild anyway, the job will probably not put you off buying the car, which should be priced accordingly.

However, it should go without saying that a car with serious rust in this vital area will be a sure candidate for MoT failure, so think carefully before buying such a vehicle!

Apart from the MacPherson struts, the anti-roll bar attachments to the bodywork, and the track control arm mountings must all be secure. If any serious corrosion exists within twelve inches of such mountings, the car will fail the MoT test.

Rear suspension mountings

The strength of the attachment points for the rear springs and the shock absorbers are also vital, of course, and any serious corrosion within twelve inches of these will, again, prevent the car from obtaining a legitimate certificate of roadworthiness.

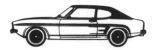

Look first at the areas around each end of the road springs, from below the car. The springs are attached to the 'chassis' by means of short hangers, and it is important that all metal in the vicinity of these hangers is sound. The rear ends are best observed from under the back of the car; the front mountings are best studied from in front of each rear wheel. When carrying out this check, pay careful attention to the channel sections of 'chassis' that sweep down each side, just inboard of each rear wheel; mud and salt from the road can accumulate here and eat into the main structure.

The rear shock absorber mountings also need to be strong, and of course the bodywork surrounding them, so pay careful attention to these areas too. All Capris employ telescopic type shock absorbers. The upper part of the top mounting is best observed from inside the luggage compartment, followed by a close survey of the underbody condition in this area, from below the vehicle. Of course it is easiest, for this and other underbody checks, to have the vehicle raised, on car ramps or axle stands.

The 'chassis'

Like most modern cars, the Capris were built on unitary construction principles, with no separate chassis as such. Nevertheless, the bodywork is reinforced by having hollow box section members running along and across the vehicle, giving strength and rigidity.

Assuming that the suspension mounting areas, already described, are sound, you should continue by looking along the length of each of these members, watching for corrosion damage, and also for evidence of twisting or other deformation,

perhaps the result of accident damage.

The underbody layouts of all the Capris are similar, and the following checks apply equally to all versions.

The danger areas to examine first are those in direct 'line of fire' from spray thrown up by the front wheels.

So, look first around each front bumper mounting, where the vertical panel meets the 'chassis' section at this point, just adjacent to the anti-roll bar attachments. Check too that the cross-member to which the anti-roll bar bolts is sound – this is often rusty along its lower edge, and rectification is tricky. Look at the main under-engine cross-member too, although this is normally less prone to serious rusting since it is very often soaked in oil, leaked from the engine!

At the rear end of the wheel arch, just inboard of and behind each front wheel, the vertical sections of the hollow, integral 'chassis' members here are particularly prone to rust damage. Also at serious risk are the rear sections of the inner wings, the jacking points (the jacking points and adjacent floor sections normally rust in unison on Capris!), and the whole of the front chassis extension channel sections, all immediately behind the wheels.

Make a very close scrutiny of the inner sill area, for moisture and mud soon enters holed channels, and rusting accelerates between adjacent sections.

Look at the continuation of the main longitudinal members, where they pass over and behind the rear axle, and be sure to examine BOTH sides of each member, as well as the bottom plate, for small holes on either side can spell a seriously weakened section. While you're under the car, look too at the main floor pan, especially in the vicinity of reinforcing beams. Again, rust in one section normally spreads quickly to

adjacent panels.

Make sure that any repairs to the floor or to 'chassis' members have been carried out only by continuous welding, around the entire perimeter of the repair section; anything less will be frowned on by an MoT examiner, and anyway may allow moisture in.

Even if all seems well from below the car, don't assume necessarily that the vehicle structure is sound. Always double check by closely examining the floor of the vehicle from above.

This often means disturbing carpets which may be very firmly attached; nevertheless the effort is well worthwhile, for many apparently sound cars have horrors lurking beneath their floor coverings! In particular, check around the seat and safety belt mountings, at the joints between the floor pan and the toeboard, and the seams between floor and inner sill panels, all favourite places for corrosion to take hold. In addition, check that all sections of floor directly above the integral channel sections of 'chassis' are sound.

It is a good idea to lift out the rear seat base, if the seller will allow this, and check the state of the floor beneath – you may find a great deal of rust here.

Look hard at the condition of both inner and outer sills, since large holes or areas of rust in either will obviously weaken the box section formed by the two panels. Small holes may not be so serious, but if several are evident, along the length of the sill, the chances are that it won't be long before gaping holes appear. New outer sill panels are available, however, and very cheaply, fortunately.

Finally, as far as the main structure on the Capri is concerned, look closely around the front door support pillars, and up into the corners between the bulkhead and the side panels, from below the dashboard, with the aid of your torch. Also examine the front edges of the

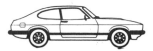

door pillar areas, from under the front wings. Serious rusting here means major repair work is needed, involving, again, removal of the front wings for access to the affected areas.

Bodywork

If all is well underneath the car, make a very thorough examination of the main bodywork. It is important to do this before moving on to examine the running gear of the vehicle, since the restoration of bodywork is, almost without exception, far more costly and time consuming than rebuilding mechanical components. If you aim to carry out a full rebuild, this may not be so important, but if you intend using your 'new' Ford for a running restoration, it pays to get one that is bodily intact!

Start by looking around the front wings. In particular, the areas surrounding the headlights are prone to rusting. The Capris are especially susceptible to holes appearing above the headlights, and around each side, due to the collection of mud and salt from the road in these areas. The upper sections at the rear of the front wings, adjacent to the bulkhead, are also danger points. Mud from the road collects on the ledge just below the wing top, and holes eventually appear. In severe cases, the bulkhead will also rot through, leaving an open passageway for water to enter the vehicle, eventually causing rust in the door pillar and front floor pan!

Therefore, even if the wing looks sound, examine it from below with the aid of your torch, for evidence of bodged repairs. Many Capris have had these areas simply stuffed with filler, placed on top of the rust – such 'repairs' seldom last very long.

Normally, filled wings will be obvious but checking with a magnet will help, as will looking carefully along the surface of the wing with the light behind it; slightly less than perfect repairs will show up as ripples.

With the bonnet open, examine the edges of the wing tops. Where rusting is serious, the wing flanges will be separating from the engine bay side panel lip; this is difficult to disguise.

Finally, look down the rear edges of each front wing, where they meet the front edges of the doors. Water trapped behind the panel can rust the wing through here, especially towards the bottom, and corrosion here will usually be obvious.

The front apron panel, below and behind the front bumper, is another area to look at closely. Strangely, some cars have suffered badly in respect of rust here, while others seem to have survived intact – even early models. So, look carefully, in case your 'guinea pig' vehicle has rusted here. It is not unusual to find dents and scrapes in this lower panel, from careless parking, for example, and it can often give a clue as to how well the car has been cared for. If the car you are looking at has had a front airdam fitted, try to check behind it – on early cars in particular, it could be hiding a damaged apron.

The bonnets are all prone to rusting along the front edge, and the extent of this is best gauged with the lid open. On some cars, there are gaping holes all along the inner lip, and it won't be long, in such cases, before the rust eats its way through to the outer panel. If the bonnet is stiff to open, or flexes from the rear edge, look around the hinge brackets, where they bolt onto the bonnet panel. Sometimes rust weakens the metal here, or, in some cases, lack of lubrication of the bonnet hinges means that the bonnet lid actually pivots by flexing, instead of opening by its hinges!

The windscreen pillars should be looked at closely; these are vital for holding the roof up,

of course, and cars which have suffered from severe rusting in the area of the bulkhead and door pillars can also suffer from spreading rot; this travels up the windscreen pillars and can almost sever them. Shoddy repairs in this area should be apparent; look for evidence of filler flaking away. Proper rectification involves welding, after removal of the windscreen.

Capri doors can be found to be rusty in several areas. First, open them wide and look around the hinge area; also check to see if the hinge pins are worn (a straightforward replacement job) by lifting the door up and down by its rear edge; if the door moves more than just perceptibly, the pins are worn, with detrimental long-term effects on the door catch, as well as increasing difficulty in shutting the door. Since the Capri doors are very large, and comparatively heavy, even fairly late cars can be found to be suffering from this problem, especially where the hinge pins have never been lubricated.

The lower door edges should be checked carefully, for water collects here and eventually rusts right through the door skin, from the inside.

Other suspect areas include the bases of the window frames, especially in the corners. In severe cases, the top section of the door can actually break off. The bootlids (tailgates on hatchback models) can also corrode, with particular problems occurring along the lower edges. If the tailgate hits you on the head a few seconds after you have raised it, the gas support struts are weak, and need to be replaced!

The rear wheel arches can suffer badly from rust, and in many cases not only does the outer flange completely disappear, but the outer section of the rear wing can part company from the mudguard panel. Once this happens, water and mud are free to travel along

the inside edges of the wing and adjacent panels, with catastrophic results. Therefore this is a very important check, best made with the aid of your torch. Even then, it is difficult to see the full extent of any damage without removing the rear wheels. However, be particularly cautious if the outer wheel arch edge looks motheaten, or has obviously been heavily filled.

The lower sections of the rear wings, behind the wheels, also suffer from serious rusting, especially on Mark Is and IIs. In bad examples, the lower edges are completely missing.

I have already covered examination of the body sills in the 'Chassis' section, so I will simply say here that any holes spell problems, and that if there are more than just one or two small ones, the best course is to replace the sills with new items.

The state of the inside of the luggage compartment can be quite revealing about how a car has been looked after through the years. If the one you are looking at is clean and tidy, it bodes well. If, on the other hand, it is full of sand, dents and rust, the previous owners may not have looked after the car too well. Not conclusive evidence, it's true, but another pointer, at least.

Anyway, lift the mat or carpet, and the 'false' floor on Mark II and III models, and make sure that the lower bodywork sections and spare wheel well are not rusty or wet, especially in the corners. If they are, the boot lid seal may be leaking, or water may be entering from the rear wheel arches, due to the rust damage already described – this of course will lead to even more problems in the long term.

Paintwork

If the paintwork on your potential purchase is merely a little dull, especially on the roof, bonnet

and boot lid, which tend to catch the sun, it may be salvageable by the use of cutting compound, followed by a liquid haze remover, and finally a good quality car polish. However, if large areas of the bodywork are affected by rust, dents, or flaking paint, a respray is the only answer to get such a vehicle looking smart again. Again, this may not be a reason for not buying the car, depending on how much restoration work you intend to carry out, and of course the asking price.

Interior

The condition of the interior trim is probably more important than many people realise, when starting out on a restoration. The seat facings and panel coverings for early cars may be almost impossible to obtain now; worth considering if you are attempting to bring the car back to original specification. Of course, motor vehicle dismantlers can provide some items of trim, but with the first Capris dating back to 1968/9, such cars are becoming increasingly difficult to come by as a source of trim parts in a decent state.

So, if the door panels and seat coverings are in good condition, so much the better. Again, the state of a car's interior can tell you much about the way in which it has been looked after. If, as many are, it is ankle deep in rubbish, with tears in the upholstery and worn out panels hanging off the doors, the chances are that it has been neglected in other areas, too.

Of course, if you are not too concerned about originality, even very tatty seats can be rebuilt, and trim panels re-faced with material which may be close to, if not exactly like, the original. The same applies to headlinings and floor coverings. The original floor coverings on early cars may be

difficult to reproduce exactly, unless you are lucky enough to find another scrapped vehicle with a good interior. While on the subject of floor coverings, it is worth checking to see whether the carpets behind the front seats are dry. If damp, the carpet will rot and so, eventually, will the floor. The problem is usually due to hardened door seals, or, on models with a sun roof, to blocked roof drain channels.

The seats on early Capris were prone to collapsing, especially the driver's seat in well-used examples. These tended to drop at the rear first, and you will soon know if your potential buy is suffering from this problem – if you sit in the driving seat and feel you are sinking, the seat needs renovation! However, even this need not be disastrous. It is a relatively straightforward job to strip a seat, and, for example, quite possible to replace the early rubber diaphragm type seat base with the sprung type base from later Ford seats. This will give improved comfort and reliability in the future.

Power units – general checks

The engines used in Capris varied widely, according to the date of manufacture, model, and country of origin. However, there are a number of comments which apply in general to all types of engine fitted, regardless of configuration and capacity, so it is worth mentioning these before looking in more detail at the individual power units employed in the Capris.

Start by looking around the engine bay for evidence of oil and coolant leaks. There is no particular evidence of either being a general problem, but, on older cars in particular, the cooling system can accumulate debris, and the resulting continuous

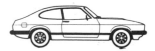

overheating can push anti-freeze mixture out of the overflow pipe. Therefore, with the engine cold, take off the cooling system filler cap, and look at the condition of the coolant. If it is murky, with muddy looking particles, it cannot do its job properly – it should be clean looking, and at least translucent, if not transparent!

If the walls of the engine compartment, as well as the power unit itself, are covered in fresh-looking engine oil, the chances are that the engine is blowing out oil fumes. The problem could be a failed crankshaft front oil seal, or excessive crankcase pressure, caused by piston 'blow-by', due to worn pistons, rings and cylinder walls. Oil and vapour can be forced out of the dipstick tube and breather, creating a real mess. Any engine showing these signs is well overdue for overhaul, no matter what excuse the seller may give!

If you can, try to hear the engine start from cold. It should fire immediately, if the engine is correctly tuned. If the weather is cold and/or wet, and the engine doesn't start, treating the high tension ignition leads to a spray of moisture-displacing fluid should get the engine running straight away. If not, it indicates the presence of a fault which will need sorting out before you can rely on the car.

The oil pressure should build up virtually instantaneously from a cold start, as indicated by the oil pressure light extinguishing as soon as the engine has started. It should also remain extinguished with the engine ticking over when hot. If an oil pressure gauge is fitted, this too should spring into life as soon as the engine fires, and the needle should not hover around the 'zero' mark with the engine hot and idling. If the engine on the car you are looking at shows reluctance to register pressure, wear will accelerate rapidly, and an early overhaul is advisable.

Specific engine types

Cross-flow engines

The cross-flow type, overhead valve units fitted to many Capris were similar to those used in the Escort and Cortina Mark II/III, with different sumps, to suit the varying position of the under-engine chassis cross-member; the Mark II Cortina had the deep portion of the sump at the front, the Mark III Cortina, Escort, and Capri had it at the rear.

The first signs of wear in these engines are fuming, increasing oil consumption, and low oil pressure. Look for evidence of fuming from the motor, particularly at speed or when under load, and, after a test run, take off the oil filler cap and watch for oil fumes emerging as the engine is revved gently. If serious fuming is evident, the chances are that the pistons, rings and cylinder bores are worn, or that one or more of the piston rings has broken. In this case, an engine stripdown or replacement will be required.

High mileage engines, or those which may have been thrashed and therefore are prematurely worn, will start to show their condition by fuming from the engine breather when hot. This occurs particularly under load, when blue (burnt oil) smoke may also be emitted from the exhaust. This smoke will be especially obvious after a long downhill section with the car on 'over-run' – when the car accelerates at the bottom of the hill, appreciable smoke means that the pistons, rings and cylinder bores are seriously worn.

The timing chains have a tendency to rattle after high mileages. This is due to wear on the chain, and on both camshaft and crankshaft sprockets. If the car you are considering buying exhibits this rattle, it is best to think in terms of replacing the

chain, both sprockets and the chain tensioner, for a complete cure.

The cross-flow engines all have five-bearing crankshafts, and there are no particular problems with crankshaft or bearing wear. However, failure of the oil pressure light to go out at speeds below around 25 mph in top gear (or an oil pressure reading consistently below 25-30 psi when hot, at normal cruising speeds) indicates wear in the oil pump (this is quite common) or crankshaft and/or bearings. Rectification of suspected pump problems involves checking first that the oil pressure sender and lamp are operating correctly – if so, remove the oil pump and check the gears for wear. If outside tolerances, a new pump should be fitted and the pressure re-tested. The pump, fortunately, bolts to the outside of the engine, and is fairly easy to change.

Another serious problem to watch for on the cross-flow engines is premature break-up of the cam followers (tappets). The faces of the cam followers wear thin, and can eventually split in two, causing a 'clack clack' noise from the engine. This may start quietly, and be intermittent to begin with. However, the intensity and frequency of the noise will increase as the trouble worsens. An engine with this condition should be attended to immediately, for if the car is driven any appreciable distance with one or more cam followers broken, the camshaft will be quickly ruined. Unfortunately rectification is not straightforward. The engine must come out of the vehicle and be inverted, and the camshaft removed, to enable the stepped cam followers to be extracted from their bores in the cylinder block. They should all be replaced as a matter of course, preferably along with the camshaft. Unless the engine has been taken out of service as soon as the noise started, the chances are that the surface of the shaft

will have been damaged anyway.

Therefore, beware the seller who advises you that the car is suffering from a 'wide valve clearance' that only makes itself heard occasionally – the chances are that the culprit is a broken cam follower, with all that it entails. A wide valve clearance in any case will be audible all the time, not just intermittently.

Overhead cam engines

Capris with the 'Pinto' overhead camshaft engines should be checked for wear in the same way as the cross-flow units, and in general, display similar symptoms when worn. In particular, though, they do suffer from heavy camshaft and follower wear, after high mileages. The problem is identifiable by a loud and continuous clatter from the top of the engine. The mileage at which the trouble starts varies according to the type of use to which the car has been put, and the frequency of oil changes. If the oil is not changed regularly, the narrow pipework supplying oil to the camshaft tends to become blocked, causing oil starvation and accelerated wear.

Rectification is not particularly easy, nor is it cheap, as inevitably it will involve the purchase of a new camshaft and followers.

Oil leaks from the valve cover are quite common.

V4 and V6 power units

The V4, two-litre Ford engine fitted in the Capri earned something of a reputation – not really warranted – for rough running and unreliability. In fact, despite its relatively complex design, with a counter-rotating balance shaft, the engine would run for many thousands of miles before major overhaul was required. Indeed I know of several such engines which have reached the 'magical' 100,000 mile mark without major attentions.

Nevertheless, look for oil leaks, especially from the valve covers, and listen for deep-throated tapping or rumbling, indicating bearing problems. In other respects, normal checks apply.

The British V6 'Essex' engines, built from many parts common to the V4 units, are also relatively long-lasting, given regular maintenance and oil changes, and providing that full use of the car's performance potential has not been made all the time. However, many three-litre cars have had a hard life, and roughness, smoking from the exhausts and metallic clatterings from within obviously spell trouble.

The 2.8 litre V6 Cologne engine has not been around for as long as the three-litre motor, but has proved to be smooth and reliable, generally. The fuel injection system too has not given any particular problems. However, a reluctance to start, lack of power and excessive smoke are, once again, indications of lack of maintenance, and/or very hard use in the past.

Transmission

The manual gearboxes fitted to all Capris were four-speed (or, late Mark IIIs, five-speed), all synchromesh units, although of varying design between the models.

On high mileage cars, whine, rumble or growling from the gearbox bearings can become evident, and, provided the synchromesh is not worn, repairs can be effected at fairly low cost, simply by changing the worn bearings, although of course this does necessitate a gearbox stripdown.

Check that the gear lever stays in the desired position – particularly when in top gear. If the lever jumps out of the selected position when under

load, until eventually the lever has to be held in position, this can be a real nuisance on long journeys! While this could just be due to a broken or weak detent or fork rod spring, it could equally be due to serious wear in the selector forks or in the gears. If this is the case, the chances are that the rest of the gearbox is also badly worn, and an exchange unit will probably be the most effective (and most economical) cure.

On 2.8i models, the layshaft bearings are the weakest point in the transmission, but, if the car is driven normally and not continuously operated 'flat out', their service life is acceptable.

The automatic gearboxes, whether the early Borg-Warner units, or the Ford 'Bordeaux' boxes fitted to the later cars, are very reliable, and give little trouble. If an automatic does misbehave, with, for example excessive slipping when accelerating, adjustment may cure the problem, but, if the car has been driven for some time in this condition, the chances are that irreparable damage has been done to the internal clutches, and a rebuild or replacement unit will be the only sensible answer. However, troubles are rare; one car that I know of has covered nearly 200,000 miles on its original Borg-Warner automatic gearbox, and is still going strong!

The clutches fitted to manual gearbox models are of conventional design, and are generally up to the job, with no specific problems. However, the three-litre cars can show rapid clutch wear, especially if the car is driven hard. On any model, to check for clutch slip, stop the car on a moderate slope and then drive away, accelerating quickly upwards through the gears. If the engine revs rise readily at each gearchange, and take several seconds to fall again, the chances are that the clutch is due for replacement.

The clutch cables can give trouble from time to time, and

difficult engagement of the gears, especially first and reverse, can often be attributed to a cable needing replacement.

Capri propeller shafts do not, unfortunately, have provision for the fitting of grease nipples. The 'sealed for life' universal joint bearings therefore have a limited lifespan, which is usually in the region of 35,000 to 40,000 miles. Fortunately the bearings fitted to the early cars are relatively easily replaced, since the joints are secured by circlips. Later types, however, have staked joints which are more difficult (and expensive) to replace.

The propeller shafts are in two sections on the larger engined models (but not USA specification cars), with a centre, rubber-insulated bearing.

Any of the bearings, when worn, give unpleasant vibrations through the vehicle, and replacement is expensive and time-consuming. If your test drive reveals vibrations which appear to come from directly below the floor, it will almost certainly be due to a propshaft problem.

The differential units fitted to Capris do not normally suffer from problems of noise, whine, or excessive wear until they have covered considerable distances – usually in excess of 60,000 miles or more. Fortunately the differential units on most Capris are easy to change, having withdrawn the half-shafts from the axle casing. The differential simply bolts into the casing, from the front. This is not the case on some models, including, for example, among others, the 2000 V4 and 3000 V6, on which the differential is removed from the rear of the integral, 'Salisbury' type axle unit; this is a rather more involved operation.

Capri rear axle hub bearings can wear, especially the outer race, giving rise to a ticking or droning noise which varies with road speed. This needs attention at once, for if the bearing should break up, the half-shaft, complete with inner race still attached, can

come out of the axle case; since the road wheel will come with it, this can be dangerous.

Replacing this bearing can be tricky, since the new one has to be pressed onto the shaft with a pressure in excess of 1,200 lbs; not really a d-i-y operation. So listen for ominous noises from the rear of the car, during your test drive.

Another, visual check to make is to look at the front of the axle and under the floor of the car, for signs of oil leakage from the differential pinion seal. A severe leak here can quickly empty the axle of oil, with obvious, disastrous effects on the gears and bearings within. Fortunately, changing the pinion seal is a job which can be tackled on a d-i-y basis.

Suspension

The suspension on all Capris comprises MacPherson struts at the front, with leaf springs at the rear.

The shock absorbers are usually the first items to wear, and the normal 'bounce' test should be applied, to gain an idea of how effective the units are. Push down hard on each corner of the car in turn, and let go. The body should rise slowly back to its original ride height. If one or more corners of the vehicle continue to bounce up and down, it indicates a worn damper.

It is also worth examining the exterior of each shock absorber. If the front struts appear to be wet with oil, especially around the point where the piston rod enters its operating cylinder, the integral shock absorber unit is leaking. Even if it is providing effective damping at the moment, which is unlikely, it will cause failure at the next MoT test. The same applies to the rear shock absorbers – if leaks are evident from the telescopic units, ride quality and handling will

deteriorate, and MoT failure is assured.

Your test drive will also tell you a great deal about the state of the shock absorbers – if the car is excessively bouncy, and leans hard on cornering, combined with a general 'uncertain' feel about the suspension, it needs new units. Fortunately, the rear ones are fairly straightforward to change. The integral shock absorbers incorporated into the front struts are a little more tricky to deal with, since the struts have to come off, and the coil springs must be compressed. Nevertheless, it is a job which can be tackled at home.

The front coil springs seldom give trouble, while the main problems experienced with the rear leaf springs are that they eventually tend to go 'flat', or they can crack.

If the car you are looking at appears to be very low at the rear – particularly if it has a tow bar fitted, the rear springs may be weakened, or even cracked, so look carefully. Older models, in particular, suffer from this trouble, and the suspension can 'bottom' when the car is heavily laden.

On any model, rattles and clonks heard when the car travels over rough surfaces can be due to a number of causes. Favourite culprits are loose MacPherson struts, worn or loose front anti-roll bar, steering/front suspension or rear spring/shock absorber bushes, or slack steering joints. Only a careful examination, by a process of elimination, will discover the source of the noise. Always check the state of the rubber bushes in the steering/suspension, since, when worn, they will give rise to ominous clonks, and a 'rubbery' feel to the steering.

Steering

The rack and pinion steering on all Capris should feel positive and

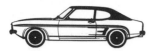

direct. Free play at the steering wheel rim should be minimal; any more than a little slack movement here will be due to wear – probably in the steering rack or ball joints.

Pin-pointing the exact source of wear is best accomplished by jacking up the front of the car and watching the relative movement of the steering links, while an assistant turns the steering wheel to and fro. However, the extent of wear present is easily assessed by a test drive. If the car tends to wander, and is easily deflected by road surface imperfections, the steering needs attention.

Finally, check that the rubber (bearing) bushes at the top of each MacPherson strut are sound.

Brakes

Only a thorough examination of the braking system, including detailed checks of the hydraulic cylinders and the brake pads/shoes, will reveal exactly how well maintained it has been. However, if serious defects are present, they may become evident during your test drive.

If excessively high brake pedal pressures are needed, even to make the car slow down, let alone stop, it is likely that some of the brake cylinders are seized, or partially seized. This problem often occurs on cars that have been standing, unused, for some time, so take care on any test drive.

On cars fitted with a servo unit, a heavier than normal pedal pressure could indicate failure of the servo itself. This can be confirmed by stopping the engine while your foot is on the brake pedal – the decreasing action of the servo as the vacuum disappears should be felt through the pedal, if the unit is working.

A tendency for the car to pull to one side under braking indicates that a hydraulic cylinder on the opposite side is not doing its job properly. Again, it is probably seized, or partially seized, or it could be leaking brake fluid. In any event, it needs IMMEDIATE investigation, for the brakes could cease to operate at any time.

A necessity for the brake pedal to be pumped before a 'firm' feel results shows the presence of air in the system, and almost certainly a loss of brake fluid. The fault, causing the air to enter and the fluid to escape, MUST be rectified before the car is driven further, as there is a real risk of sudden and complete brake loss.

It is well worthwhile making a detailed visual check of the state of the brake fluid pipes and hoses underneath the bonnet, and under the bodywork, looking for corrosion damage in particular. Of course, you may be lucky in finding a vehicle which has already had the brake pipes replaced. If they are of long-lasting copper, so much the better. Rusty steel pipes should obviously be replaced forthwith.

Wheels and tyres

Look around the car at the wheels and tyres; bent wheel rims and scuffed tyre side walls indicate a careless owner, and if the front wheels show signs of serious kinks around their rims, there is always the possibility that the steering system may have been bent as well, by a hefty clout or two.

Tyre tread depth is important, of course; ideally all the tyres should have plenty of 'meat' left on them, but just as important, wear should be even, across and around the tyre. Tyres worn on one side only, or in patches around the circumference, show that there are problems, with tracking, worn suspension or steering, or with the brakes.

It may sound obvious, but check that all the wheels and tyres match in size (I've come across cars where they don't!), and with regard to tyre type. They should be all radials or all cross-plies, ideally, but if a mixture has been fitted, the ONLY legal (and safe) combination is to have cross-plies on the front, and radials on the rear. This is acceptable, but then you really need two spare wheels.

On your test drive, make sure that the car feels smooth at all speeds. Any unevenness could be due to a damaged wheel or tyre. Any regular vibrations felt through the steering wheel could well be due to the front wheels being out of balance. Fords with MacPherson strut front suspension have always been very sensitive to precise wheel balancing, and it is best to have the wheels (and therefore the hubs and brake discs or drums) balanced ON the vehicle, for smoothest results.

General

Provided that you check all the bodywork and mechanical systems in the way described in this chapter, you should be able to avoid buying a rough vehicle, if you are looking for a car to use, and to keep for a long time. If, on the other hand, it is your intention to buy a cheap car for total restoration, the checks outlined here should at least give you a very good idea of exactly how much work you are letting yourself in for.

Whatever condition your prospective purchase is in, it is best to assume the worst about any doubtful aspect, until you can prove otherwise, and that is usually only after you have parted with your money. This applies particularly in the case of long-static non-runners, where the owner, for example, might

talk enthusiastically about the seized engine, clutch or brakes being 'easy to free off' . . . I've heard it all before!

Finally, if you are buying a running vehicle, take heed of what the instruments tell you, rather than what the seller might tell you. For example, if the temperature gauge shows 'hot', there is probably good reason for this – it may not be 'just the gauge at fault'. Another potential problem can be the oil pressure gauge which 'always runs near the zero mark' – again, it could just be the gauge, but it is more likely that the oil pressure is very low.

Of course, it's nice to think that you can trust everyone, but when buying a car, and laying out YOUR hard earned cash, it always pays to take the greatest care.

B1. ▼ *The state of the bodywork structure is vitally important on Capris, as with most vehicles built on unitary construction principles. At the rear of the car, check the main 'chassis' members, especially in the vicinity of the suspension mountings. Check too for evidence of rusty pipework – in particular brake pipes.*

B2. ◄ *Examine the 'chassis' members where they lift up over the rear axle, and look hard at the shock absorbers, to make sure that they are not leaking, and that the support rubbers are intact.*

B3. ▲ *Under the front of the car, make sure that the cross-member, immediately below the radiator, is sound, and that the anti-roll bar mountings (including the rubber bushes) are in good condition.*

B4. ◄ *The longitudinal 'chassis' sections, along each side of the car, together with the jacking points/outriggers, plus the inner and outer sills, call for particular attention. Rust in any of these panels needs to be dealt with as soon as possible.*

B5. ▲ *Capris often rust in the vicinity of their headlamps. This Mark I was quite badly holed between the headlamp and the front valance, although the bumper was hiding much of the rot. Look carefully in this area.*

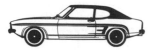

B6. ▲ Capris seem to be prone to accidental damage at all four corners. This generally tidy Mark I 'Facelift' 1600GT had a nasty dent on the nearside front corner, and this is not uncommon.

B7.◄ Another dented front wing, but this time from a Mark II two-litre 'S', owned by Chris Martin, and which we used as one of the project vehicles for the 'Bodywork' chapter of this book. This car showed the classic signs of rusty bubbles emerging from behind previous, hastily filled repairs. When we 'attacked' the leading edge of this front wing for the 'Bodywork' chapter, we found filler on the outside, on top of a layer of rust, behind which was road mud and salt – and very little sound metal. Mud often sits on top of the headlamp ledge, above the lamp unit, and causes rust to eat its way through adjacent panelwork, in all directions!

B8.◄ Look closely at the rear upper corners of the front wings, too, especially on early cars. This Mark I exhibits the danger signs – a few bubbles, and tiny holes, caused by mud sitting on the bodywork ledge below this point.

B9.◄ Mark II cars are similarly affected; the rust nearly always proves to be worse than it looks, as we discovered when we started prodding these patches, in preparation for repairs to be carried out.

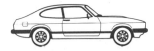

B10.► Minor rust in the wing tops and at the rear edges can be patched, but when corrosion damage is as severe as on the front wing on this Mark I 3000, the best answer is a new panel. This particular car is owned by Capri Owners' Club Chairman, John Hill, and features extensively in the 'major' bodywork surgery photographs, included in Chapter 3. This wing is shown being replaced in that chapter.

B11.► Further wing problems often show up when the bonnet is opened. Angry looking rust patches, or large areas of hastily-applied filler, indicate that the wing seams are well past their best. Check beneath the lip at each side of the engine bay, by hand (feel for holes) and by eye. If extensive rust is present, new sections need to be welded in.

B12.▼ Front airdams (spoilers) are often fitted for aerodynamic reasons, or simply to make the car look better. They can also hide rust, so check behind the panel, as far as possible, to ensure that the front valance has not been eaten away. The valance collects salty mud from the road, and is frequently found to be rusty.

B13.▲ The bonnet lid is another target area for rusting to occur, especially in the front corners, as on John Hill's car.

53

B14. ►If a bonnet shows rusty bubbles near the centre, as on this Mark I, it is almost certainly near the point of breaking out in large holes, all the way along the front . . .

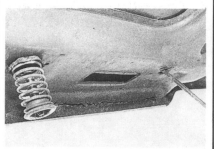

B15. ▲. . this situation can be confirmed by opening the bonnet and checking the leading edge, from behind. The same Mark I was suffering from rust damage all along the lip, due to moisture eating its way through the enclosed section of the bonnet frame.

B16. ►Always check the condition of the narrow metal cross-bar, just below the grille, and of the glass fibre Ford airdam, where fitted. This Mark II showed signs of surface rust on the cross-bar, requiring urgent attention, and cracks in the airdam – these are often found, since the panel is vulnerable to attack when parking, or on rough roads.

B17. ◄Mark I cars suffer from rust along the extreme rear edge of the bootlid, although this car was quite sound in this area. Check a prospective purchase for accidental damage such as the minor knock in the offside rear panel on this Capri. Missing or damaged sections of bright trim can be quite difficult to obtain for the earliest cars.

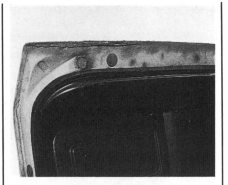

B20. ▲ *The tailgates too need checking – they can fill up with water, due to leaking window seals, and show signs of rust along the bottom edge.*

B21. ▲ *Lift the tailgate and examine the reverse side of the lower lip, to see how bad the rust is. This tailgate was flaking here, although the main part of the panel was quite solid.*

B18. ▲ *Look at the panelwork from all angles. This Mark I 'Facelift' was quite tidy, but close inspection revealed a fairly severe dent in the nearside rear wing, which could easily be missed from a casual inspection.*

B19. ► *The hatchback models can exhibit nasty rust in the vicinity of each tailgate hinge. Although the hinge mountings are normally sound, such damage as this needs rectification as soon as possible, to stop the spread of the rust to the main roof panel.*

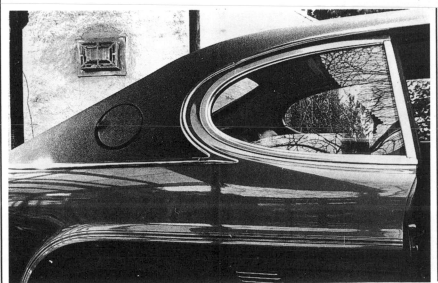

B22. ◄ *If the car you are looking at has a vinyl roof, like this Mark I, make sure that it is sound, and that the edges are all firmly stuck down. Major tears are almost impossible to rectify neatly.*

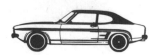

B23.► *The rear wheel arches require the closest of inspections. From a distance, a problem like this may appear to be just one of flaking paint. It may be, but always look hard at the arch, and feel behind it to see how much metal is intact.*

B24.▲ *The rear arch on the 'project' Mark II looked as if it might be reasonably solid, from a brief examination . . .*

B25.► *. . however, always look at the arch from below – there may be lengthy sections missing, as on our car. Check that the inner wheel arch hasn't rusted away, leaving a gap adjacent to the outer wing, through which mud and water can pass, to wreak further havoc in the lower sections of the rear bodywork. Rectification of such problems is fully covered in Chapter 3.*

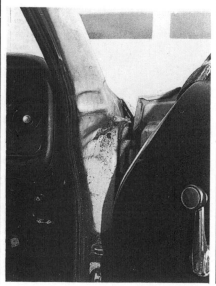

B26.◄ *On all models, open each door to its fullest extent, and check the pillars for rust damage. Some at least will usually be evident on most cars more than a few years old.*

B27.► *While the door is open, check for wear in the door hinge pins, by lifting the door up and down. Just perceptible movement is acceptable; any more, and the pins need to be replaced as soon as possible, or the door will not shut easily, and may cause further damage.*

B28. ▲ Always look in the luggage compartment, whichever model of Capri you are examining. The general condition can tell you a great deal about how the car has been looked after. On Mark I cars, lift the floor mats and examine the metalwork all around the boot. Look closely at the spare wheel (and tyre) and its compartment, and at the insides of the rear wings, for rust damage and signs of water leaks. This car was remarkably clean here.

B29. ▲ On hatchback versions, lift out the false floor and make a thorough examination of the area below. Always remove the spare wheel, and check its condition, as well as that of the floor of the vehicle. Although this Mark II looked clean and tidy from a brief inspection, we found that the spare wheel well contained water, mud and a fair amount of rust, all of which needed to be banished.

B30. ► As already mentioned, it is always a good idea to examine the spare wheel and tyre, since doubtful articles are usually consigned to the boot! This check is especially important on models, such as the 2.8i, with expensive alloy wheels.

B31. ◄ The condition of the interior should be carefully examined. Some trim items are virtually impossible to obtain for early cars, and restoring a rough interior to good condition can be time-consuming and expensive. This particular Mark I GT had a tidy, clean interior.

B32. ► The Mark III cars, like this smart 2.8i, are still relatively young. Therefore severe wear and tear of interior trim suggests either very hard use, or a careless owner. Bear this in mind when checking the rest of the car.

B33.►*Sagging seats – especially the driver's – are common features in Capris more than a few years old. This seat, in a Mark II, was stripped and rebuilt; the details are included in Chapter 5.*

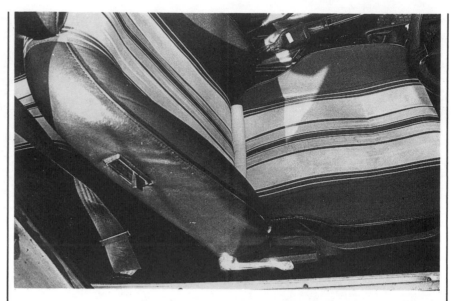

B34.◄*Check the seat fabrics very carefully for signs of tears or stains. Rectifications in either case can be tricky and expensive, so it is a cause for celebration if you find a car with a pristine interior, like this.*

B35.►*Examine the rear seats, too, and the state of the carpets throughout. A tatty carpet may be cheaper to replace than a worn seat, but it depends on the model, and on the extent of the damage.*

B36.◄*It is important to look at the power unit, and to watch (and listen to) it when running. Smoke emission, oil leaks or clatters from within all spell trouble. Negotiate a lower price, or find another car. This Mark I 'Facelift' 1600GT engine was in good condition, and fairly clean.*

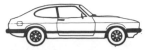

B37. ►Look at the engine, of whatever type, from the front, and from each side. Always check for oil or water leaks from the cylinder head gasket(s), and for oil leaks from the rocker/cam covers, especially on overhead camshaft engined models. Make sure that the exhaust manifolds are firmly attached, and are not cracked, if of the cast iron variety. This Mark I was tidy in every respect, under the bonnet – even the suspension mountings/inner wing tops were sound.

B38. ►Try to establish where engine oil is coming from, if looking at a car with a leak; it may be just a leaking gasket or seal which is quite easily fixed, but it is advisable to find out before you buy the car. This engine bay of our Mark II features again in Chapter 4, when being tidied up.

B39. ►The engine bay on the V6 engined cars is rather crowded, as typified by this 2.8i. Nevertheless normal checks apply. The fuel injection system is in fact generally quite reliable, but d-i-y overhaul is not recommended unless you are very keen!

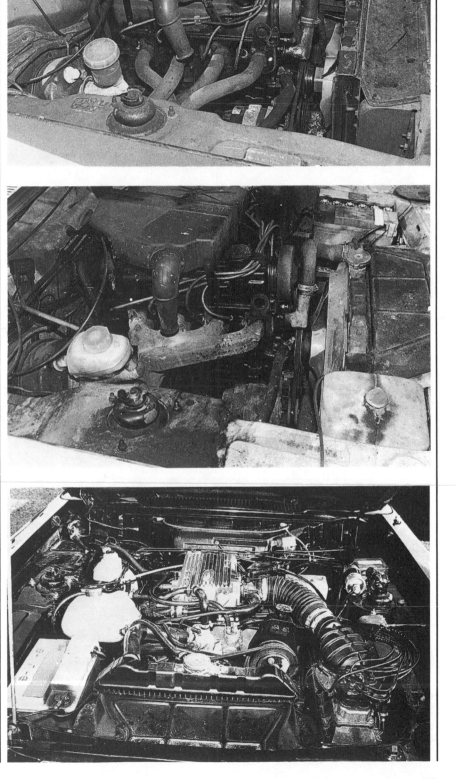

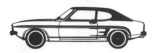

B40.►The steering and front suspension components require careful checking. Look for leaking shock absorbers, worn bushes and ball joints, uneven tyre wear and leaking or damaged steering rack gaiters.

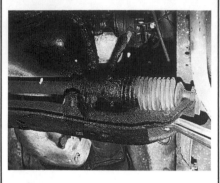

B41.▲ The oil on this steering rack gaiter was in fact running down from an engine oil leak, higher up. Such leaks need urgent attention.

B42.►Alloy wheels are very expensive to replace as are low profile tyres on faster models, so examine their condition carefully before parting with your cash. Poor condition will be obvious; look for pitting and scuffing of the wheel edges.

B43.◄'One careful owner . . . never raced or rallied . . .' If you are very enthusiastic you may prefer to buy a 'kit' of parts like this and to restore and assemble the car bit by bit. At least then you will know exactly what has gone into your Capri!

All of the problems displayed in the foregoing photographs were within the sensible boundaries of d-i-y- rectification. Details of how to overcome these, and other common Capri ailments, are described in the following chapters.

③ Bodywork

Introduction

The restoration of most 'modern' cars (in this context I am referring to post-war vehicles) hinges around the state of the bodywork. With very few exceptions, 'everyday' cars (as opposed to some luxury vehicles and limousines, etc.) of this era have been built on the 'chassisless' construction principle, where the car's bodywork is 'fully stressed', and has integral strengthening members, rather than having a separate backbone, or chassis. Therefore the vehicle's inherent strength, and ability to stay in one piece, is dependent on the major part of the body shell, and in particular its 'load-bearing' sections, being in good condition.

This applies to all Ford Capris, and should be borne in mind when looking for a vehicle to restore, taking into account your own facilities, abilities, and the size of your bank balance, as outlined in the 'Buying' chapter. If you are restoring a car with a view to keeping it long-term (as opposed to driving it just until the MoT runs out), it is essential to tackle the body repairs very carefully – particularly those which affect structural rigidity. For such repairs, welding is the

ONLY acceptable method of rectification, so you will need the necessary equipment (more about which later). Alternatively, you may prefer to prepare the car as far as possible yourself, leaving the welding operation to an expert. For example, very often, by removing trim, carpets, etc, you can save a great deal in labour costs, even if you cannot undertake the actual welding yourself.

Ways and means

The Capris covered by this book will be found to vary greatly in condition. Methods of restoration vary too, of course. What may seem 'sacrilege' to a perfectionist may be quite acceptable to someone trying to keep his car on the road at minimum cost. There are no definitive rules to cover this, unless you are seeking to win prizes in certain concours competitions where originality is the prime yardstick; in such cases, of course, nothing short of perfection, and with the car completely 'as original', will do. In other cases, departures from original specification may be considered in order – for example the use of anti-rust paint or wax on the underbody, or the hand-painting of a particular part

of the car. In the final analysis, the decision is yours. It is, after all, your car, and if you are happy with the end result, then this is the main concern. The only note of warning that I would sound in this connection is to say that, in general terms, the more departures from 'standard' which are made, particularly where the bodywork is concerned, the lower will be the vehicle's intrinsic value to enthusiasts. This problem takes on greater proportions as the car ages. Of course, if the value of the car in sheer monetary terms does not concern you, then this will obviously be of less importance.

To what extent you intend to restore a car will depend, largely, on what use you intend to put it to. For example, you may buy a car which is structurally sound, but which needs cosmetic surgery to 'tidy it up', for everyday use. On the other hand, you may have bought a completely rusted out wreck, and hope to restore it to 'concours' condition. In this chapter we cover jobs ranging from fairly simple 'patch-up' operations to full-scale bodywork rebuilding. So, whatever the state of your particular vehicle, and whether you are carrying out a 'running' restoration when time and cash permits, or an all-out rebuild, there is plenty of information to help you.

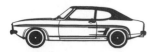

Before you start, though, you should form a plan of action. This is especially important where you may rely on the car as transport during the week, for example; whatever you do to it on Saturday and Sunday, you must make sure it's back together for Monday morning! So, don't try to be too ambitious; tackle only what you think you can handle in one go.

Another, vital, point, is NEVER to cut ALL the rusty metal out of a wreck, in one session – the car will almost certainly collapse. The metal may be rusty, but it might be all that's holding the thing together. Therefore, tackle one section at a time, preferably leaving one side of the vehicle intact so that you have patterns to work to.

Another, important point, for cars requiring total bodywork renovation, is that it is always best to tackle the major work first, before carrying out the 'cosmetic' jobs.

Whether you are carrying out minor 'touch-up' work only, or more serious, structural operations, time spent on the bodywork is time well spent – a car with a solid, attractive body shell looks better, feels better to drive around in, and is worth more!

Equipment

Basic bodywork restoration can be attempted with a very few basic tools, with the range of jobs extending as the number and variety of implements are added to.

A hammer, bolster and cold chisels, universal tin snips, a file and a range of spanners and screwdrivers are handy items to start with. An electric drill is also useful for any number of jobs, and, for patching non load-bearing panels, a blind riveting gun is helpful. It is worth pointing out here that it is

ESSENTIAL for all cutting tools and drill bits to be SHARP. Trying to cut or drill metal with blunt tools is inviting disaster – panels can be torn or dented, in some cases severely, by the use of worn out implements. There are also safety risks, with the possibility of perhaps a chisel skating across the surface of a panel and into your hand. So check the cutting/drilling edges of your tools before you start work, and have them sharpened, if necessary. It is also advisable, where possible, to support any panels being cut, using a panel-beating dolly or a heavy hammer behind the panel. Make sure that fingers are kept well clear of the action.

For bending and shaping metal panels, various tools can be used. For straightening bent bodywork, on or off the vehicle, it is worth investing in a small set of panel beating tools, such as those made by Sykes-Pickavant, who also make an excellent slide hammer type 'Panel Puller' for removing dents from inaccessible bodywork sections. If your vehicle is even half as dented as the ones restored for this book, such tools are invaluable. The company also make a wide range of other useful tools (including those in their 'Speedline' series) to help the d-i-y body rebuilder, ranging from metal benders and cutters, to welding clamps. The following Sykes-Pickavant items are particularly useful for d-i-y bodywork repair:

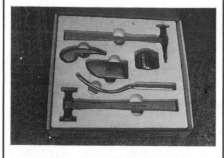

E1. ▲ This panel beating kit contains all the tools required for dealing with any dents likely to be encountered on your Capri.

E2. ▲ This hand-operated 'Edge Setter' is an invaluable tool for flush-fitting repair or replacement body panels. It lets a 'step' into the edge of one panel, so that the new section sits on the step and forms a flush surface, for a more professional finish.

E3. ▲ A bench or vice-mounted version of the edge setting tool is available, for dealing more easily with larger panels. The lower roller is adjustable, to allow for varying thicknesses of steel. Like the hand-held model, this handy tool will cope with mild steel of up to 18 gauge (1.2 mm thickness).

E4. ▲ *If you should need to fit a replacement door skin to an otherwise sound door frame on your Capri, this 'Door Skinner' will help to create a neat, sturdy finish. It features nylon pads which prevent damage to the door skin, while it is being tidily crimped to the frame.*

E5. ▲ *One of the most useful tools for general panel repair work is an adjustable body file. This Sykes-Pickavant model consists of a sturdy holder and a blade – several types are available to suit different surface materials – which can be adjusted in profile from convex to flat to concave, to suit varying bodywork curves. The tool is a great asset for quickly removing excess body filler, for example, to achieve the correct surface profile in readiness for final rubbing down. This particular tool has seen much service on one of the Capris featured in this book!*

It is always worth arming yourself with plenty of abrasive materials before you attempt any bodywork. Minimum requirements include a supply of steel wool and fine emery paper (for surface rust removal), and wet and dry paper in varying grades. Grades designated 80/100, 150, 240, 360/400, 600, 1000 and 1200 can all be used effectively for varying roles in cleaning up metal and in bodywork preparation. If you are going into restoration on a fairly large scale, it is well worth spending money on an electric grinder; invaluable for cleaning up rusted metal flanges, it is also ideal for smoothing off welds, where a level surface is required, and for a number of other jobs, including preparing doors for re-skinning, grinding through spot welds in inaccessible areas, etc. etc.

E6. ▲ *This electric grinder should last for many years, given a little care. For prolonged use, it is worth spending a little more to get a 'professional' or 'heavy duty' unit, like this one.*

For working underneath a car, where much of the corrosion damage occurs, a trolley jack and axle stands are the easiest means of getting and keeping (respectively) the vehicle airborne. The jack (of whatever type) should only be used to get the car off the ground, never for holding the vehicle up while you work on it; the stands are for that job!

E7. ▼ *This well-used Draper trolley jack has lifted many cars, and the inexpensive, secure axle stands alongside have worked equally hard in holding many a wreck airborne as it has gradually been 'sewn' back together!*

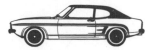

Welding

It is well worthwhile learning how to weld, even if the thought appears daunting to start with.

The many benefits of being able to weld a rusty vehicle yourself include 1) you don't have to pay anyone else to do the job, 2) you don't have to wait for someone else to do the work and 3) you will have the satisfaction that the job has been well done – by yourself!

So, how does one learn? Well, if you buy any kind of welding gear, comprehensive instructions are normally included with the set. Failing that, the supplier should be able to supply you with basic information at least.

You may also know a welder who is willing to instruct you, or a friend who is proficient in welding, who may be able to help. Make sure, though, that they really do know what they are talking about, particularly when it comes to safety. Far better, in my opinion, to learn by attending evening classes at a local college or school, where thorough instruction is given on safety and correct methods of working. Contact your local adult education centre for details of courses held near you.

Knowledge thus obtained can, of course, be backed up by reading, and there are many interesting books about welding to be found in your local library or bookshop, and even comprehensive videos on the subject. The theory complements the practical work, and vice versa.

Welding kits

Electric, or arc welding kits can be purchased very cheaply, and are ideal for work on heavy gauge metal, for instance as employed on 'chassis' sections below the car. The problem as far as work on outer panels is concerned is that most d-i-y welders are too fierce. It is therefore very easy to burn holes through the metal, and to cause distortion. You really need a machine which operates at 20 amps (or less) to weld body panelwork. There are adaptors available for larger capacity machines, to enable them to weld such metal successfully. The alternative is to use a carbon arc brazing attachment, which is fine for non-structural areas, but which cannot be used on 'structural' sections of the car body.

E8. ▲ A small arc welding set like this is inexpensive and can tackle all the 'structural' repairs necessary below the car. It's a bit fierce for outer panelwork, though..

Gas welding is more useful as far as general bodywork repairs are concerned, and there are a number of small gas kits available. Choose carefully, though, for some of the cheaper sets do not produce a flame which is hot enough for successful welding. Another problem, if you intend to do a lot of welding, is that the cylinders, being small, are exhausted fairly quickly, and can be expensive (or difficult) to exchange. For just occasional use, such disadvantages may not be so important.

For someone carrying out a full-scale restoration, a small oxy-acetylene welding kit, such as the well-known 'Portapak' is ideal. The gas bottles, although small in comparison with industrial bottles, hold enough gas for a weekend's welding, for example, and can be exchanged at BOC gas centres. The cylinders can in fact be exchanged for larger items, if required, on payment of the required extra rental. The welding kit is purchased by the user, while the cylinders have to be rented (on a seven year basis) from BOC.

The beauty of such a welding kit is that the gun is the same as used in the trade, and will accept the full range of nozzles, etc., to give maximum flexibility in use, to cope with materials of varying thicknesses, for example. In addition, the gun can be used for cutting out rusty metal, as well as for welding in new sections.

Slightly cheaper alternative systems are available these days, and it is worth shopping around, and talking to welding equipment suppliers and users, before you purchase.

E9. ▲ This Portapak set, purchased secondhand, has already saved 11 cars from the scrapyard! Spares are readily available and gas supplies are fairly easily obtained around the country.

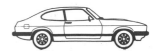

a reality, and these are now available to d-i-y enthusiasts.

As with most equipment, the level of sophistication obviously rises in line with the price ticket, when it comes to welding machines. A MIG welder such as the SIP 'Ideal' 120N or 150 – both designed for the rigours of industrial use – is the ultimate for d-i-y restorers.

E10.◄ This SIP Ideal 150 MIG welder is an excellent piece of equipment for any car restorer. The smaller 120N model will produce equally good results. It takes a little bit of getting used to after arc or gas welding, but the different technique is soon mastered, and then seems easier! A form of spot welding can also be achieved using the SIP machines. All aspects of the weld (wire speed, voltage selection, etc.) are easily controlled, to suit particular conditions and materials.

The revolution in welding today centres on MIG (standing for 'metal inert gas') welding. This employs a continuously fed wire, which is melted onto the workpiece within a shroud of inert gas (normally argon or carbon dioxide). The gun can be operated with one hand, and distortion to surrounding metalwork is minimal – far less than with gas or arc welding. A clean weld results, which needs no 'de-slagging', as with arc welding. In addition, the process is at least three times quicker than oxy-acetylene welding. Once the technique is mastered, MIG welding is excellent for restoration purposes (and, for many newer cars, built with special steels, it is in fact the only acceptable method).

There are a number of small, comparatively cheap MIG welders on the market today, all doing the same basic job. The current ranges of portable 'miniature' MIG welders produce first class results. Recent innovations have allowed 'gasless' MIG welders to become

E11.▲ These days the 'miniature' MIG machines have come into their own. SIP's Migmate Super gives performance formerly associated with larger machines, but in an easy to use, portable package.

With six power settings, trigger-controlled supply and all ancillaries needed for 'instant' welding, the machine is ideal for dealing with thin car body panels.

E12.◄ One of the most recent innovations into the field of d-i-y welding is that of 'gasless' MIG operation. SIP's Gasless 150 Migmate is a result of this new technology.

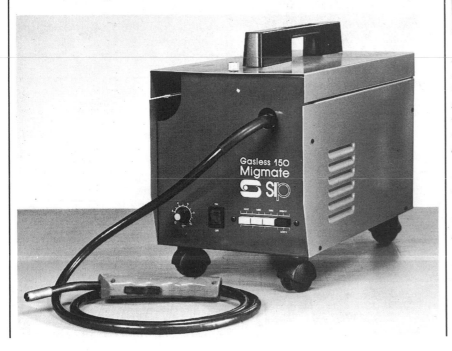

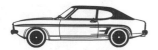

It is of course possible that you cannot afford to buy new equipment of the type described. Much good equipment can be purchased secondhand, but always take someone with you to make sure that it is safe, before you buy. Many welding centres can supply used welding gear at reasonable prices, so it is worth asking.

Spraying

Another aspect of bodywork restoration is applying the paint to the prepared bodyshell. If you are reluctant to have the car resprayed professionally, there is no reason why you cannot do an excellent job yourself. The choice of equipment is enormous. Cheap, electric sprayguns can produce excellent results, and, as an example, the author still uses a fourteen year old Wagner 'airless' gun for spraying, and is pleased with the results. Alternatively, there are many compressor type sprayguns on the market, with prices which vary enormously. Shop around, and ask the opinion of spraygun sellers AND users before you buy. For optimum performance, it is worth considering buying a

compressor with an air receiver tank, to supply a smooth supply of air which is free from pulsations, which can affect the finished result.

As with many aspects of car restoration, the quality of paint spraying varies not only with the sophistication of the equipment, but more often than not with the degree of determination and patience of the operator!

Whatever equipment you use, it needs to be kept scrupulously clean for good results.

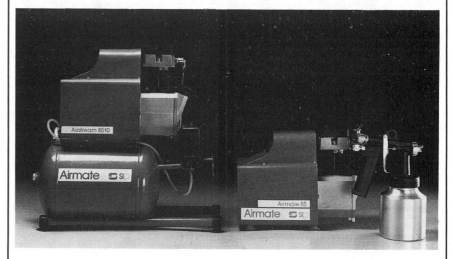

E13. ▲ SIP make a range of spray compressors, including the fully portable Airmate 85 (supplied complete with a spraygun and hose) and the Airstream 8510, which has a 10 litre air receiver tank. The compressors can also run air tools such as air brushes, blind rivet guns, staplers and nailers.

E14. ◄ The larger capacity Hurricane produces more compressed air than the models already mentioned, and the range continues upwards to encompass industrial duty units, where required. SIP also make a range of high quality spray guns.

Read all about it

If you are unfamiliar with basic bodywork rebuilding techniques, it pays to read up about the various methods which can be used. Workshop manuals don't normally cover this area in detail, but there are many books about bodywork repair. Try your local library or book shop. One of the most comprehensive books available on this subject is the *Haynes Car Bodywork Manual*, written by Lindsay Porter – it is a complete, easy to follow guide to all aspects of car body repair, including sections on welding and spraying.

Plan ahead

Once you have made a thorough examination of the car, you should have a good idea of which major panels need replacing, and it is always a good idea to arrange for the purchase of these, before you start work. That way, you will avoid the delays which sometimes occur, especially when dealing with the early Capris. With panels for the older cars ever more difficult to get through Ford dealerships, 'pattern' panels, or old 'unused' stock available through specialist

suppliers, are increasingly becoming more relevant to restorers' needs. The panels ARE about, but you may need to look for them harder than you might at first imagine, and it is essential that you start well in advance of when you need the particular sections.

Safety

NEVER take chances when working on your car. Extensive notes are included in Appendix 1 – PLEASE READ THEM NOW. Of course, these cannot cover every eventuality, and it is up to each individual restorer to take commonsense precautions at every stage of the job. No responsibility for the effectiveness or otherwise of advice given here, nor for any omissions, can be accepted by the author. 'Safety' notes are intended to include some useful tips and no more.

ALWAYS wear goggles when working underneath the car, particularly when poking dirty and rusty sections, and when using any form of grinding or cutting tools – hand operated or power tools.

Wear protective overalls, fully buttoned, at all times, and 'gauntlet' type gloves when welding. Never weld without the correct shielding goggles for the type of welding you are carrying out – 'arc eye' is a painful result of watching welding with the naked eye. In addition, there are serious risks from flying molten metal and sparks – the results are horrific to contemplate.

Take particular care when dealing with jagged – and, particularly, rusty – edges, or freshly cut metal; the razor sharp edges can inflict devastating wounds.

Always try to make sure that someone else is around when you are working on the car. Then if anything unfortunate should occur, there is someone else to help you, or raise the alarm.

PLEASE TAKE CARE – YOU KNOW IT MAKES SENSE. The whole point of restoring a car is to be able to enjoy it when it's finished – the whole thing would turn very sour if lack of a few simple precautions, or the thought that 'It'll never happen to me' led to a serious accident.

Initial work

It is almost always necessary to remove items of trim from the vehicle, prior to work on the body. The extent to which you have to go depends on the nature of the damage, and which part of the car you are tackling. Inevitably, however, areas of bodywork round the grille, lamp units and bumpers tend to suffer from corrosion damage, and so, to start with, it is worth looking at how these items come off.

It is always wise to disconnect the battery before attempting to remove lamp units or their wiring, or any of the vehicle's electrical components . . .

IW1.▼ To remove the headlamp units from Mark I cars, first take out the four screws (two at the top, two at the bottom) securing the bezel to the car. The four screws securing the sealed beam lamp unit can now be removed. The assembly is then pulled forward a little way, so that the wiring plug can be withdrawn from the rear, also the sidelight bulb, which lives just below this plug. The indicator cable can now be disconnected, to allow the headlight assembly to be removed from the car.

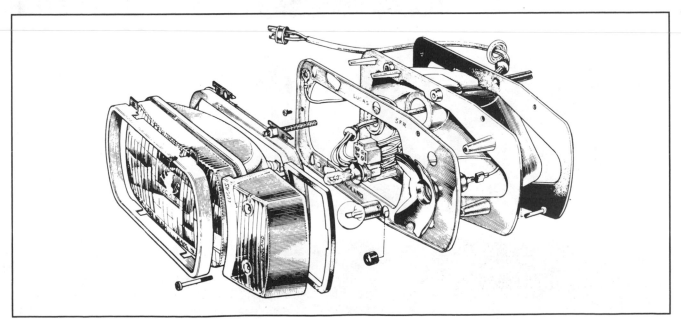

IW2.►On Mark II cars, the
indicator lens has to be taken off
before the headlight unit can be
withdrawn. The lens is held by
two Phillips screws. These can be
very tight, and the use of a
hand-held impact screwdriver will
allow greater leverage. Try not to
resort to hitting the screwdriver
with a hammer or the lens may
shatter!

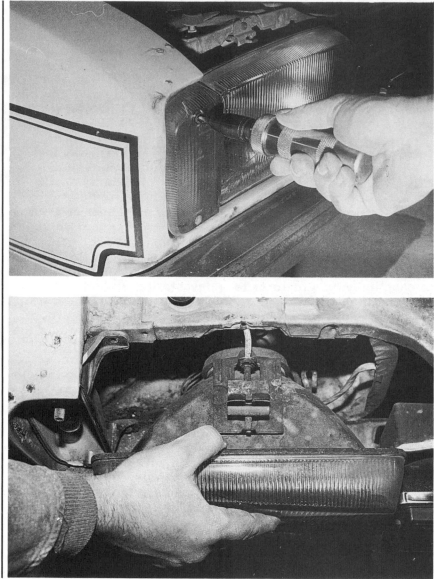

IW3. ▲ The headlamp assembly is
then unscrewed from the
bodywork; it has a single
retaining screw at the top, sitting
on twin clips at the bottom. The
upper securing screw of the
indicator unit can also be taken
out at this stage.

IW4.►Carefully pull the headlight
unit forward, taking care not to
strain the wiring.

IW5.◄The connector plug can
now be released from the rear of
the unit . . .

IW6.◄ . . . as well as the sidelight bulb holder – gently twist the unit anti-clockwise, and withdraw from the headlight assembly.

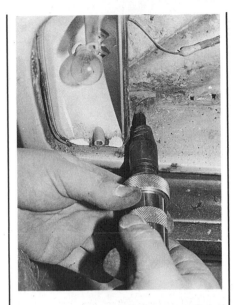

IW7.►The lower screw securing the indicator unit can now be taken out, and the complete assembly withdrawn, after labelling and disconnecting the wires.

IW8.◄On all Capris the grille is released by taking out the securing screws around the perimeter. On some models, like this Mark III 2.8i, the grille must come out before the headlamp units can be removed.

IW9.►Carefully lift the grille away, and take particular care that you put it in a place of safety, NOT on the ground near to where you are working – it is all too easy to tread on it accidentally!

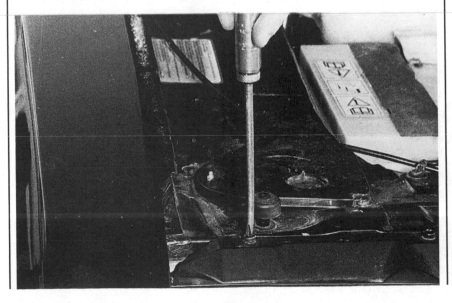

IW10.◄To remove the headlights, start by taking out the four Phillips screws securing the surround.

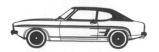

IW11. ►*With the screws safely clear, extract the moulding, taking care not to damage it or the 'lipped' corner of the front wing.*

IW12.◄*The individual lamp units can now be removed – start by releasing the screws holding the retainer rings.*

IW13.►*The lamp units can now be pulled forward and away, after disconnecting the wiring.*

IW14.◄*Whichever model you are tackling, it pays to keep all screws, nuts, bolts, etc. in a safe place, and precisely labelled. This saves a lot of time later on, when trying to reassemble the vehicle.*

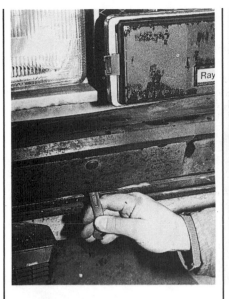

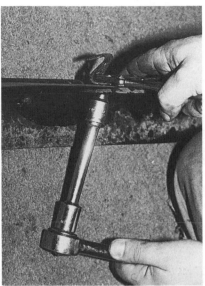

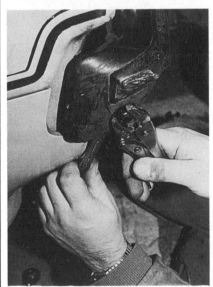

IW15. ▲ The one-piece bumpers on Mark I and II Capris are bolted onto their brackets, and removal should be just a case of taking out the nuts and bolts. However, lack of space between the bumpers and bodywork makes life awkward, and the inevitable rusty bolts don't help. Soak the threads in penetrating oil a day or two before you start, and repeat the process immediately before the job.

IW16. ► A pair of self-grip pliers may still be needed to 'capture' the rounded bolt heads, since these often start to turn with the nut! If all else fails, remove the bumpers complete with their brackets. The use of copper-based grease on the bolts, on reassembly, will help to prevent seizure in the future.

IW17. ► Patience pays off! It took us over an hour to remove this bumper, but it was worth the effort so that we could get better access to the scruffy bodywork beneath it!

IW18. ◄ The front number plate support brackets are mounted directly to the bumper and are notorious for rusting. They can be unbolted once the bumper is off the car.

IW19. ▼ Mark III Capris have three-piece bumpers. To remove the front units, start by prising off the black plastic disc from each side section, then release the Phillips screw beneath.

IW20. ▲ The complete section is then unclipped from the wing, and carefully pulled away from the main part of the bumper.

IW21. ▼ The full-width central section of the bumper is then simply unbolted from its brackets at each end, and in the centre.

IW22. ►Capri rear bumpers are removed in a similar fashion to the front units. On Mark I models, the number plate lamp can be removed first, if desired. On Mark II and III cars, the bumper bracket attachment bolts are reached from inside the luggage compartment. Start by lifting up the false floor and taking out the reservoir for the rear screen washer (if fitted), for easier access to the bolts.

IW23. ►The bolts can then be released from the rear panel, allowing the bumper to be removed.

IW24. ▼ On Mark I Capris, the rear lamps can be removed after unscrewing the cover panels from inside the boot. The lamp assemblies are unscrewed (again, from inside the boot), and can then be gently prised away from the outside of the vehicle.

To remove the rear number plate lamp from the bumper, first disconnect the live and earth wires (inside the boot), then pull the wires through the hole in the floor. Now, from below the bumper, push the lamp unit retaining levers inwards, and carefully extract the assembly.

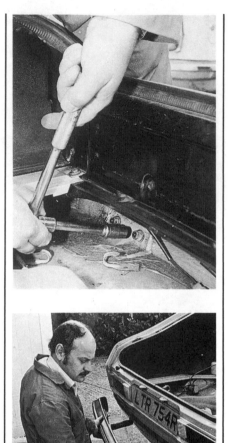

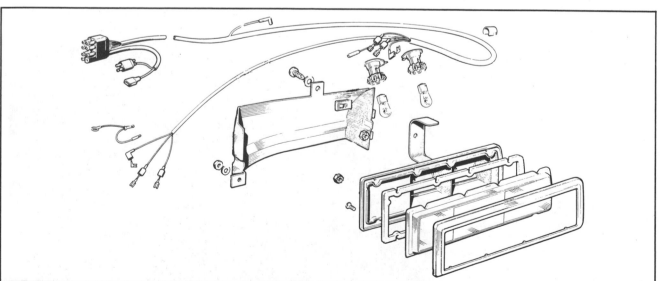

IW25.► On Mark II and III cars, the rear lamp lenses are simply unscrewed from the outside of the car.

IW26. ▲ The lenses should then be lifted away, and carefully stored out of harm's way, since they can easily get broken and are not cheap to replace.

IW27.► The lamp holders on the Mark II and III models are released from the bodywork from inside the hatch area, by releasing the retaining screws. The lamp assemblies can be gently prised away from the bodywork, but make sure that you don't scratch or dent the paintwork during this operation. On refitting, make sure that the lamp units are effectively sealed to the bodywork; apply a little sealing compound if necessary, to keep out moisture.

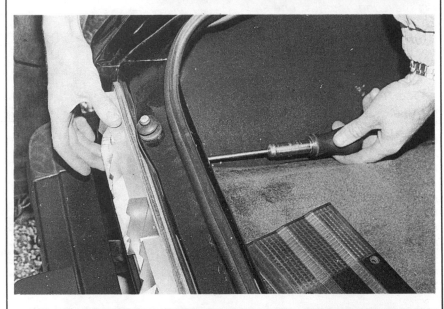

IW28.► The number plate lamp lenses on Mark II and III cars are released by taking out the two Phillips screws. If removing the body of the lamp, disconnect the wiring from within the luggage compartment, and attach a stout length of cord to the electrical cable. The cord can then be pulled through the bodywork as the wiring is withdrawn, and will help guide the wiring on its return journey, on re-assembly.

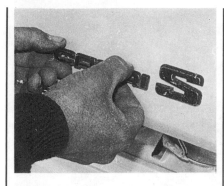

IW29. ▲ *Badges of all descriptions – especially on rarer Capris – need very great care to avoid damaging them during removal. Gentle prising with a screwdriver, at intervals around the edges, is far less likely to cause damage than levering from just one end. The securing clips normally remain in the bodywork as the badge is lifted away.*

IW30. ► *When removing a bonnet, bootlid, or hatch tailgate, it is a good idea to mark the position of the hinges on the relevant panel, before you start. Use a soft ('B') grade pencil or a ball-point pen to mark the hinge outline, if you are not going to respray the panel, or use an old knife or screwdriver (or other sharp implement) to scribe the metal if you are intending to apply paint before the panel is re-fitted. Your marks will then still be visible when you need them!*

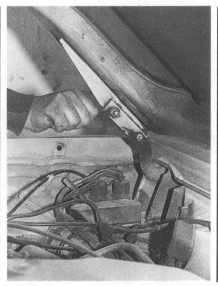

IW31. ◄ *Use a ring or socket spanner to loosen the securing bolts, and have an assistant (or two, in view of the size and weight of Capri bonnets and tailgates!) on hand to take the weight of the panel as the bolts come out. Take care not to scratch surrounding paintwork; it is a good idea to cover the wings and bulkhead areas with cloth, unless they are going to be changed/resprayed anyway.*

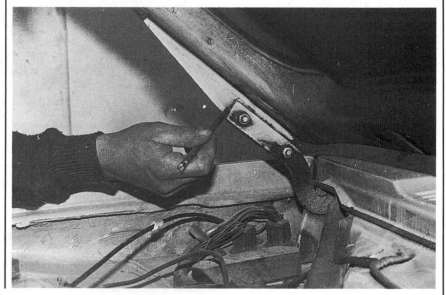

IW32. ◄ *If you are intending to carry out any more than just minor bodywork restoration, it is safest to remove the battery from the vehicle, rather than just disconnecting it. Slacken the retaining plate securing bolt, and lift this, and the battery, clear, after taking off the battery leads. Store the battery in a safe place, away from heat, sparks, animals and children.*

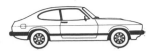

IW33. ▲ It is worth applying penetrating oil well in advance, to any nuts and bolts which have to be shifted to allow work on the body to take place. This could save hours of struggling later on!

Fuel tank removal

Before carrying out any major reconstruction work on the body shell – especially at the rear of the vehicle, or underneath it, and in any event when welding is involved – it is wise to remove the fuel tank and fuel pipes, having first disconnected the car's battery. It is advisable, where possible, to run the fuel level in the tank as low as possible, leaving less petrol to drain off. Avoid having the car over a pit, where petrol vapour can accumulate, and, for the same reason, do the job outside, if possible. Obviously keep naked

flames, cigarettes, etc. away from the vicinity.

One of the easiest and safest ways to drain the petrol is to raise the rear of the car, on axle stands or ramps, then disconnect the fuel feed pipe at the fuel pump, directing the fuel which emerges into proper, marked petrol containers, designed for the job. Seal any cans used, and store them well out of the way of the working area, and away from the reach of children.

FTR1. ▼ On Mark I Capris, the tank can be removed after releasing the flexible filler pipe fitted between the tank and the fixed filler neck, in the offside rear wing. The flexible pipe is secured by wire clips. The two nuts and bolts (later Mark Is have four bolts and spring washers) holding the tank to the rear bulkhead can then be taken out, and the tank pulled a few inches backwards, and into the boot. Before withdrawing it further, disconnect the wire from the fuel gauge sender, at its snap connector, and release the petrol supply pipe (to the pump), and any vapour lines (note where they fit) from the tank. The tank can then be lifted clear.

If you need to take out the fixed section of the filler neck, from the rear wing, simply take out the three securing screws.

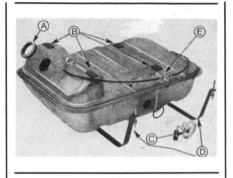

*FTR2. ▲ On Mark II and III Capris, the fuel tank is held to the vehicle's chassis by two support straps. After disconnecting the fuel pipe from the front of the tank, unclip the pipe from the retaining clips, found along the front edge of the tank. Disconnect the two wires from the sender unit **marking where they fit**, then unclip the vent pipe from the chassis, and disconnect the breather pipe at the 'T' connector (mark the connections to aid re-assembly). Late Mark II and Mark III cars also have a fuel return pipe, which should be disconnected from the gauge sender unit.*

Support the tank from below, and release the two support straps. With the clamp between the filler pipe and the tank loosened, the tank can then be removed, complete with guard (if fitted) – the filler pipe remains in position on the vehicle. On re-fitting, make sure that the four rubber insulation pads are correctly attached.

To aid re-assembly, lightly grease the filler pipe base so that it slides more easily through its seal in the tank – make sure that this is re-fitted! Check too that the filler pipe is properly located within the tank, once this is in position.

Re-attach the fuel and vent pipes in their original positions, and re-fit the tank support straps, so that approximately 1½ inches of thread is protruding through each nut. Make sure that the fuel feed and vent pipes are properly clipped into position, and are not kinked or trapped.

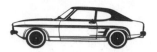

On Mark II and III cars, the fixed fuel filler pipe can be removed, once the fuel tank is out of the way, after taking out the right-hand trim panel in the load area, and the spare wheel cover panel. On Ghia versions (only), peel back the insulation, clear of the pipe cover panel. Take out the nine bolts securing the internal filler pipe panel, and then slacken the clamps between the floor and the pipe gaiter, finally lifting the gaiter clear of the floor.

Take off the filler cap, and release the screw securing the filler neck to the body; the pipe and gaiter can now be removed.

On re-assembly, don't tighten the pipe securing screw or the gaiter clamp, until the tank is correctly positioned.

FTR3.➤ On USA model Capris, the procedure for removing and re-fitting the tank is similar, except that you may encounter a fuel feed 'return' line, which will also need to be disconnected before the tank can be removed. On re-assembly, both feed and return pipes should be re-attached to the clips along the front of the fuel tank.

On re-fitting the tank, make sure that the vent pipe passes behind the fuel tank support straps.

On all models, check very carefully for leaks on re-assembly, and, in the case of hatchback versions, do this before you re-fit the trim panel.

From experience, I would also advise you very strongly to clean all electrical connections (to the fuel gauge sender) *thoroughly, before you re-fit the tank*, especially following a lengthy rebuild. This could help to avoid non-operation of the fuel gauge, which means taking the tank out *again!*

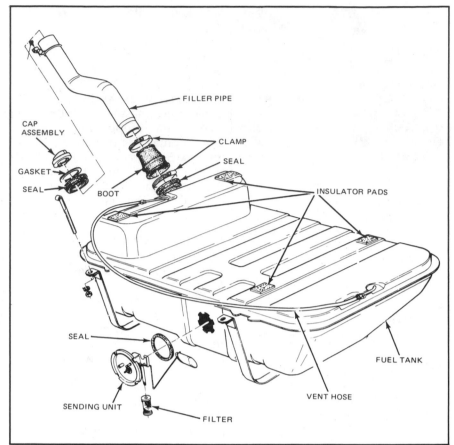

Minor bodywork repairs

Introduction

Later in this chapter I shall be dealing with major bodywork restoration operations, involving replacement of complete panels, fabricating large metal sections and so on. However, you may be lucky, and your Ford may only need comparatively minor cosmetic surgery to put it to rights. As already mentioned, complete information on all aspects of bodywork restoration is contained in *Haynes Car Bodywork Manual,* and it is well worthwhile purchasing a copy if you have not tackled bodywork repairs before, or indeed if you want to improve your technique.

However, in the following sections, I shall be outlining how to tackle typical bodywork 'tidy up' jobs, on a budget basis. This can be useful where perhaps time and/or funds are limited, and where repairs are a practical alternative to changing a complete body panel. It is appreciated that not everyone has full bodywork restoration facilities at home, and the aim here is to show what can be achieved using readily available and relatively inexpensive tools and materials. The idea is to enable you to keep your car on the road and presentable, without having to spend a great deal of time and money, or invest in expensive equipment.

The techniques illustrated can be applied equally to any of the outer bodywork panels. It must be stressed, however, that these methods are ONLY appropriate for cosmetic body repairs, and MUST NOT be used to patch areas of structural importance. For these, rectification by welding in new metal is the only acceptable method.

Minor Surface Damage

MSD1. ►*Stone chips are common on most cars, and Capris are particularly vulnerable along the lower edges of the doors, since they 'fold in' towards the road. The first step is to remove any rust from affected areas. Prise loose flakes off with a screwdriver, then employ fairly coarse (100 or 150 grade) 'wet and dry' paper, used dry, to rub down the surface. Aim to get as near as possible to completely bright, clean metal, and 'feather' the edges of the surrounding paintwork so that they slope gently towards the centre of the damaged area.*

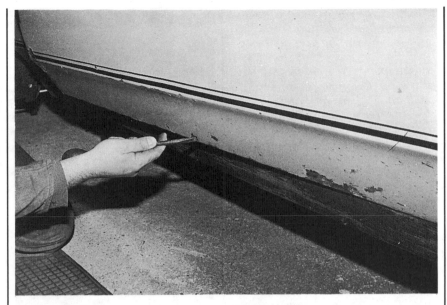

MSD2. ▲ *Inevitably there will be tiny 'pinhole' sized pits of rust remaining, so treat the surface of the metal with a rust killer – use as directed on the bottle to achieve good results.*

MSD3. ►*Now use an anti-rust primer to give the surface a protective base for the final paint finish. Two coats of the primer are often required – again, read the instructions carefully, and follow them to the letter. After drying and 'curing', the surface of the anti-rust primer should be smoothed down with wet and dry paper; use medium (280 or 320), followed by fine (400) grades. Finally, cellulose primer, then top coats of paint, can be applied by aerosol spray. Full details of these operations are included in the 'Rear Wheel Arch Repairs' section, which follows this one.*

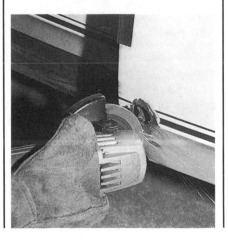

MSD4. ◄*If holes appear when you scrape off the loose rust, use a round file, a flap wheel in an electric drill, or an angle grinder (CAREFULLY, and using protective gloves and goggles) to rid the edges of the hole of all rust.*

MSD5. ►*Tap the edges of the hole slightly inwards (to accept an appropriate filler), and apply rust killer, followed by an anti-rust primer, for long-term protection.*

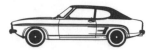

MSD6. ►The methods available for filling holes are numerous, and depend on the size of the hole. For large ones, over a few square inches in area, rivet, braze or weld suitable plates in position. For smaller holes, like this one, reinforced glass fibre paste can be used. Smooth the reinforced paste into the hole, so that the surface comes to just BELOW that of the surrounding metal, for this paste is incredibly difficult to rub down. It is designed to be used as a waterproof reinforcement, not a surface filler.

The final finish can be achieved by using plastic body filler, as described in the 'Rear Wheel Arch Repairs' section.

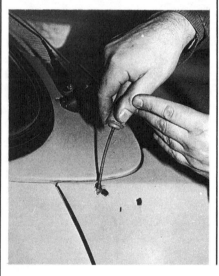

MSD7. ◄Tiny holes like these, often found at the rear upper edges of the front wings, do not warrant being attacked with an angle grinder. Instead, use a small round file, to rid the edges of rust, then . . .

MSD8. ►. . . use the rounded end of a ball pein hammer to tap the edges inwards. Rust killing, priming and surface rectification can then be continued as already described.

MSD9. ◄Dents can be straightened on a d-i-y basis, using hammers and dollies as supplied in the Sykes-Pickavant panel beating kit. Full, step-by-step instructions are included in the excellent booklet which comes with the kit. Their 'panel puller' (slide hammer) can be used to remove the worst creases first, where necessary.

This front wing had already been repaired and painted when a 'hit and run' driver buckled the wing when the car was parked!

Mud and dirt is first removed from the back of the affected area, then, by holding a dolly at either side of the panel . . .

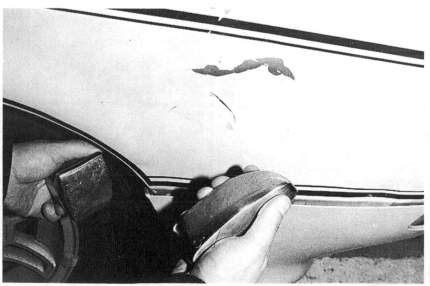

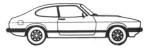

MSD10.➤ . . the dent can be 'encouraged' out by gently tapping the dolly on the concave side, while keeping the heavier dolly held firmly against the opposite side of the panel.

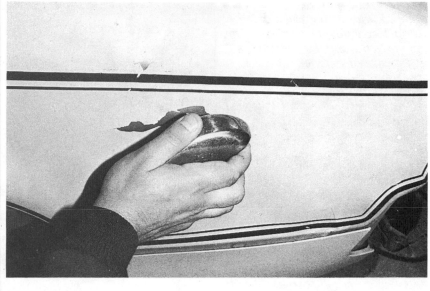

MSD11.▲ We used similar techniques to remove creases from the rear panel of the car – apparently this Capri had used a telegraph pole as a brake, when travelling backwards! Final surface filling may be necessary to obtain a perfectly smooth repair, depending on how good you become at using the panel beating kit.

Rear wheel arch repairs

Capri rear wheel arches are prone to gradual disintegration once rust has taken a hold around the lip of the arch. If damage to the rear wheel arches on your Capri is severe, you will have little option but to replace the outer arches, as described later in this chapter, together with rotten sections of the inner arches, if these are holed. The deciding factor is how much of the original metalwork remains intact. However, the following sequence shows how to patch an existing arch, assuming that rust has not destroyed the major part of the lip, and that you have a good 'edge' to work to. The only 'special' tools required for these repairs are an electric drill, and a 'blind' rivet gun. Alternatively, the repair panels could be welded into position.

Although this section deals specifically with a rear wheel arch, the working methods described here, particularly those relating to bridging gaps in the bodywork, filling and painting, can be applied to most outer panelwork on Capris.

Where possible, carry out all such operations in dry conditions, and when the ambient temperature is above 15°C (60°F), to get the best results and fastest 'curing' times from fillers, paints and so on.

RWR1. ◄ Start by removing the road wheel, having first jacked the car and secured the bodywork on axle stands. Use a wire brush to rid the inner surfaces of the wheel arch of mud and loose rust, so that a proper inspection can be carried out.

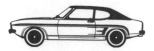

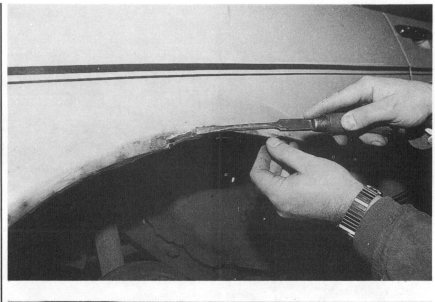

RWR2.►*Loose flakes of rust can then be prised from the surface, using a screwdriver or chisel. This enables you to get a better idea of the size of patches required.*

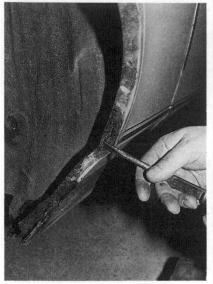

RWR3.▲ *The offside rear arch on this Capri was good in places, but, at intervals around the perimeter, rust had eaten right through the metal.*

RWR4.►*WEARING PROTECTIVE GOGGLES AND GLOVES, use an angle grinder, or a sanding attachment in an electric drill, to carve away the remaining rust and 'motheaten' metal. Stop when you reach clean steel.*

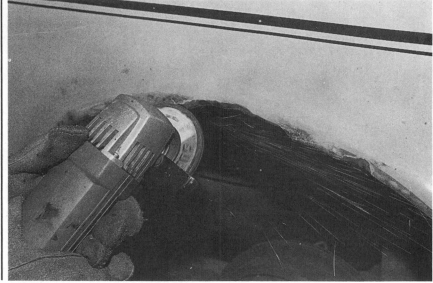

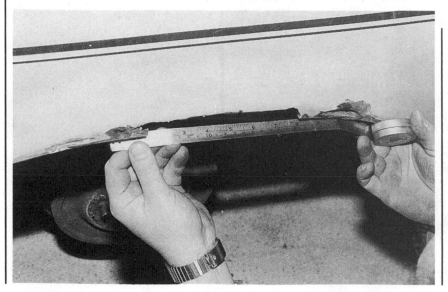

RWR5.◄ *Measure the length and depth of missing sections, allowing at least an inch at each end, to overlap the remaining good edges.*

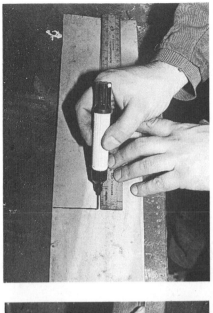

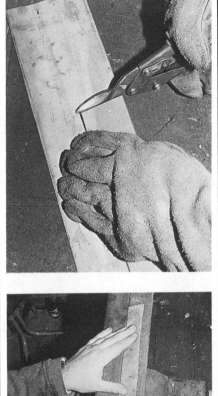

RWR6. ◄ Transfer these measurements onto steel plate, using a felt-tipped marker pen. As we were intending to rivet our plates into position, we chose to use zinc coated steel, to give extra anti-rust protection. This is not so suitable if you intend to MIG weld the plates in place – the zinc will prevent the weld from 'taking' unless the edges of the plate are ground back.

RWR7. ► Use tin snips to cut out the repair sections from the new metal. It is advisable to wear thick gloves during this process, and to dispose immediately of any sharp off-cuts of metal. Don't leave them lying around, especially if children or animals are nearby.

RWR8. ◄ The metal strips must now be shaped to give the correct right-angled lip. Two lengths of angle iron or aluminium, clamped in the jaws of a vice, are suitable to grip the strips along their length. Measure the depth of the lip, and mark it on your repair section. The flange can then be bent over by the required amount, a little at a time, using a hammer.

RWR9. ► A few deft taps with a hammer along the angled adge will give a clean finish.

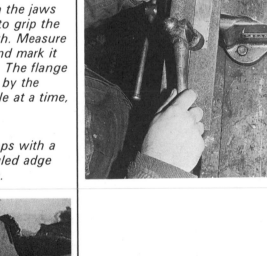

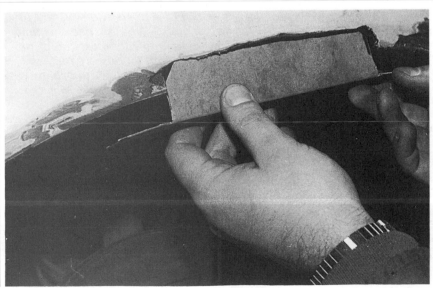

RWR10. ◄ Trim each repair patch approximately to shape, then offer up to the vehicle, noting where any minor 'adjustments' need to be made.

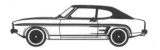

RWR11.►It is necessary to cut slots in the vertical surface of the repair panel, so that it can assume the natural curve of the wheel arch – space them equally, every few inches, and ensure that they don't quite reach the right angled bend in the panel.

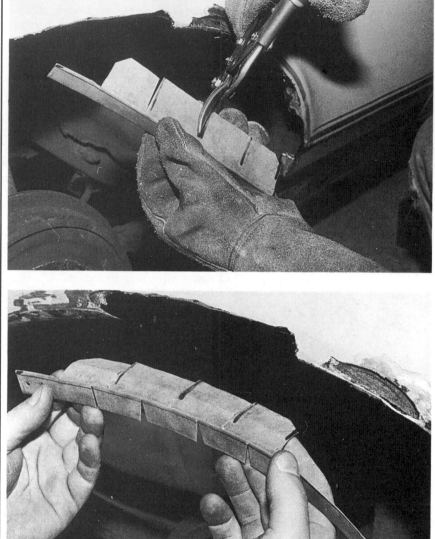

RWR12.▲Drill two ¹/₈ inch holes in each end of the metal strip, to accept 'blind' rivets. It is far easier to make these pilot holes now, than to wait until the panel is clamped in position on the car. Use an old block of wood beneath the drill bit, rather than the bench!

RWR13.▲It is also necessary to cut slots – 'vee' shaped this time – in the horizontal section of the wheel arch lip repair panel, so that this can follow the shape of the original arch, otherwise the contours will be incorrect.

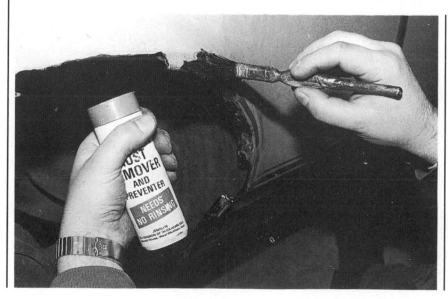

RWR14.◄Before attaching the new metal, treat the original lip with rust killer, to reduce the chances of problems in the future.

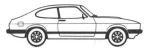

RWR15.►Once more, offer up the repair panel to the vehicle, and carry out any final trimming found to be necessary.

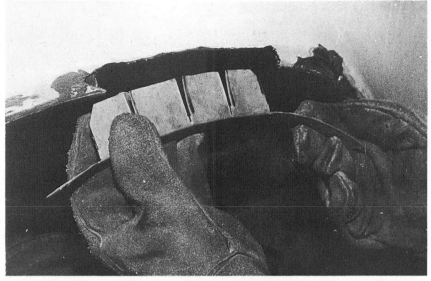

RWR16. ▼The new panel is then clamped in place, using a pair of self-grip wrenches.

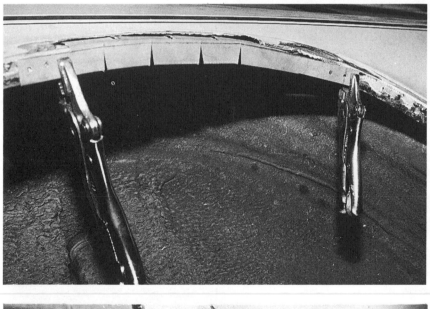

RWR17. ▲By using the guide holes, already drilled in the patch, and by keeping the electric drill as close as possible to the self-grip wrench, holes can be drilled accurately through the good sections of the wheel arch, ready to accept the rivets.

RWR18.◄A rivet gun and blind rivets can then be used to secure the new metal permanently in position. If you can obtain countersunk rivets, so much the better, to give a flush surface to the repair. In any event it is a good idea to countersink the holes in your repair panel, so that the rivet heads protrude as little as reasonably possible.

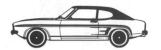

RWR19. ➤With the new section riveted firmly in place, the bare metal in vulnerable areas can be treated to an anti-rust paint. When this has cured, waterproof reinforced glass fibre paste can be used to fill the deeper holes, and to bridge gaps in the metal. Leave the top surface of the paste just below that of the surrounding bodywork, to allow for final surface filling.

We ran a fillet of the waterproof paste around the inner surface of the entire wheel arch lip, to help keep the elements at bay.

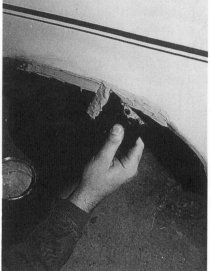

RWR21. ▲ Build up the filler in several thin applications, and try to keep the surface as level as possible.

RWR20.➤Once the fibre paste has fully hardened, plastic body filler can be used to bring the surface of the repair to the same level as the rest of the wheel arch. Don't mix up more filler than you can apply in ten minutes or so, or it will harden into an unworkable lump before you are ready to use it!

RWR22. ▲ Inevitably the filler will need to be shaped to give the correct profile, and an adjustable body file, like this one from Sykes-Pickavant, will save hours of tedious rubbing down. It is extremely useful on curved sections of bodywork, such as wheel arches, for its profile can be changed from concave to . . .

RWR23. ◄. . convex, to suit the contours of the panel. Excess filler is quickly shaved off, ready for final rubbing down. At this stage the surface of the filler should be just proud of the adjacent panelwork.

RWR24.➤Use 100 or 150 grade wet or dry paper, used dry, to level surface 'hills and vales'. A smoother finish will result from using a flat support block behind the paper. A cork block gives excellent results, although wood can be used. Use progressively finer grades of paper – probably 280 or 320 grade, then 400 grade, until the surface is perfectly smooth to the touch. Any small craters discovered can be re-filled at this stage, and further rubbing down operations carried out. Rubbing in a circular motion, or diagonally from varying directions, will help to smooth all the rough edges, to blend the filled area into the original bodywork.

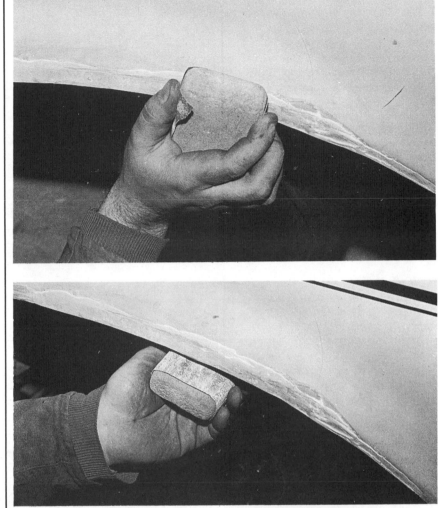

RWR25.➤Don't forget to rub down rough areas beneath the wheel arch lip, or these will show up when the paint is applied, and spoil the overall appearance of the job.

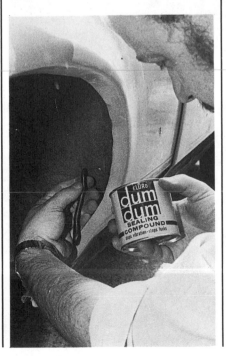

RWR26.◄Before completing restoration work on the outer wheel arch, it is worth sealing the inner arch against moisture. In addition to the fillet of glass-reinforced paste already described, lengths of flexible sealing compound can be moulded into position between the inner arch and the outer flange, around the perimeter of the arch. Shape the sealant so that water and mud flow away from the lip, rather than being allowed to sit on it, causing further rust problems!

RWR27.➤An application of two good coats of a rust-resisting paint to the entire inner wheel arch/lip joint will help to further protect this area from corrosion attack.

RWR28.►Before applying paint to the outer wheel arch, cover the wheel and tyre to protect them from overspray. We used an old car seat cover, which had elasticated edges and therefore gripped the tyre perfectly. Before applying paint, ensure that the bodywork surface and surrounding areas are free from dust, by wiping them clean using a 'spirit wipe' solution and/or 'tacky cloths' – available from most car accessory shops.

RWR29.► For localised areas like this, the use of aerosol cans is probably the easiest method of applying paint. For maximum economy and to ensure that you have enough paint available, the larger (375 ml upwards) cans are the best bet. Apply primer first, moving the can smoothly and at a fixed distance from the panel, to give an even coat, and overlap the edges of the repair by a few inches all round. Allow the paint to harden – after about 20 minutes at temperatures above 15°C (60°F) – before rectifying any minor surface imperfections.

Apply at least three coats of primer, then allow to dry before starting final preparation for the top coats.

RWR30.►When the primer has dried – allow at least half an hour after the last coat – use fine (600 grade) wet and dry paper to carefully smooth out any 'nibs' in the surface of the primer. Use the paper wet; a bucketful of warm water, to which a little washing-up liquid or soap has been addded, is ideal. The warm water will evaporate from the bodywork surface more quickly than cold water, and the soap will help keep the paper clean.

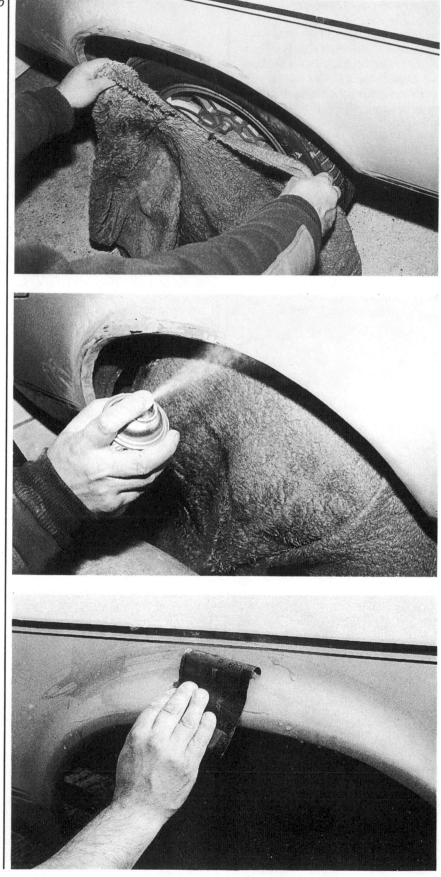

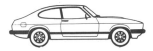

*RWR31.►The final job is to apply the top coat. Try to choose a calm, dry, warm day if spraying the car outside. For best results, the can needs to be held fairly near to the surface of the bodywork, to give a good gloss, but **not** so close that the paint runs. Again, keep the can moving at a steady speed, and constant distance from the vehicle. After the paint has been allowed to dry for a day or two, the surface of the paint can be very carefully 'cut back' (if necessary) and polished. Full details of these operations are included in the section entitled 'The Respray', later in this chapter.*

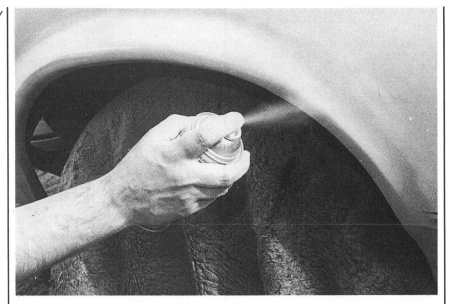

Front wing top repairs

The tops of the front wings are susceptible to rust on all Capris, and it is likely that any Capri undergoing restoration will need at least some reconstruction around the headlamp areas, or at the extreme rear edges of the wings.

If damage is very severe, the most sensible option is of course to fit a new wing, and full details of how to do this are included later in this chapter. However, if rust damage, for example, is confined to small areas, or is not too extensive, the alternative is to repair the existing wing. This can be easier than it sounds. To start with, and looking on the positive side, in most cases, around 90 per cent of the wing will be in good condition, so it's only the other 10 per cent that you will have to deal with!

In addition, repairing an existing wing is obviously cheaper than obtaining a new one, and is usually less involved, since Capri wings are welded to the body shell. Another advantage of repairing rather than replacing, is that you are less likely to have problems with realigning door shuts, bodywork

lines and trim mouldings, on completing the job. The decision on whether patching will suffice will depend on your facilities and abilities, and on your assessment of the overall condition of the wing, having made a detailed examination of it.

The repairs we show in this section were purposely carried out without using welding gear or expensive special tools. However, there is of course no reason why repair patches cannot be welded into place, prior to surface filling, if you have the necessary equipment.

Indeed, if rust is so extensive that the inner wing panels or

bulkheads are seriously affected, rectification by welding in new metal is the only acceptable repair method.

If welding on a Capri equipped with an alternator, the battery should be disconnected first. Always cover the windscreen and door windows when welding or grinding near them, or the sparks will burn into the glass.

FWT1.▼ Initial probing into rusty looking craters around the headlamp area will give a good idea how severe the rust problem is.

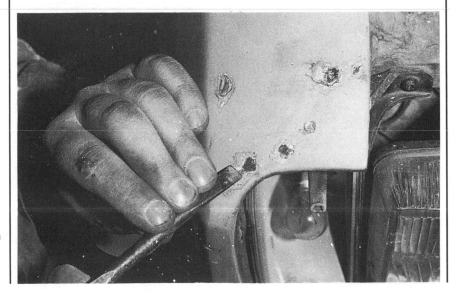

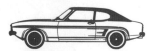

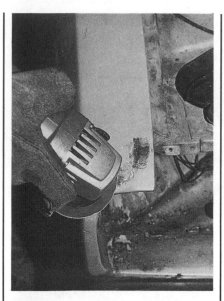

FWT2.◄ Clear the area of loose rust and paint by using an angle grinder, or a sanding attachment in an electric drill – WEAR GOGGLES AND PROTECTIVE GLOVES. Luckily this wing was only affected by comparatively minor rust. However, we removed the headlamp (as described in 'Initial Work') to check the areas below, which were showing signs of imminent trouble!

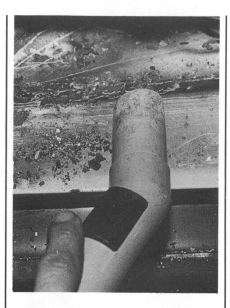

FWT3.► A vacuum cleaner is the most effective tool for ridding the working area of loose rust and dirt, especially in awkward shaped corners, which abound in the headlamp areas. Alternatively, a soft brush can be used to rake out all the debris.

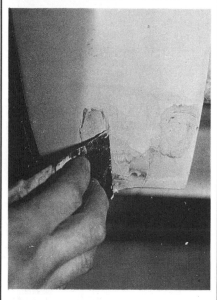

FWT4.◄ Once the affected areas are clean and de-rusted, surface filling can be carried out, as already described in the 'Rear Wheel Arch Repairs' section.

FWT5.► On this Capri, our attentions then turned to the opposite front wing, which was showing signs of more serious rust damage, as well as a number of minor parking scrapes, and evidence of earlier half-completed repairs! In such situations, the first step is to establish how far the corrosion extends, so that a decision can be taken on the most effective repair methods. We attacked a flaky-looking piece of body filler, to find extensive rusting underneath.

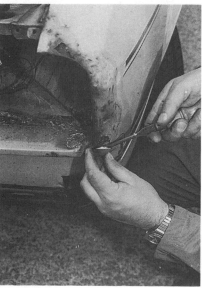

FWT6.◄ Worse still, the area immediately above the headlamp was riddled with rust, due to an extensive accumulation of mud and salt on the 'ledge' above the lamp unit.

FWT7.► It is always wise to leave fragments of the edges of such areas intact as long as possible, since, although damaged beyond repair, these edges of rusty metal can be invaluable as guides to where the repair panels should fit.

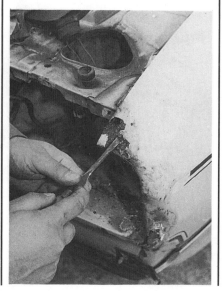

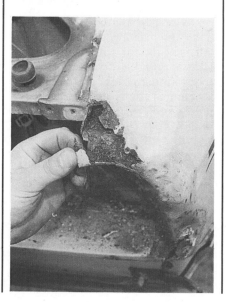

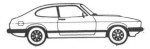

FWT8.►*Probe the adjacent panelwork, too, to see how far the damage extends. Things always look worse before they can look better! Now is the time to decide whether to patch the wing or to replace it . . .*

FWT9.►*. . . in this case the owner wasn't keen to disturb the wing, which in any case was generally sound, so he elected to repair it.*

Start by cutting out repair sections to cover the affected metal, using cardboard templates as necessary. The profile of the repair section is traced from the vehicle to paper or card, then transferred to sheet steel, which is cut to shape with a pair of tin snips. Make the repair patch around half an inch wider and longer than the damaged area. This allows for overlapping the edges of the remaining good metal when fitting, if you are intending to rivet the patch in place.

FWT10.◄*It is a good idea to work on just one side of the car at a time, so that the opposite side may be used as an accurate reference for measuring, for example, the depth of the lip above the headlamp . . .*

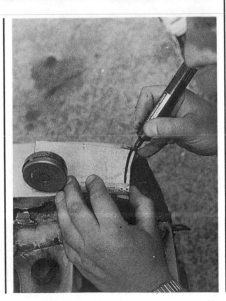

FWT11.►*. . . this dimension can be transferred to the repair plate, using a felt-tipped pen. Take your time to get such measurements accurate, to achieve good results.*

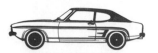

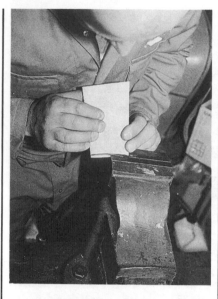

FWT12.◄The flange can be bent a little at a time, by hand to start with, by placing the repair panel in a vice. Move the metal along a fraction of an inch at a time, to obtain a smooth, uniform profile.

FWT13.►A soft-faced hammer or mallet can then be used to accentuate the bend, and, by tapping along the fold line, to give a neat 90 degree angle.

FWT14.◄Try the plate in position on the vehicle; any minor adjustments to the 'set' of the flange may then be made using a self-grip wrench or even a pair of pliers.

FWT15.►The section of rusty metal, already marked on the wing (and, as previously described, smaller than the repair panel by about half an inch or so all round) should now be removed. This can be done with a hammer and sharp chisel or bolster, or using a cutting disc in an angle grinder – WEAR GOGGLES AND PROTECTIVE GLOVES. Take care only to remove the metal from the top of the wing, leaving sound metal (if any!) above the headlight intact.

FWT16.◄Still wearing the gloves, since the edges will be very sharp, and probably still hot, lift away the damaged metal. The areas beneath, so exposed, can now be cleaned up, prior to carrying out rustproofing operations.

FWT17.➤The edges of the surrounding metal can be tidied up using a flat file.

FWT18.➤We were intending to put a 'step' in the edges of the repair plate, using the Skyes-Pickavant Edge Setter tool, so that when in position, the surface of the repair panel would be level with the surrounding bodywork. In order to get the dimensions absolutely correct for 'setting' the edge of the plate, first measure the exact width and length of aperture in the top of the wing. It is a good idea to mark the positions of the existing edges of the repair plate on the wing, so that, during 'trial' fitting at this stage, the plate always goes back in the same place.

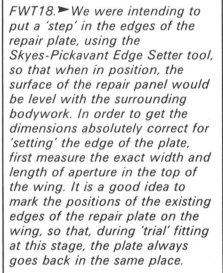

FWT19.◄The next step is to transfer the dimensions of the aperture in the wing to the repair panel, checking again with the steel rule to make sure that the measurements are accurate.

FWT20.➤Clearly mark the lines along which the set will be made, then trim the outer edges of the plate very precisely, so that, when inserted in the tool, the plate will be bent at the correct points.

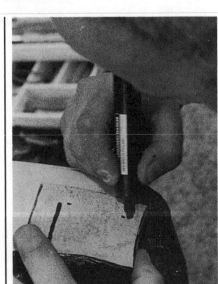

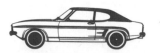

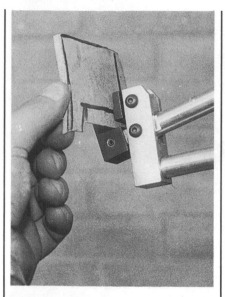

FWT21.◄It is then a very simple matter to step the edges of the panel using the Sykes-Pickavant Edge Setter. We used a hand-held model, but, for coping with larger panels, a bench-fitting version is available. This is equally easy to operate, and very effective.

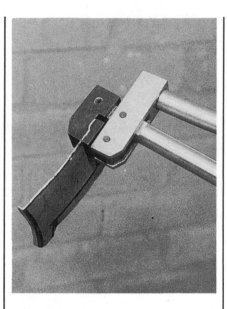

FWT22.►By squeezing the handles together, on the hand-held tool, a neat step is formed in the repair panel.

FWT23.◄Final trial fitting can now take place; we tapped the repair plate into position using a rubber hammer, and, much to our delight, it fitted perfectly first time. If you aren't quite so lucky, minor trimming is normally all that is required.

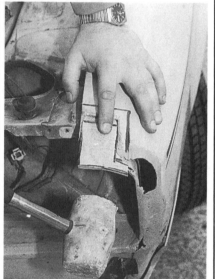

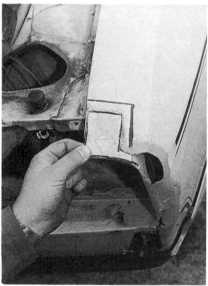

FWT24.►When all is well, remove the panel for the last time, so that the metal beneath the new panel can be inhibited against future rusting.

FWT25.◄We used a rust killer, followed by two thick coats of an anti-rust primer, as initial protection . . .

FWT26. ►... and followed this up with two coats of rust-resisting Hammerite paint, to give as much protection as possible.

FWT27. ◄ The repair section can now be finally fitted, and clamped into position, using a self-grip wrench. Making sure that the plate is still in the correct position, drill in $1/8$ in. hole as close as possible to the wrench, to accommodate a blind rivet.

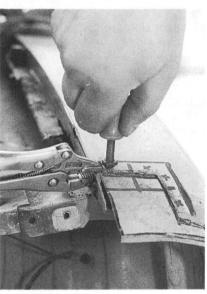

FWT28. ► Countersink the hole, so that the rivet head is pulled flush with the surrounding bodywork. Where possible, obtain countersunk rivets, although these are not always readily available.

FWT29. ◄ Use a hand-held rivet gun to fix the rivet in position – by squeezing the handles firmly together, a strong joint is made. Work around the edges of the plate, attaching rivets at strategic intervals so that the two sheets of metal are pulled together.

FWT30. ► Once the plate is in position, the usual rust-prevention and surface filling steps can be taken, to give a smooth surface for the final paint coats.

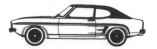

FWT31.▶ *If rust extends 'around the corner' to the wing panels just inside the bonnet, they too can be plated in a similar manner. However if rust is serious, and extends to the inner wing panel, repairs should only be made by welding in new metal. In either case, the first step is to rid the area of lacy, rusty metal, and cut out a suitable steel plate with which to repair the area.*

FWT32.▶ *The vice can again be used for shaping the plate – we used two right-angled lengths of aluminium here (clamped in the vice jaws), since a sharp 90 degree angle was required. The aluminium will help prevent the repair plate from becoming damaged by the vice jaws, too.*

FWT33.◀ *The neat 90 degree angle required along the length of the repair plate was again achieved by hammering. This time we used a fairly heavy hammer, and flattened the metal a little at a time against the aluminium formers.*

FWT34.▶ *After rust-proofing and painting exposed metal, the plate can be attached. Even if you intend to weld the plate in position, it can be riveted in place first, to hold it during welding operations. This method can be especially useful if you are working on your own.*

FWT35. ▲ *Final surface filling can now be carried out to the repaired areas. With care, the result will be indistinguishable from a new panel, and should last indefinitely.*

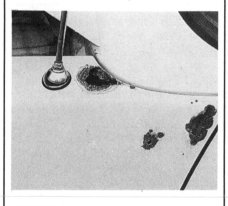

FWT36. ▲ *The rear upper corners of the same front wing were the only other damaged sections – mud had collected beneath the wing. This is a common problem on all Capris.*

FWT37. ► *Once again, suitable steel plates can be fabricated and attached by riveting or welding.*

FWT38. ▲ *Following initial surface filling with waterproof, glass-reinforced paste, the repairs can be completed using proprietary body filler, primer and top coats.*

Door hinge pin replacement

Capris are particularly vulnerable to wear in the door hinge pins, since the doors are wide and fairly heavy. Serious wear is common after a few years, especially if the hinge pins have not received regular attention from an oil can. The doors will creak when moved, and will eventually drop at the rear, while becoming increasingly difficult to open and close.

The top hinge pin wears more rapidly than the lower one, and very often replacement of just the upper pin will cure the trouble completely. The techniques for removing the old pin and fitting a new one are similar for either hinge, and a 'special' tool is required. However, this can easily be made at home, as described later.

The main problem with removing the old pins is that the

top edge of each door folds inwards, over the top of the upper hinge pin, while the lower edge of the door, adjacent to the sill, also folds inwards, below the bottom of the lower pin. In either case, therefore, access with the tool, for knocking out the pins, is VERY restricted! Patience is needed, but in fact the job is far easier than might be imagined.

New hinge pins are available from Ford dealers, and cost just a few pence each.

HPR1.▼ *Start by making your 'special' tool, which, once fabricated, can be used again and again – it can also be used on other Fords, for example Escorts. You need two lengths of ¹/₄ inch diameter round steel bar – one, about 2³/₄ inches long, the other, bent at 45° for the last half-inch at one end, about 2¹/₄ inches long. You also need a length of flat steel bar, approximately 14 inches long, 1 inch deep and ¹/₂ inch wide.*

Drill a ¹/₄ inch diameter hole, approximately ¹/₂ inch deep, ¹/₄ inch from one end of the flat bar, so that it will just grip either of the short, round steel rods.

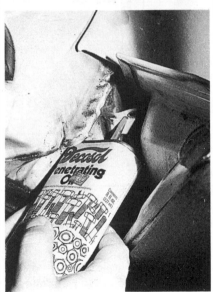

HPR2.◄ *Open the affected door (the hinge pins on the driver's side normally wear more rapidly than those on the passenger door), and carefully prise off the dust cover from the top of the hinge, using a flat-bladed screwdriver.*

HPR3. *Apply copious quantities of penetrating oil to the hinge pin, opening and closing the door several times, so that the oil works its way around the pin. Then leave the oil to do its work for at least an hour or two* ◄ *(preferably overnight).*

HPR4.▼ *The upper hinge pin MUST come out downwards, since the upper edge of the door prevents it from moving upwards very far. However, the pin on our Capri was more than reluctant to move downwards, to start with. We therefore attacked it from below, using our special tool and the straight length of round steel rod. This encouraged the pin to move upwards a little way – we coated the exposed section of pin with more penetrating oil, then tapped it back down again, and repeated the process several times.*

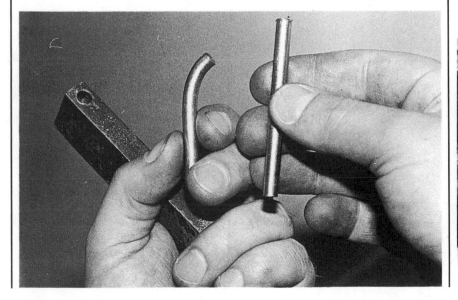

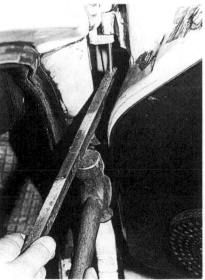

HPR5.►When the pin was moving more freely up and down, we had another attempt at dislodging it downwards from the hinge, this time using the length of round rod with the angled end. In the early stages, a spacer – such as an old socket bar – is required, between the hammer and the corner of the special tool. Great care is needed at all times to avoid hitting the surrounding bodywork with the hammer! Get an assistant to take the weight of the door as the pin is removed; alternatively the lower edge of the door can be supported on blocks of wood.

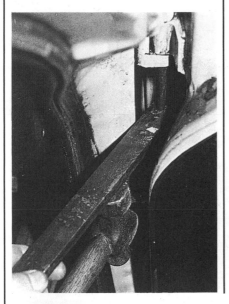

HPR6.◄ The new hinge pin should then be greased, and can be very carefully tapped into place from below. We used our length of flat bar to help with this operation, as it is impossible to hit the pin directly with anything but a very tiny (and ineffective in this application!) hammer.

HPR7.►Always give the new pin a good squirt or two of engine oil to keep it moving freely; again, open and close the door several times to work the oil in. Repeat the lubrication every month or so to prolong the life of the pin indefinitely. Don't forget to refit the dust cover to the top of the hinge.

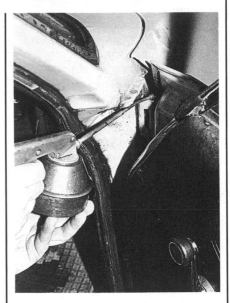

HPR8.◄Once the new hinge pins have been fitted, you may have to adjust the height of the door catch/striker plate to allow the door to close as it should. First apply a little engine oil to all the moving parts of the catch assembly (wipe off excess with a clean rag), to help the door shut easily and quietly.

New hinge pins normally remove all free play from the hinge assemblies, since, fortunately, each pin tends to wear more rapidly than the body of the hinge.

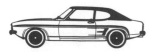

Rear bodywork/roof repairs

It is not unusual for rust to appear around the rear window, bootlid or tailgate areas, particularly on older Capris.

The Mark I cars often suffer from rust around the perimeter of the bootlid, and the patching techniques already described can be applied to this area. However, if rust is extensive, the easiest solution is probably to find a bootlid in better condition than the one on your car (they can still be found), and simply swap panels. This is a straight-forward spanner job.

The hatchback models seem to be especially prone to rusting in the vicinity of the tailgate hinges, as illustrated in the 'Buying' chapter, and along the lower edges of the tailgate. In either case, rectification is far easier if the tailgate is first removed from the car. This should be done very carefully indeed to avoid damaging the paintwork, and it is essential to have another person around to help you when removing and re-fitting the hatchback door. Even then, it is only too easy to damage the freshly repaired roof, when fitting the tailgate (guess how I know . . . ?).

It is a good idea to tackle just one side of the car at a time, so that the original, opposite side can be used as a reference throughout the repair operations.

RBR1.► Before attempting to remove the tailgate, mark the position of the hinges in relation to the panel, using a ball point pen or a pencil. This only takes a moment, and will ensure that the tailgate goes back onto the vehicle in precisely the correct position. This therefore saves a great deal of time being spent on re-aligning the tailgate (in its aperture), the lock, and so on.

RBR2.◄ With the hinges thus marked, loosen (but DON'T yet remove) the bolts securing the hinges to the tailgate. A ring or socket spanner should be used, especially if the bolts are tight, to avoid 'rounding' the bolt heads, thereby rendering them extremely difficult to remove.

RBR3. ▼ Use a large Phillips screwdriver to slacken the screws securing the support struts to the tailgate – they can be left attached to the vehicle at their lower ends. We found that an impact screwdriver, operated by hand, was ideal. It gave enough leverage, without having to hit it with a hammer.

An assistant is required, to take the weight of the tailgate, as the screws are removed.

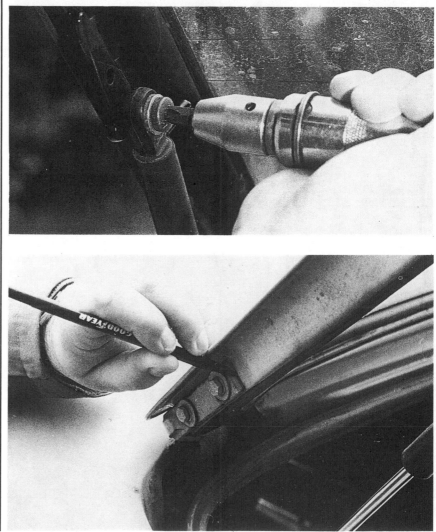

RBR4.◄ *The hinge bolts can now be taken out, and the tailgate VERY carefully lifted clear of the car. This is very definitely a two person operation!*

It is a good idea to lay newspapers or an old blanket on the floor, well clear of the working area, so that the tailgate will not be scratched by contact with the ground, or trodden on by passing people!

RBR5.► *With the tailgate out of the way, it was clear that on this Capri the rust above each of the tailgate hinges was fairly extensive, although fortunately the main roof panel was not holed to the extent that water could enter. The hinge supports, too, were sound, thankfully. Fortunately they seldom suffer structural disintegration.*

RBR6.◄ *It is vital that ALL rust is removed from the affected areas, as far as humanly possible, or the problem will re-appear at a later date. It is therefore necessary, in the first instance, to chisel away all loose rust and lacy metal from around the hinge area. We laid a large sheet of paper across the hatchback floor area and rear seats, before starting work, to keep dust and rust at bay.*

RBR7.► *An angle grinder, or sanding attachment in an electric drill, can then be used to grind back remaining rust, until clean, bright metal appears.*

RBR8.◄ *Before proceeding further, a vacuum cleaner can be used (ask permission first, where appropriate, to avoid undue wrath!) to rid the zone of dust and debris. A soft brush can be used if permission to use the vacuum cleaner is not forthcoming, but this takes longer.*

RBR9.► *When all the dust has been removed, apply rust killer to search out any remaining corrosion buried in pits, etc. Allow to cure as directed on the container.*

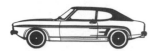

RBR10.► Cut a small metal plate to fit the aperture, so that when secured in position, it will give the correct profile to the edge of the roof. The techniques for measuring and cutting such plates have been covered in earlier sections of this chapter.

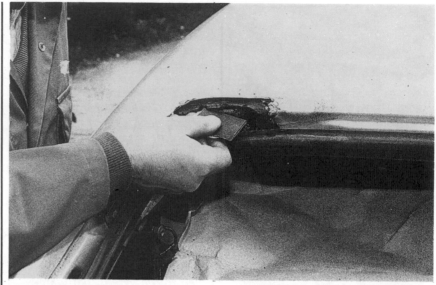

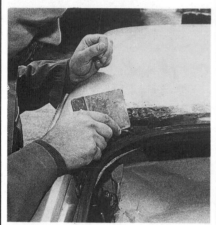

RBR11.▲ The repair plate can be riveted in place, or welded – but in this case the interior headlining and tailgate seal will need to be removed first.

Alternatively, the plate can simply be positioned and held with glass-reinforced paste, which, once hardened, is extremely strong. The area is non-structural, and does not take any direct load from the tailgate hinges, so the repair, which is purely cosmetic, does not need further reinforcement.

RBR12.▲ Final surface filling can then be carried out, building the filler up in thin layers until the correct profile begins to emerge. Stop when the surface is just proud of the surrounding roof line, to avoid unnecessary rubbing-down.

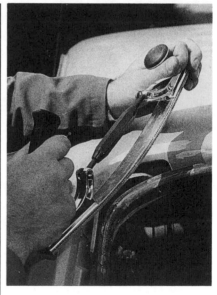

RBR13.▲ We used the Sykes-Pickavant Adjustable Body File once again to shape the filler. This quickly restored the correct lines of the roof panel at this point, so that . . .

RBR14.◄ . . . a minimum amount of rubbing down with wet and dry paper (used dry) was required. We used coarse (100 grade) paper initially, gradually working down to 400 grade for final smoothing. The finished repair was then cleaned, primed and sprayed using the techniques described fully in the 'Rear Wheel Arch Repairs' section of this chapter.

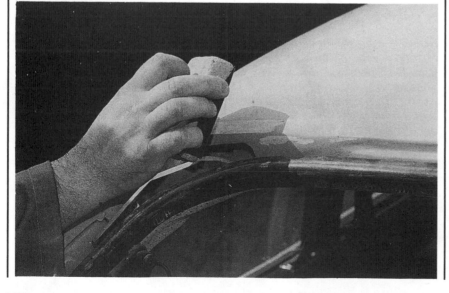

RBR15.►While the tailgate is off the car, it gives an ideal opportunity to sort out the corrosion which almost inevitably seems to be present along the lower edge of the panel. Start by chiselling off loose, flaky rust. We used an old screwdriver for this, since it was handy for getting into the smaller pits.

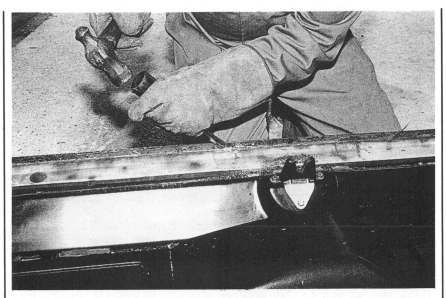

RBR16.►A sanding disc can then be used, fitted to an angle grinder or electric drill, to rid the flange of any remaining rust. Stop when bright metal is reached, then treat the surface to a chemical rust killer, filler (as necessary), primer, and top coats. Such measures will help preserve the tailgate indefinitely.

On completion of repairs, the tailgate should be re-fitted to the car (taking great care of the paintwork in the process), referring to the alignment marks made prior to dismantling, as described in RBR1.

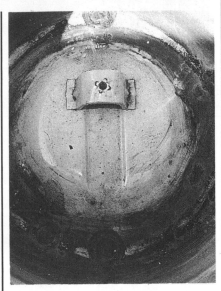

Below decks

An area which is often ignored during major restorations is that of the luggage compartment, and especially the 'below decks' area beneath it. The Capri is no exception to this, and very often the only time that anyone looks beneath the 'false' floor in the luggage area is when the spare wheel has to be fitted!

However, it is worthwhile making positive steps towards tidying this part of the car. This is not only to make this area 'look pretty', but also to preserve it indefinitely. The chances are that the spare wheel well and surrounding metalwork will have suffered from water ingress due to a leaking boot or tailgate seal, or even through condensation. Replace any damaged seals discovered, to avoid similar problems in the future.

It is often the case that the steel boot floor of the car is found to be very rusty, so the earlier steps are taken to tackle the problem, the better.

Although the detail rear end design differed between the Mark I cars and later, hatchback, Capris, rectification principles apply equally to all models.

BD1.▲ Lift out the 'false' floor of the luggage compartment, the rear screen washer reservoir (where fitted) and the spare wheel, to make a close examination of the metalwork below. This Mark II Capri is a typical example, and displayed condensation and a fair amount of rust here. The steel 'bungs' in the spare wheel well had almost completely disintegrated.

Remove the rusted bungs, and use a sanding disc or flapwheel to rid the surrounding steelwork of all traces of rust. Treat the damaged areas to a chemical rust killer, followed by two thick coats of anti-rust primer.

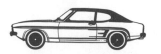

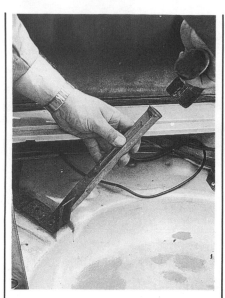

BD2. ◄ *The bracket securing the rear screenwash reservoir is very often found to be severely corroded, as in this Capri. The screws holding the bracket to the car were seized solid, and the heads were damaged, so we simply chiselled them away, to release the bracket.*

BD3. ► *Early hopes of 'cleaning up' the original bracket soon disappeared when it broke in half upon receiving its freedom (this often happens). So we scoured the local scrapyard and discovered a 'low mileage' bracket from a late Mark III. We invested 50 pence (money no object!) and brought the 'new' item home.*

BD4. ◄ *We treated the replacement bracket with two generous coats of glossy anti-rust paint, to protect it for the future. This treatment is worthwhile, even if you intend to re-use the original item.*

BD5. ► *By this time the anti-rust primer in the spare wheel well had cured, so we rubbed down the surface with 400 grade wet and dry paper (used dry), then coated the entire area with three coats of grey primer. This gives a good base for the final paint coats.*

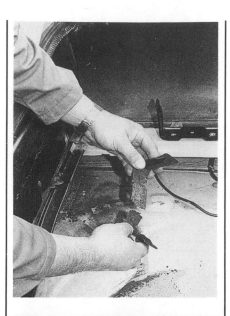

BD6. ◄ *After half an hour, the area was ready for top-coating – the boot floor was beginning to look smart once again. Apply several coats to give lasting protection.*

102

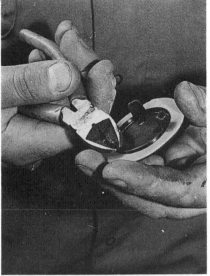

BD7.◄ Since the steel bungs are usually past saving, it is worth buying new ones. The replacement bungs, supplied by our local Ford dealers, were made of plastic, and had hooked feet, which made them stand proud of the panelwork. We therefore used a pair of side cutters to trim the feet so that the bungs sat flush with the floor.

BD8.► A bead of sealing compound can be used to bridge the gap between the bung and the boot floor. Make sure that the sealant is spread evenly around the base of the bung . . .

BD9.◄ . . . and then push it firmly home, in the spare wheel well. Repeat the process for all three bungs in this area.

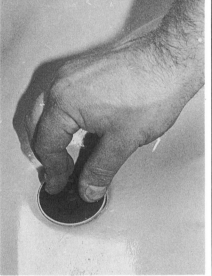

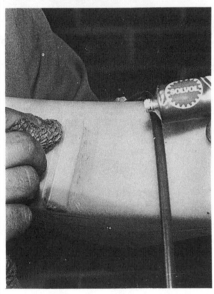

BD10.► It is worth cleaning the rear screen washer reservoir before re-fitting it to the car. We used a paste type chrome cleaner, which works wonders on some types of plastic – try it on a small section first.

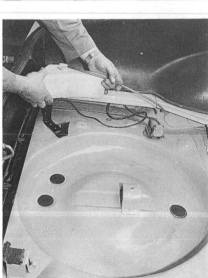

BD11.◄ With the spare wheel well repainted, the replacement screenwash reservoir mounting bracket installed, and the restored reservoir itself re-fitted, the 'below decks' area of the luggage compartment will take on an 'as new' look.

Body panels

Before undertaking any major vehicle restoration, it is useful to know the availability of body panels for your car, since these are usually more difficult to find than mechanical spares.

Luckily, the Capris covered by this book were built in considerable numbers, which at least helps the supply situation, and, to a certain extent, keeps the prices competitive.

Generally speaking, the later the car, the easier it will be to obtain bodywork sections for it. Therefore Mark III Capris present few problems, and even the Mark I models, dating back to 1969, are still provided for.

Fortunately, there are several avenues to explore in your search for new panels. It is worth trying your local Ford dealer, although it has to be said that, by now,

103

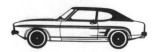

many of the bodywork spares for early models will have long since gone. If you do strike lucky, however, the panel will, of course, be a genuine Ford item. Autojumbles are another useful source of 'original' type panels.

There are also, now, several specialist suppliers of Ford parts, listed in Appendix 6, and they often have body sections for sale; it's worth a 'phone call.

Another source could be your 'High Street' motor accessory shop, or local parts factor – they often supply body panels, as well as mechanical spares.

Several firms specialise in producing vehicle body sections and complete panels, and, for example, LMC Panels can supply a number of bodywork components for the Capris, and indeed have recently extended their range of panels for these models.

BP1. ▼ *The diagrams illustrate just how many panels can be obtained for the models covered by this book, from one supplier alone – LMC Panels, of Westbury, Wiltshire. It pays to buy good quality panels, for ease of fitting and durability. (Reproduced by kind permission of LMC Panels.)*

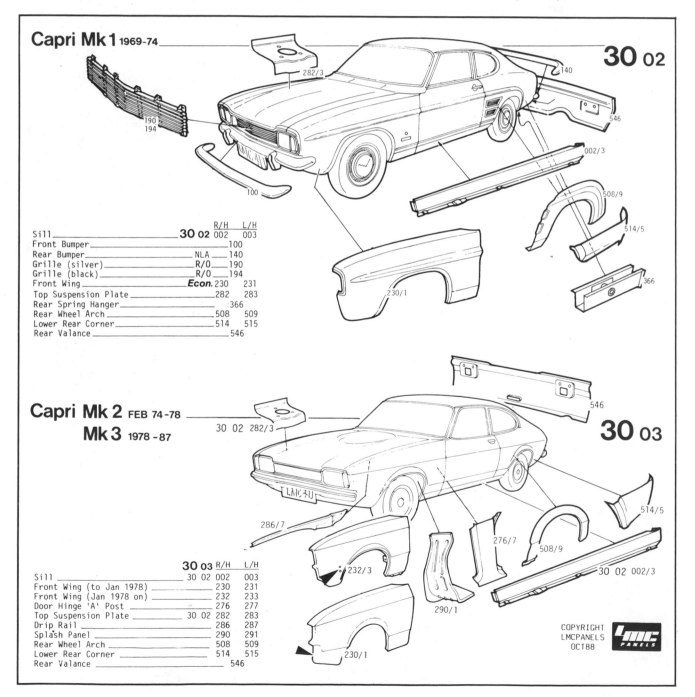

Capri Mk 1 1969-74

30 02

Sill	**30 02**	R/H 002	L/H 003
Front Bumper			100
Rear Bumper		NLA	140
Grille (silver)		R/O	190
Grille (black)		R/O	194
Front Wing	**Econ.**	230	231
Top Suspension Plate		282	283
Rear Spring Hanger			366
Rear Wheel Arch		508	509
Lower Rear Corner		514	515
Rear Valance			546

Capri Mk 2 FEB 74-78
Mk 3 1978-87

30 03

	30 03	R/H	L/H
Sill	30 02	002	003
Front Wing (to Jan 1978)		230	231
Front Wing (Jan 1978 on)		232	233
Door Hinge 'A' Post		276	277
Top Suspension Plate	30 02	282	283
Drip Rail		286	287
Splash Panel		290	291
Rear Wheel Arch		508	509
Lower Rear Corner		514	515
Rear Valance			546

COPYRIGHT
LMCPANELS
OCT88

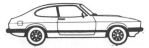

Major bodywork restoration

Earlier in this chapter we dealt with many of the routine, minor bodywork challenges which you are likely to encounter on any well-worn Capri. However, many cars – especially early examples – are found to be suffering from more serious rot, or have been accident-damaged. In such cases, often the only sensible option is to replace the relevant panels, or, if these are not obtainable, to fabricate sections and weld them in place on the vehicle. Repairs to any structural areas of the vehicle MUST be carried out by welding, and not by the 'cosmetic' methods covered earlier.

Although, for easier reference, we have dealt with the various repair and replacement jobs under appropriate headings to cover individual sections of the vehicle, in practice you will often find that several areas of the car rust in unison. Therefore it is seldom that you will, for example, be able to replace a front wing without at leat some attentions to the sills. We have therefore cross-referenced the relevant sections, where appropriate.

MBR1.► *If you are already aware that much of the panelwork on your Capri will need to be replaced or repaired by welding in new metal, it is a good idea to relieve the body shell of as many components as possible, before you start work in earnest. This applies particularly to interior trim, which is best stored safely out of the way. Not only will this prevent damage to the trim, but it could also help to avoid a fire, for example when welding. If you haven't already done so, drain and remove the fuel tank, as described in detail earlier in this chapter. Store all components removed from the car in a dry place, where they cannot be damaged.*

MBR2.▲ *Once the lamp units, grille, and so on are removed, it is easier to see areas of rust at the front of the car, especially around the wings. We also suspected that the front spoiler on this 'guinea pig' Capri would be concealing a rusty front valance.*

Front wing (and valance) replacement

The front wings on all Capris are of the welded-on variety, which, unfortunately, means that they

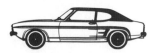

have to be cut off, and new ones welded on in their place. Removing the old wings is not a difficult operation, although care needs to be taken to ensure that sufficient metal is left along the wing support flanges to weld the new wing to. If in doubt, cut more of the old wing away than you need, leaving surplus metal to be later cleaned from the body shell. If you cut too much away from the car's body shell to start with, you will then have to weld in new metal, to form a support for the new wing!

We have included in this section details of how to change the front valance, and the front 'chassis' cross-member, since these are often found to be rusty, along with the wings, and are best dealt with in conjunction with the wing change. Of course, if damage is confined to individual panels, these can be replaced on their own.

You will need to have access to welding equipment when attaching the new panels to the vehicle, together with the necessary safety goggles and gloves.

It is important to appreciate that, almost inevitably, removal of the wings will reveal further corrosion, which needs to be dealt with before the new panels can be fitted. This is especially true of the areas surrounding the suspension leg turrets, the inner wings, the bulkheads and the front bumper mountings. Therefore, always allow far more time than you think you will need, to tackle a wing change. This is important if the car is required as daily transport – far better to start a wing change on a Friday evening, for example, than at Sunday lunchtime, if the Capri has to take you to work on the Monday!

It is a good idea to leave the bonnet in position, assuming it is correctly aligned, while the wings are changed – it will help to gauge the correct wing gaps at each side, when the new panels are fitted. It is also well worth

painting the hidden surfaces of new panels or repair sections with two good coats of anti-rust paint (except around edges to be welded), before they are attached to the car.

FWR1. ▼ A close inspection of the wing will reveal how badly rusted it is. If it is as severely eaten away as this – and this wing was just as rotten in most areas – the only sensible answer is to replace it with a new wing, having first rectified any corrosion damage discovered beneath the wing.

FWR2. ▲ A chisel or a sharp bolster can be used to separate the wing from the vehicle; start at the rear and upper flanges of the wing, cutting into the wing, rather than the main body shell, as already described. Any surplus metal can be cleaned off afterwards using a chisel or an angle grinder. In fact if your Capri is as rusty as this one, you will find that the rust will offer little resistance to your attacks on it!

FWR3. ▼ Continue your assault at the front of the wing, taking great care to separate the outer wing flange from the headlamp surround without causing damage to this panel, which can be re-used if sound.

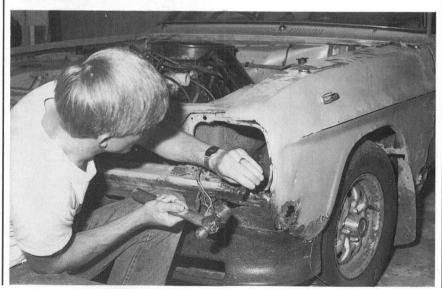

FWR4.➤ After a few minutes, the wing should be ready to remove. Always take care when lifting it – the recently cut edges will be very sharp. It is best to dispose of the rusty metal as soon as possible after removing it from the vehicle, once any trim items, etc. have been salvaged.

FWR5. As the wing comes away from the vehicle, you will be able to gauge the true extent of corrosion beneath. Even if your car looks as bad as this Mark I did, don't despair – things always look worse before they can get better! ➤

FWR6.▲ The offside wing on our 'guinea pig' Capri had in fact been replaced by a previous owner. However, the inner wing was so badly rusted that the job had to be done again – so off came the recently-fitted wing.

FWR7.➤ With the outer wing removed, it is necessary to make a very thorough inspection of the inner wing – especially along the top, and in the vicinity of the upper mounting for the MacPherson strut. The three-litre cars have this triangular reinforcement plate fitted, to stiffen the upper mounting. Check this very carefully for rust.

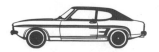

FWR8.►*Check the lower areas of the inner panelwork, fore and aft of the front wheel, also the door pillar, using a screwdriver to prod the metal with, where necessary, to establish how bad things really are. Only then can you formulate an exact plan of attack.*

FWR9.▲ *If rust at the rear of this area is severe, as on this Capri, it is worth buying a complete new scuttle/door pillar ('A' post) panel. This will cost around £50, from a Ford dealer, but has complex shapes, and must be strong to support the weight of the door.*

FWR10.►*First of all, of course, the old panel has to come off, and to allow this, the original spot welds have to be broken; this can be achieved using an electric drill . . .*

FWR11.◄ *. . . then by carefully driving a bolster or slim chisel between the inner and outer panels at this point. Take particular care not to wreck the inner panel in the process.*

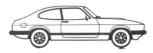

FWR12. ◄ The forward section of this panel can be removed in a similar fashion, until the car looks like this. The original panel was completely rotten on this Capri.

FWR13. ▲ Clean up all the bodywork flanges, using an angle grinder (AND WEARING SAFETY GOGGLES). If necessary, the edges of panels can be 'dressed' back to shape, using two hammers.

FWR14. ◄ In order that the new welds can be 'dropped' into place, a hole punch (or an electric drill) can be used to make a series of holes, equidistant from each other, around the outer edge of the new panel. The windscreen pillar section was removed from this large, original Ford panel, since the pillars were sound on the project Capri.

FWR15. ◄ The next job is to transfer the small brackets from the old to the new panel. Note the heavy duty hinge mounting plates on the new panel.

FWR16.►*Make quite sure that any brackets transferred from the original panel are fitted in EXACTLY the same position on the new one – mark this before welding in place. This particular bracket is to hold the outer end of the parcel tray. Before attaching the new panel to the car, it obviously makes sense to repair any holes in the front end of the inner sill, while this area is open for access.*

FWR17.►*Normally if the outer sill needs to be changed, this would be done before fitting the scuttle/door pillar panel. However, during fitting of the sill, the relative position of the door to its surrounding panelwork has to be constantly checked, and this is difficult if the door post is very weak, as on this Capri. In such cases, it makes sense to install a new door pillar section before changing the sill.*

ALWAYS, before starting to weld, clamp the new panel into position, then check that it fits precisely, and that the existing flanges on the vehicle mate with it. Use welding clamps or self-grip wrenches, to hold the panel in place.

FWR18.►*Only when the panel is in exactly the right position should welding be carried out. Apply a few tack welds, at intervals, initially, then double-check that the panel is still correctly aligned. Try the door on the panel to make sure that the gaps all around the door are equal, before finally welding the panel in place, all around its edges.*

FWR19.►You may find that you will have to fabricate small repair panels to bridge any gaps between the new metal sections and the existing bodywork. The area at each side of the lower windscreen support panel is a favourite for rust, and small plates like this may need to be cut out and welded into position.

FWR20.▲ Once again, re-fit the door to ensure that it still fits correctly, before proceeding further . . .

FWR21.▲ . . . it should align perfectly with the existing bodywork, including the sill.

FWR22.▲ If you are lucky, you may only require small repair panels, like this one, for fitting just ahead of the forward end of the sill, or . . .

FWR23.◄ . . . this slimmer, vertical door pillar ('A' post) panel. These are available commercially, and do not need to be fabricated. They are also, of course, far cheaper than the complete repair panel we showed being fitted to the nearside of this Capri, but their use will depend on only minimal rust damage being present in the vicinity. Having offered up the smaller repair panels to the offside of this car, it was decided, after all, that the larger, full scuttle/door pillar section would be required. Although the original offside pillar was still fairly sound, the metalwork further forward was very thin.

FWR24.► *As already mentioned, where the door pillar is comparatively sound, it is preferable to replace the sill, if necessary, before attacking the post (full details of sill replacement are given later in this chapter). This will then ensure the correct relationship between the door post, the sill and the door itself. This is difficult if the door post is weak, as it had been on the nearside of this car, which is why, on that side, the door post repair panel was fitted first. On the offside, which had a sound pillar, the sill was replaced before the scuttle/door pillar.*

FWR25.► *Much of the front end of each sill is concealed behind the outer panelwork when the wing is fitted. Ideally, to do the job properly, it is best to remove the front wings if you are intending to replace the sills, so that better access can be gained to the areas at the front of the sills. The new sills can then be fitted, followed by the wings. However, since the front wings are usually destroyed in the process of removing them, this course is normally practical only where you are changing the wings anyway.*

FWR26.► *It is very likely that the reinforced areas, surrounding the upper strut mounting, will be rusty. If the inner wings are also bad, it may pay to purchase a complete panel, like this, which incorporates the webbed support and upper mounting turret for the strut, as well as new bumper mountings. It should be said, though, that this complete inner wing panel is expensive, and EXTREMELY difficult to fit, without a jig. It is hardly a d-i-y job, unless you are very experienced with major bodywork reconstruction. This panel is for the three-litre models, and incorporates an extra bracing member between the top of the inner wing and the upper strut mounting.*

FWR27.➤ If rust damage is comparatively localised, repair plates can be fashioned and welded into position, once the rusty sections are removed. Poking the area with a screwdriver will reveal whether the metal is sound. In this case, only the central area of the turret was damaged, so the corrosion was cut out and a neat repair plate made. It is important, for such load-bearing areas, that any repair panels are made from steel AT LEAST as thick as the original metal.

　Note that, on this Capri, which had previously had a new wing fitted, the wing-mounting flange, at the top, had almost disappeared!

FWR28.➤ Having cut the repair plate from a suitable sheet of steel, offer it up the vehicle, to ensure that it will fit correctly. Trim the patch until it is a perfect fit in the aperture.

FWR29.▲ Tack-weld the repair plate(s) in position, using a hammer to tap the steel into the correct profile, where necessary.

FWR30.➤ Finally, weld the plate all along its seams, so that it forms an integral part of the vehicle's structure. Clean up the welds, if necessary, using an angle grinder (AND WEARING GOGGLES), then treat the area to two good coats of an anti-rust paint. Similar repair sections can be made and fitted to deal with other localised areas of rust in the vicinity of the inner wing.

FWR31. ▲ The next step is to remove rusty metal from the upper wing support flange. This can be achieved using a hacksaw, to start with. The flange on this Capri was too thin to hold the new wing.

FWR32. ▲ Tin snips are more convenient to deal with some parts of the flange; remaining rough edges can be removed by using an angle grinder (WEAR GOGGLES).

FWR33. ▲ If the headlamp support panels are found to be very rusty, new ones are obtainable. Offer the new panel up to the original, to ascertain exactly how much metal needs to be removed from the vehicle. Once again, when cutting off the old panel, take very great care not to destroy any of the metalwork which needs to be left on the vehicle. If the front valance on your Capri is sound, and you are not intending to replace it, the new headlamp panel can be clamped in position and the new wing trial-fitted. When the fit is perfect, the headlamp panel can be welded into position.

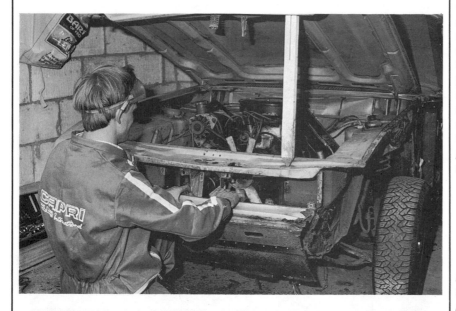

FWR34. ◄ The front valance on this Capri was, as expected, very rusty, and was removed after drilling out the spot welds, using the method shown earlier in this section. The flanges can be cleaned up, using an angle grinder, once the main panel has been removed.

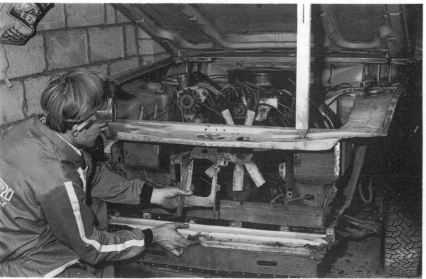

FWR35. ◄ DON'T throw away the **old valance**, for the reinforcement brackets on the old panel need to be transferred to the new one. Carefully cut these away from the original valance, and weld into position on the replacement.

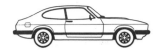

FWR36.◄ The 'chassis' box section across the front of the car often suffers from rust along its lower edge, to which are bolted the anti-roll bar support brackets. The box section is formed by the joining together of the two panels shown, which are fairly expensive, but which are available if required. Of course, if rust is minimal, and localised, small repair patches can be fabricated and welded in place.

FWR37.◄ If corrosion damage is extensive, the panel should be replaced. Start by cutting through the centre section of the member, using a junior hacksaw.

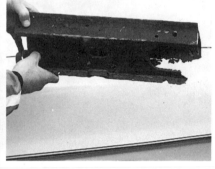

FWR38.▲ With this section removed, it was evident that the remaining metal was becoming thin and, even if it had been patched, would have given further problems in the future.

FWR39.◄ With the centre section removed, further trimming is required to remove all the original metal. The car needs to be carefully jacked and supported on axle stands, for easy access to each end of the chassis member.

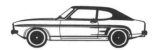

FWR40. ►The next job is to unbolt the anti-roll bar supports from the remains of the cross-member, before finally cutting this out, using a hammer and bolster. Take care not to damage the chassis side rails in the process.

The various models differ slightly in this area; for example, the three-litre cars like this one have extra reinforcement for the side chassis rails – even so, holes are likely on older Capris!

FWR41. ▲ The inner wings on both sides of this Capri were quite badly holed; in all such cases the rust must be totally removed, by cutting and grinding, and later (please see FWR43), appropriate repair patches can be fabricated. Note the flanges on the chassis side rails – these were cleaned up using an angle grinder, ready to accept the two panels comprising the new chassis cross-member.

FWR42. ◄ The rear/top section of the cross-member is fitted first, tack-welding it into position, to start with.

FWR43. ◄ Now, using the techniques described in the 'Minor Bodywork Repairs' section of this chapter, a repair plate can be fabricated from sheet steel, for the side rails/inner wings. The repair plates must be of at least the same thickness as the original panel. Make sure that the holes in the new panels are pre-drilled to the exact positions; the two large holes at the front of this plate are for the bumper brackets, while the smaller two, at the rear, are for the anti-roll bar bracket.

FWR44. ▲ Similar repair sections can be made for the inside faces of the inner wings. The panels can be held in place using welding clamps or self-grip wrenches, prior to welding.

FWR45. ▲ The front half of the box section can now be added, and welded to the rear half, already in position, to complete the cross-member.

FWR46. ▲ With the panels now welded all along their edges, the front of the car will have regained its strength. The vehicle will now have enough new metal for the valance panel to be welded on at all the correct points, to give a solid, long-lasting assembly.

FWR47.◄ Offer up the valance to the car, to make sure that it fits flush, and that the brackets line up correctly with the body shell.

FWR48.◄ The valance can be clamped in position for final alignment checks. Temporarily 're-hang' each of the front wings, to help to gauge correct fitment. It is helpful to have a friend or two to assist you when checking alignment.

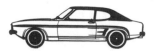

FWR49.➤When satisfied that all the major panels will easily fit together, remove the wings again, also the clamps and the front valance.

FWR50.▲ Now is the time to offer up the headlamp mounting panels, making sure that they will fit flush with the surrounding metalwork. If necessary, 'dress' the support flanges on the vehicle, until smooth, using two hammers.

FWR51.➤When the headlamp panels fit perfectly, clamp them in position, prior to trial-fitting of the front valance panel and the new front wings.

FWR52.➤If you find it difficult to clamp these panels without the clamps fouling the surrounding bodywork, they can be temporarily attached by using blind rivets, to hold them in the correct position. On no account start welding yet – the wings and the valance MUST first be trial-fitted, and checked to ensure that their fit is perfect before committing yourself to installing them permanently!

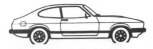

FWR53. ►*The next few stages are tricky and time-consuming, but care here is vital to ensure that the car looks 'right' when all the welding has been carried out. Start by hanging each of the new wings onto the car, checking for fit all around their edges, and at each of the contact points. The gaps between the doors and the wings should be equal all the way down, each side. The wings must also line up with the bonnet (with equidistant gaps each side), the headlamp support panels, and the front valance, when this is offered up. Again, the more helpers you have during these operations, the better.*

FWR54. ▲ *Only when you are completely satisfied that all is well should you tack-weld the valance in place.*

FWR55. ▲ *Check once again that the fit between all the panels is perfect – look at the gaps at each side of the bonnet . . .*

FWR56. ▲ *. . . and the alignment between the wings and the valance – this MUST be correct. Only then can the valance be finally welded securely into place.*

FWR57. ◄ *The headlamp support panels too can be welded into position, so that they are firmly attached to the inner wings, at the top, and the front valance, at the bottom. Use tack welds to start with, then . . .*

119

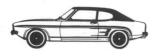

FWR58.►. . . trial-fit the wings once more, to ensure that all is well. The wings can then be removed and the headlamp panels finally welded around their edges.

FWR59.▲ The wings can now be clamped into position. The doors, having been fitted during the alignment procedures, have to be removed . . .

FWR60.►. . . to allow access for welding the wings at their rear edges. Again, make tack welds only, initially, completing the welding after double-checking that the alignment is still correct.

FWR61.►The wings must be clamped and welded at their lower rear corners, to attach them to the floor/sills. They also require welding at the front, to the valance, and to the headlamp support panels. Finally, the inner wing panels must be built up to the inner flanges of the outer wings, filling any gaps with appropriate repair panels. These cannot be installed until the outer wings are in position (in perfect alignment at front and rear, and at the same height as the bonnet, when closed). Repair sections for the joints between inner and outer wings can be purchased, and trimmed to size as required, before welding in place, to finish the job of attaching the wings.

Seam sealer can afterwards be applied to keep the elements at bay from exposed joints – push well into any small gaps between the panels.

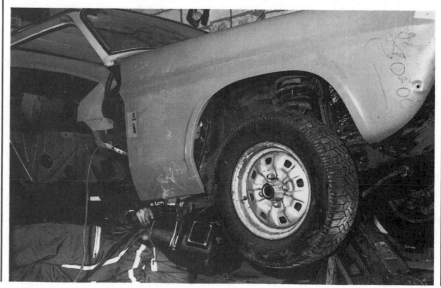

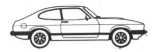

Sill change (with front wing on)

Ideally, it is best to replace a rotten sill panel on a Capri with the front wing removed from the car. This allows better access to the front end of the sill, and to the hidden sections, behind the lower rear edge of the front wing. We show the stages of replacing a sill while the wing is removed, in the next section of this chapter.

However, Capri front wings are almost always destroyed by the process of removing them, so, unless the wings on your car are particularly rusty, or accident-damaged, you may naturally be reluctant to cut them off just to change the sills! It should be made clear though that if the bulkhead/door pillar panels are rusty, the wings should in any case come off for repairs to be made to these vital structural areas, as detailed earlier in this chapter.

To change a sill you will need cutting tools (hammer and bolster or slim chisel), an angle grinder, and of course welding equipment.

As with most such jobs, you may find that the inner sills and floor require patching, once the outer sill has been removed. Check these areas as far as possible in advance of tackling the sill, by looking inside the car, with the carpets removed, and by examining the floor/inner sill from beneath the car. It is also advisable to allow far more time for the job than you think you will need, to cope with any 'extra' tasks which almost always crop up. Typically, you should allow at least a whole day per side, in any case.

Of course, if rust damage is restricted to small areas of the sill, it can be rectified by cutting out repair sections from sheet steel, and welding them to the sill. The basic procedures for these operations are similar to those shown for repairs to other parts of the car, earlier in the chapter. Very often though, visible rust on a sill is just the 'tip of the iceberg'. If holes are present in one area, it usually won't be long before they crop up further along the panel, so make a detailed investigation of the sill before deciding whether repair or replacement is appropriate.

Always tackle one side of the car at a time; NEVER remove both sills at once – even if rusty, they will still be holding the car together. Leave the doors on the vehicle while changing the sill – their lower edges can be used to gauge correct alignment when fitting the new sills.

SCW01.▼ This Capri was in tidy condition, generally, and in particular, the front wings were very sound. Even the sills looked good – from a distance.

SCW02.◄ However, close inspection from below the nearside of the car revealed that the forward end of the sill was rusty, and holed. It was evident that the metal further back was becoming thin, too. So the decision was taken to replace, rather than to patch the panel. However, in view of the excellent condition of the front wings (and the fact that the under-wing structural bodywork components were sound), the owner was unwilling to remove them (and almost certainly destroy them in the process), so elected to fit a new sill while leaving the wings in place.

SCW03.►*The first step is to separate the upper edge of the existing sill from the vehicle. Using a bolster or slim chisel (WEAR PROTECTIVE GLOVES AND GOGGLES), very carefully slice the sill just below its upper edge, all along its length, leaving approximately $1/8$ inch of metal at the top. This area is normally sound.*

SCW04.◄*Similarly, open up the lower part of the sill, by using the bolster/chisel just outside of the lower flange.*

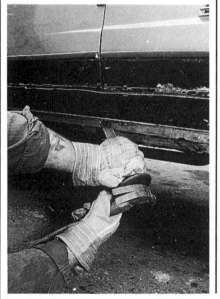

SCW05.►*Each end of the sill panel requires a vertical cut, to free it from the car – just behind the front wing, and immediately ahead of the rear wheel. Towards the end of the cutting operations, the sill can be carefully pulled downwards (WEAR PROTECTIVE GLOVES – the raw edges of the steel will be VERY sharp) to allow access for cutting through any particularly tough sections. As the sill on this Capri was pulled away, the extent of rust within the panel was evident.*

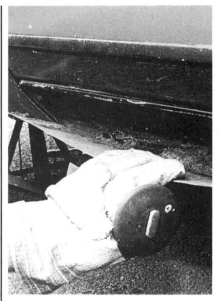

SCW06.◄*When all the cutting is complete, the outer sill can at last be parted from the car. Note how flimsy this one was, once detached around its edges. It would not have been long before holes had appeared all along the lower edge of this panel.*

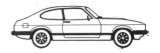

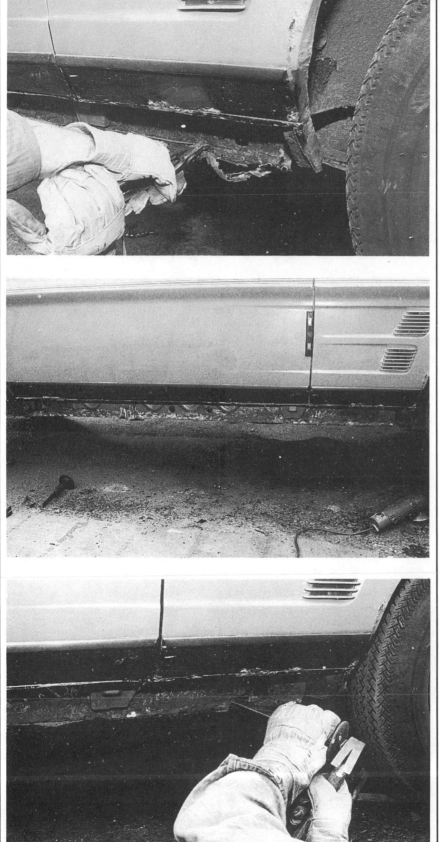

SCWO7. ◄ The inner sill must now be cleaned up and prepared for the new outer panel. The first step is to remove the remains of the lower flange of the original outer sill. This can be carefully chiselled from the bottom of the inner sill, or 'wound' away from the spot welds, using a pair of grips or a self-grip wrench. This is time-consuming but essential.

SCWO8. ▲ Once the strip of metal has been removed, use an angle grinder to grind off each of the spot welds along the lower edge of the inner sill. WEAR PROTECTIVE GLOVES AND GOGGLES during this operation. If the lower edge of the panel is distorted, 'dress' it back to shape using a hammer and dolly, or two hammers.

SCWO9. ◄ The next job is to sweep up all debris accumulated so far from the working area, and from below the car. This includes dust, rust, and lethal off-cuts of sharp metal. Next, look closely at the condition of the inner sill panel. This one was suffering from a few small holes just forward of the rear wheel, but was otherwise sound.

SCWO10. ◄ It is pointless to leave rust on the panel, so use the hammer and bolster/chisel to cut around the damaged area, until you reach sound metal.

123

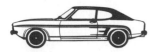

SCWO11.► The angle grinder is useful for cleaning up surface rust from the vicinity.

SCWO12.▲ Select a piece of steel sheet slightly larger than the required patch, and of AT LEAST the same thickness as the original panel, and use a pair of tin snips to trim the steel to size.

SCWO13.► Offer up the patch at each stage, to ensure that you don't remove too much metal. Make sure where possible that the lower edge of the patch finishes just above the bottom flange of the inner sill, or it will add an extra layer of metal (which will encourage rust) at the point where the new outer sill is to attach. In addition, the extra thickness of steel would prevent the new sill panel from fitting flush with the inner sill.

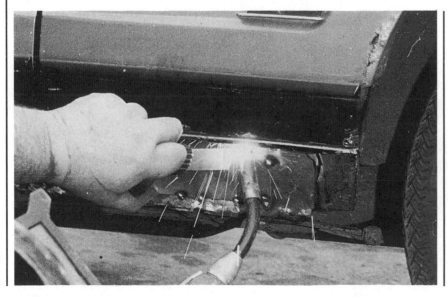

SCWO14.◄ Remove the carpets and interior trim, if still fitted, from inside the car, then weld the plate in place, using the bolster/chisel or a long screwdriver to hold the patch in the correct position, initially. Use tack welds to hold the plate firmly, then weld all around its perimeter.

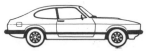

SCWO15. ►When all the welding is finished, rub down (with medium grade wet or dry paper, used dry) the surface of the inner sill, and any other exposed metal, and apply two good coats of preservative, anti-rust paint. Avoid painting the lower flange, since the new sill must be welded along here, and MIG welders, especially, do not like paint!

SCWO16. ▼ Next, carry out any necessary repairs on the opposite side of the inner sill assembly (inside the car), and, again, treat them with anti-rust paint upon completion. The procedures for cutting out the rust, making repair patches and welding them in place are identical to those covered already in this chapter. The entire inner sill/floor area will then be sound, and ready to accept the outer sill panel.

SCWO17. ▲ Offer up the new sill to the vehicle. You will probably find that the rear end of the sill is proud of the bodywork. This is because the upper flange of most new sill panels is too deep at the rear, where the sill must sit tight against the rear quarter bodywork panel, just forward of the wing.

SCWO18. ►This problem can be overcome by careful trimming (a little at a time) of the top of the new sill in this area, so that it will fit around the rear quarter panel. Take care not to cut off too much metal, and . . .

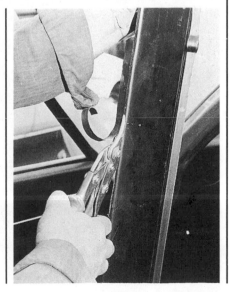

SCWO19.► . . . offer up the panel to the car after each cut. Stop when the sill flange fits neatly into the groove in the quarter panel at this point, while allowing the sill contours to blend with those of the main bodywork. Make sure too, that the sill remains a close fit at the front. Before continuing further, pre-drill a series of small holes (approximately $1/8$ inch diameter) in the lower flange of the new panel. This will facilitate easy 'spot' welding, through these holes, to the inner sill, when the outer sill is welded onto the vehicle.

SCWO20.► Use the angle grinder to remove paint from the outer edge of the door step (at the top of the original sill), where the top flange of the new sill will be welded. This is especially important if you are intending to use a MIG welder.

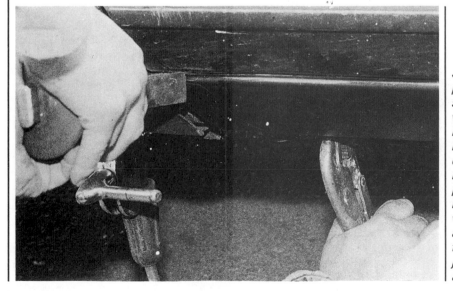

SCWO21.◄ Check that the sill fits perfectly, and that, with the door shut, it remains level with the wing and door panel. Use the bolster/chisel to 'adjust' the fit, if necessary, and use welding clamps or self-grip wrenches to hold the outer sill to the inner sill panel, along their lower flanges, in the correct position for welding. It helps to have an assistant available during this tricky operation. Don't rush this job – take your time to get the alignment perfect.

SCWO22.► Use tack welds to attach the sill at intervals along the upper edge. You may find it necessary to have your assistant pushing the sill against the car, at least initially, while the welding is taking place – the panel often attempts to 'spring' out.

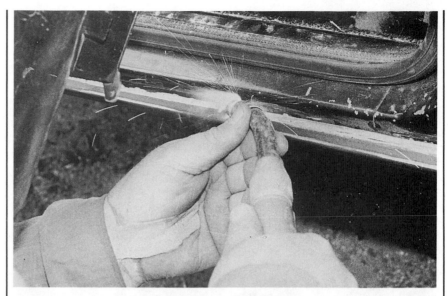

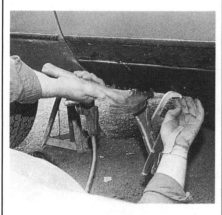

SCWO23.▲ Minor 'adjustments' to the fit can be made at this stage using a hammer, against the lower flange of the sill.

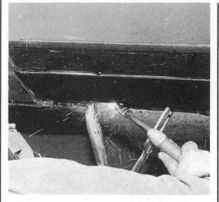

SCWO24.▲ Only when the fit is perfect should the sill be 'spot' welded along its lower edge, using the pre-drilled holes described in SCWO19.

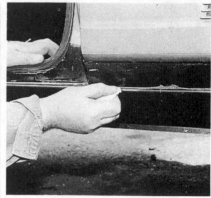

SCWO25.▲ Make sure that the paint is removed from the upper edge of the rear end of the new sill, and the lower edge of the rear quarter panel, then . . .

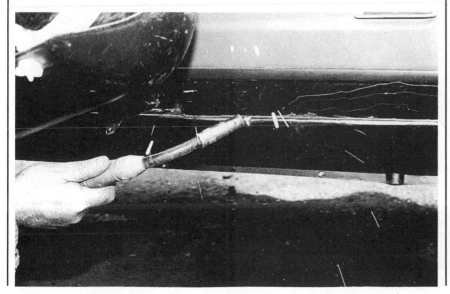

SCWO26.◄ . . . carefully tack-weld the sill to the vehicle along the groove at this point.

Re-check the sill for alignment along its entire length, and only then complete the welding along all the seams. Final cleaning-up of the welds can be carried out using the angle grinder (WEAR PROTECTIVE GOGGLES AND GLOVES), making sure that the welds are not weakened by grinding too far, Take great care to leave a neat finish along the seam on the rear quarter panel, as this is highly visible!

Sill change (with front wing removed)

In this section we show how to change a *full* outer sill panel – including the door 'step' and the extension piece which fits beneath the lower rear edge of

the front wing. It is only possible to fit this full sill panel if the front wing is removed from the vehicle, so that access can be gained to the 'hidden' area behind the front wing. It therefore makes sense to time a full sill change so that it coincides with removal of the front wing(s).

As mentioned in the previous

section (on changing a sill with the wing still fitted) it is ESSENTIAL that only one side of the car is tackled at a time, so that the body shell doesn't distort. Fit the door to the vehicle and align this with the bodywork mouldings, BEFORE attempting to fit the sill. The lower edge of the door can then be used as a gauge for alignment, as the new sill is fitted.

SCWR1.◄ You will need a selection of tools to carry out the sill change, including a bolster or slim chisel, hammer and dolly (or two hammers), tin snips, an angle grinder, and welding clamps (or several self-grip wrenches). You will also need an electric drill.

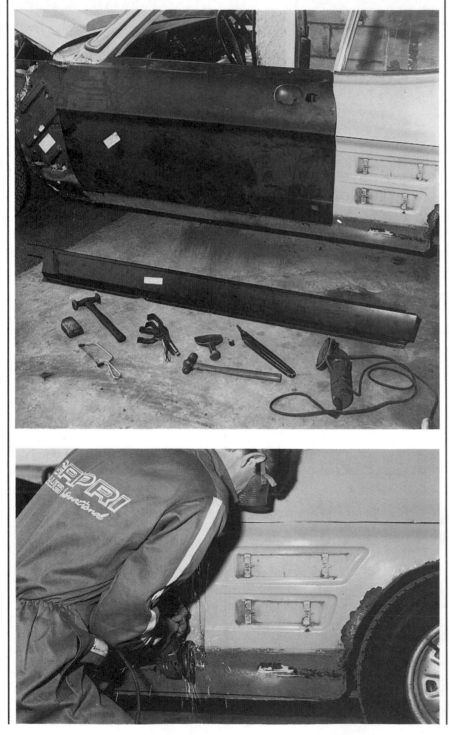

SCWR2. ▲ Start work by drilling through the spot welds along the top joint between the inner and outer sill panels, having first removed the trim around the door aperture. The drilling will weaken the welds, prior to their removal, described in SCWR4.

SCWR3.◄ Use an angle grinder (WEAR SAFETY GOGGLES) to cut the original sill away from the bottom of the rear door pillar and separate the sill from the rear bodywork. This is achieved by cutting just below the horizontal groove in the quarter panel, ahead of the rear wheel. Make sure that the cutting doesn't damage the door pillar, the inner sill or the main part of the quarter panel.

SCWR4. ▲ A hammer and bolster (or very slim chisel) can be employed to finally break the spot welds along the top of the sill, already weakened by drilling.

SCWR5. ▲ The sill can now be 'unrolled' from the top, using the lower joint as a hinge. The true state of the inner and outer sills becomes apparent as the outer panel is pulled away.

SCWR6. ▲ The angle grinder (or a hammer and chisel) can now be used to cut the lower edge of the sill away from the inner panel, by cutting just outboard of the lower flange, from above.

Normally this is quite a weak area, but this Capri had already been fitted with 'oversills' – that is, replacement sills had been attached ON TOP OF the originals, making a repair which was perhaps strong but certainly unsightly.

SCWR7. ◄ While the inner sill is exposed, check it for damage and plate it as necessary, as described in the previous section of this chapter. The surface can then be rubbed down and painted with a rust-resisting paint, or treated with an anti-rust preparation, then painted. Try to avoid getting paint on the flanges to be welded.

SCWR8. ◄ Trial-fitting of the new sill can now take place. Almost inevitably, a certain amount of trimming will be required so that the new panel sits flush with the surrounding bodywork, and is sufficiently high to give a neat gap beween the bottom of the door and the upper edge of the sill. Only trim very small pieces at a time, and re-check the fit after each cut is made.

SCWR9. ►*Make sure that the front end of the new sill fits neatly into the bottom of the scuttle panel. Only minimal trimming (if any) should be necessary here.*

SCWR10. Use clamps or self-grip wrenches to hold the sill in position, then make strategic tack welds, at intervals along top and bottom of the panel, before re-checking and finally welding the sill firmly into position. The 'spot' weld holes can be pre-drilled in the sill panel, as shown in the previous section.

Note the cardboard sheets placed over the rear side window, to prevent the glass from being damaged during welding and subsequent grinding operations. ►

Rear wheel arch replacement

Earlier in this chapter we showed how to patch-repair a rear wheel arch. This is practical where corrosion damage is not too severe. However, if rust has really taken a hold, and much of the flanged lip is missing, it is best to admit defeat and change the entire wheel arch – repair panels are available. Before starting work, check the inner arch for damage, too, after wire-brushing all dirt away from the area (USE PROTECTIVE GOGGLES). It is almost certain that, if the outer wheel arch and its lip are eaten away, the inner arch will be holed or at least very weak, too. If the car has been used for very long in this condition, expect problems too at the base of the rear wing, since water and salt will have entered between the inner and outer arches, where damaged, to attack the inside surface of the main wing panel.

Welding equipment will be required, in addition to an angle

grinder, hammer and bolster (or slim chisel), and welding clamps or self-grip wrenches. A sharp knife or scribing instrument will also be needed. A Monodex cutter or similar is useful for removing the old wheel arch.

RWAR1. ►*Using the new wheel arch panel as a template, hold this firmly in place and scribe the outline of the panel onto the vehicle. You may find it easier if you have a companion on hand to hold the panel in the correct position, while you scribe the line.*

130

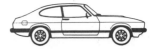

RWAR2. ►*The scribed line can then be used as a guide for cutting, using an angle grinder and/or a Monodex cutter, to give a neat finish. Since the arc scribed should be exactly to the profile of the new panel, it should be possible to achieve a very neat 'butt' joint between the new arch and the existing bodywork. This will give a smoother surface, requiring less filling, than an 'overlap' joint.*

Clean all paint from the exposed edge of the quarter panel, using the angle grinder.

Note the rust present in the inner wheel arch – this of course must also be cut out. A repair section is attached to the inner panel AFTER the outer arch has been rebuilt, so that the OUTER arch is used as the datum to work to.

RWAR3. ►*Check that the new panel fits correctly, and carry out any minor trimming which is required, until the new arch is a perfect fit.*

RWAR4. ▲*With the new wheel arch clamped in position, apply a few tack welds, at intervals around the perimeter of the arch, to hold it in place. Check once again that the fit is still as it should be, before adding further tack welds.*

RWAR5. ►*It will probably be necessary to 'dress' the adjoining edges of the panels to ensure a perfect butt joint, since even with MIG welding, a little distortion often occurs.*

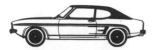

RWAR6.▲ When all is well, the welding can be completed.

RWAR7.►Unfortunately it was not possible to buy a repair panel for the inner wheel arch, so improvisation was called for. An extra outer arch panel was purchased, and marked so that surplus metal could be removed from it. This must leave enough steel to bridge the gap between the sound part of the original inner arch, and the outer flange of the new arch. This can be measured by reference to the vehicle, and the dimensions transferred to the home-made repair panel.

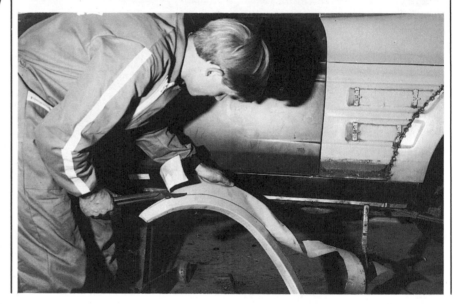

RWAR8.►The extra metal can then be trimmed off, using a pair of tin snips, to give the required panel. This will already have exactly the same curve as the outer arch, of course, and should fit perfectly.

RWAR9.►The repair panel for the inner wheel arch can then be clamped and welded into place, to fit as shown. The lower edges of both outer and inner arches are welded together, to form a neat joint, and the inner edge of the repair panel is attached to the sound metal of the existing arch, to complete the welding operations.

After welding, it is wise to apply seam sealer all around the joints, and to protect the area with a generous application of anti-rust paint.

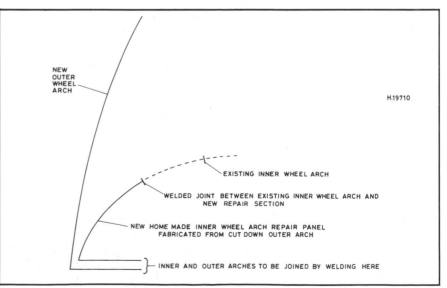

NEW OUTER WHEEL ARCH

H.19710

EXISTING INNER WHEEL ARCH

WELDED JOINT BETWEEN EXISTING INNER WHEEL ARCH AND NEW REPAIR SECTION

NEW HOME MADE INNER WHEEL ARCH REPAIR PANEL FABRICATED FROM CUT DOWN OUTER ARCH

INNER AND OUTER ARCHES TO BE JOINED BY WELDING HERE

RWAR10.► *Similar operations were carried out on the opposite side of the car, before applying coats of primer, to protect the bare metal. This should always be done if final surface filling cannot take place immediately.*

Sundry bodywork reconstruction

The techniques covered so far in this chapter can, of course, be applied to any areas of the body shell, with the proviso that structural sections MUST only be repaired by welding in new steel. This applies to the underbody/'chassis' of the vehicle, for which some commercially made repair sections are available. However, in some cases it is necessary to fabricate your own repair panels and weld them into position, using the methods already described.

SBR1.► *Carefully examine the floor and underbody from above and below, to gain a good idea of what repairs are necessary. It is best to remove all the seats and carpets/mats, since areas of corrosion are often hidden.*

SBR2.◄ *Before cutting out any rusty metal, check beneath the floor to ensure that petrol pipes, brake lines and exhaust systems are well clear of the area to be worked on. If in doubt, remove all such pipework before you start. When all is clear, use a hammer and bolster, oxy-acetylene gas torch or angle grinder to cut around the edges of the damaged/missing section, to give a neat aperture with boundaries of sound metal. Always do the cutting from above, where possible, and ALWAYS WEAR SAFETY GOGGLES.*

SBR3. ►*After cutting out a repair patch, from steel of at least the same thickness as the original panel, this can be welded into place. If welding from above, always re-check the weld from below the car, on completion, to ensure that the seam is strong, waterproof and neat. If necessary, run another seam along the joint between the new patch and the existing floor, from below, to 'tidy up' the weld.*

The respray

The chances are that you will have to apply paint to at least some of your vehicle, even if it only amounts to using an aerosol can or two, to cover repaired areas on wings and wheel arches, etc.

Once the bodywork is intact, as far as rectification of rust and dents are concerned, the aim must then be to get it in the best possible state to accept paint. This can just mean rubbing down the old paint and body filler which has been applied, so that they present a perfectly smooth surface on which to spray a primer-surfacer, or it could mean stripping the existing paint right back to bare metal, and starting again. So, how do you decide which is best?

There are several factors. In some cases, you really have little choice. For example, if the vehicle has been painted (usually hand-painted) with an oil-based household paint, there is no way that you will ever get a cellulose vehicle paint to stick to the old surface, even assuming that you could get it smooth! Other possibilities could be that the existing paint finish is covered in tiny lumps, about 1 mm across

('micro-blisters'), or that the paint surface has lots of tiny cracks running around it ('crazing'). In either of these cases, it is honestly a waste of time and money trying to apply paint on top; the new surface will soon suffer from the same underlying problems that affected the original paint. Therefore, in all these cases, and where the original paint is peeling, don't waste any time thinking – strip the old paint right off the car, back to bare metal. Tedious though this may be (and, believe me, it IS tedious!), it is quicker, cheaper and far better in the long run. You end up with a better surface, for a longer-lasting result that looks right; in short, a proper job.

Another advantage of completely stripping the paint from the vehicle is that this operation will reveal any areas that have been filled previously, since the paint stripper will react with the filler. You can then deal with such areas as appropriate, putting in new metal where this is desirable – for example where rust damage has been simply covered with body filler in the past!

There are two notes of caution to sound in connection with paint stripping.

Firstly, the job will take about a week of evenings, plus a

weekend, for a car the size of a Capri. During this time, the bare metal MUST NOT be allowed to get damp. This means that either the car should be garaged in a dry place, for the whole time the job takes, and then painted, at least in primer, before being used, or, as each panel is stripped, it should be primed straight away, if the car is to be used, or even parked outside overnight. Just one shower of rain, or a night out in damp air, will cause surface rust over the whole of the bare metal areas. This is difficult to remove, and you stand to leave at least some of the rust behind, which will then work away at the metal under your new paint.

Secondly, strictly speaking, bare steel should be coated with an 'etching' primer, prior to normal priming and the application of top coats. However, the fumes created by such primers can be dangerous to inhale, and a proper respirator (NOT just a gauze face mask) MUST be worn when working with them. Check with your paint suppliers – normally 'Health and Safety' information sheets about each type of paint sold are available from the suppliers.

If in doubt, use a standard primer, suitable for the top coats you will be using, direct onto the bare metal surface. In practice, the finish should be durable even

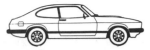

when an etching primer is not used on the bare metal.

This brings us onto the choice of the type of paint to use on your car. There are arguments for and against the use of, for example, cellulose, acrylic, or synthetic paints. For general use, to respray the models covered by this book, any would do the job satisfactorily. Cellulose finishes are the 'traditional' respray material. For d-i-y use they are comparatively easy to apply, are durable (if applied properly!), and, even if the 'gloss from the gun' is not fantastic – and that depends a great deal on the sprayer, and on temperature, paint mix, and so on – they can be 'cut back' to give a deep shine. They can also be applied without the need for special safety equipment – apart from a face mask and perhaps goggles. Some of the acrylic and synthetic finishes available are very hard wearing, give better initial gloss when applied, and are perhaps more forgiving in some ways to the manner in which they are sprayed. Disadvantages can be, depending on the paint, that cellulose cannot be applied over the top of some finishes (for example when repairing minor scrapes, etc.), that they often respond less well to polishing, after application, and – especially some of the 'twin pack' paints, with chemical hardeners – they can be poisonous to inhale, and need very careful handling. Special respirators are required for some paints.

Whatever material you choose, talk to your paint supplier before you buy, and in particular find out about the safety implications, and the correct methods of applying and polishing the paint you intend to use. Data sheets are very often available, and these give a wealth of useful information about the product, which helps you make a better job of your restoration project. As the paintwork is the part that most people see first this is obviously important.

Paint stripping

Assuming that 'the worst' situation prevails, and that you have to strip the paint from your vehicle, you will need about five litres (perhaps a little more) of paint stripper, so this should be purchased before you start. It is pretty strong stuff, and burns if it touches your skin. Therefore take particular care when stripping paint. Cover your arms and wear rubber gloves; always wear old clothes which don't matter, or an old pair of overalls. It is especially important that you don't get any stripper in your eyes, so don't splash the stuff about. Normally, for the odd spot of paint stripper on your hand or arm, copious quantities of water, applied straight away, will help, If you should splash paint stripper in your face, seek medical aid immediately. Keep paint stripper also out of reach of children and pets.

Start by taking off any rubber trims and water deflectors, for any spots of paint stripper falling on these will cause damage. The same applies to tyres; it is best to cover them.

Apply the paint stripper with slow, even strokes of an old paintbrush. Give the entire surface a thorough coat, then go over it again, especially where the car has several layers of paint on it.

Allow the stripper several minutes to percolate through the old paint, until the surface has bubbled, then use a paint scraper to peel the paint away from the metal. Rubber gloves are handy at this stage, since bits of paint falling from the vehicle, will still be soaked in paint stripper, and will burn your skin.

On a car which has had several coats of paint, some of them quite thick, you may need two or three applications of paint stripper, to lift all the paint. It is best to tackle the large, flat panels first, moving onto the smaller, complicated bodywork sections later. A small, stiff hand brush can be useful for 'agitating' the paint stripper on the surface, to make it work more quickly, and an old tooth brush is useful for getting into tight corners. Stripping the paint from a large vehicle is one of those jobs where the more friends you have, the better.

When the bodywork is finally back to bare metal, wipe off all the stripped surfaces, using a little cellulose thinners on a clean rag. This will ensure that the surface is free from paint stripper and paint fragments.

Prepare for painting

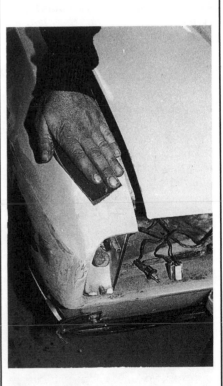

PP1. ▲ With all the filling finished, the entire surface of the body should be rubbed down, using 400 grade 'wet and dry' paper, used dry. This will smooth out minor imperfections, yet give a key for the primer.

PP2. ►It is sensible to take off as many as possible of the easily removable components on the body shell. This will avoid the need to mask them, and allow a better job to be carried out.

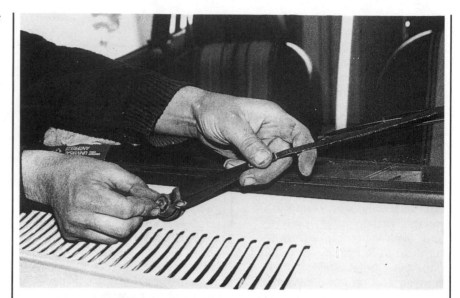

PP3. ►It is a matter of choice whether you feel that the main door handles should come off the car or not. They are relatively easy to mask up; the tape is first wrapped neatly around the handle, adjacent to the bodywork, then the outer section of the handle is enclosed. Leave the doors on the 'latch' if just spraying the outside of the car, so that the door edges will be adequately covered with paint.

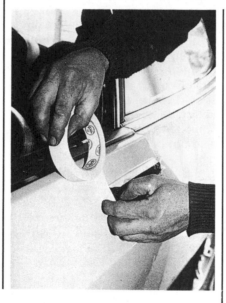

PP4. ▲Continue masking up all items remaining on the car, that you don't want painted! Masking tape often doesn't like sticking to rubber window seals, but, if you wipe the seal using a rag with a little cellulose thinners on it (don't overdo it, or you may soften the rubber), the masking tape will adhere a lot better.

PP5. ◄Start masking the windscreen and windows by applying a single strip of masking tape, all around the sealing rubbers. It is vital that the tape fits right to the outer edges of the seals, to give a neat, clean line when spraying.

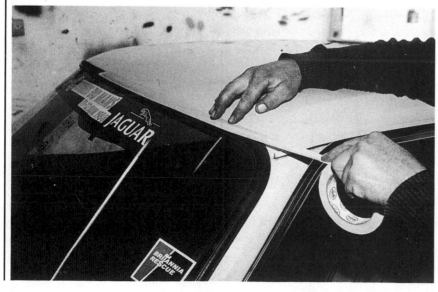

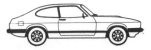

PP6.►Be especially careful at the corners of screens, where it is easy to leave sections of the rubber unprotected. If necessary, excess tape can be trimmed off in the corners, using a very sharp knife.

PP7.▲ Using several thicknesses of newspaper, cover up the exposed glass areas, by taping the newspapers to the previously laid single strip of masking tape.

PP8.►If is often quicker to mask large areas of glass, like the windscreen, by attaching the tape to the newspaper first, then applying the sheet direct to the screen, rather than the more fiddly method of trying to 'join' the newspaper to the outer screen seal with a length of masking tape – the paper inevitably moves!

PP9.►Completely cover the wheels and tyres. There are several ways of doing this, but we used some old car seat covers. These are easy to fit, and paint spray doesn't pass through them.

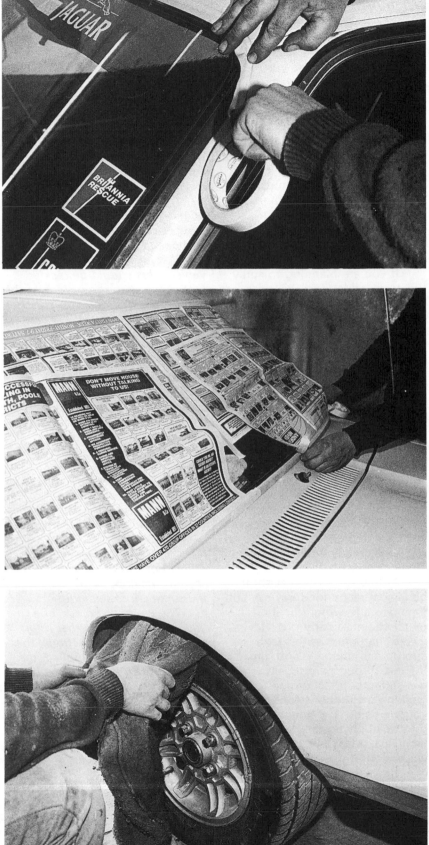

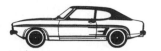

Applying the paint

If possible, choose a warm (but not scorching), dry day for spraying the car. Generally speaking, if working outside, or in an unheated garage, the minimum temperature for paint to go on 'properly' is around 15° Centigrade (60° Fahrenheit). It is not impossible to spray a car successfully at temperatures below this, but you are more likely to encounter paint runs, and 'blooming' of the surface. The paint also takes far longer to dry.

If you are planning to spray the car outside (and this does have some advantages – mainly that you can move around the vehicle more easily, and the paint fumes are not contained in a confined area), you need a CALM day. Any more than the slightest breeze will blow the paint spray all over the place, and whisk specks of dust onto your newly sprayed car. This is more than annoying.

Another problem with spraying outside can be insects – they often land on wet paint, and this obviously causes havoc with the finish (it doesn't do the insects much good either!), so try to choose a day when the gnats are not about!

At this stage, the car should be almost ready for spraying, but there are a few more final preparations to carry out. Having mixed the primer with the appropriate thinners, and 'timed' the mix through a viscosity measuring cup, according to the working instructions for the paint you are using, the final steps prior to applying the paint involve 'anti-dust' measures. The floor areas around the car should already be swept clean, but applying a little water will help dampen flying dust. The surface of the car, too, will need wiping. Start by using a 'spirit wipe' solution – obtainable from your paint suppliers. This removes grease, grime and dust from the surface. Don't touch the car again by hand before spraying. Give a final wipe over the vehicle with a 'tacky' cloth (a sticky cloth designed to collect fine dust particles from the surface – again, these can be bought, in packs of ten, from your paint supplier), and the car is ready. Give the primer a final stir before loading the spray gun, then don a suitable mask, and goggles.

ATP1.►We used a 'high build' primer-surfacer, applied in several fairly thick coats, over repaired sections of the car.

If spraying the interior of the vehicle, this should be tackled first, along with the insides of the doors, and the door shut panels. Tackle any underbonnet areas, such as the inner wing tops, at this stage, too. These areas should always be sprayed before the outside of the vehicle.

If the car has been completely stripped of paint, it will of course be necessary to prime the whole of the bodywork. However, where only localised damage has been repaired, only these areas need to be primed, unless there are so many of them that it makes sense to cover the whole of the car!

ATP2.►Continue applying the primer until all the repaired sections have been covered, and the surface looks smooth.

The main advantage of a 'high build' primer is that it fills minor surface imperfections; the more coats that are applied, the better the tiny holes, etc. will be filled. Allow the paint to harden in between coats. Apply the paint in smooth passes of the spraygun, overlapping each stroke just a little, by the same amount on each stroke, to get a smooth, even finish. The gun needs to be kept at the same angle to the car throughout each pass. If you swing the gun in an arc, you will finish up with more paint on the car at the centre of each stroke, than at either end!

If priming all the vehicle, spray the roof, the upper edges of the doors, and the rain channels, before moving on to the sides of the car, and large, flat panels, like the doors and wings. Keep the spraygun moving all the time, to avoid runs, and apply paint to the panels in strict sequence, the same for each coat. That way, you can't miss any part of the car! It is important that body ridges and sharp edges get more than their fair share of paint, both with primer and top coats.

Opinions vary regarding the correct sequence for spraying, some prefer to start with the roof, bonnet and boot lid, while others

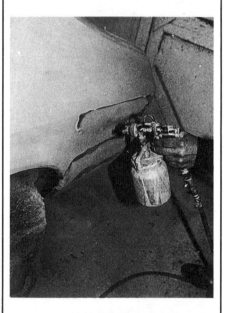

leave these until last. Personally, I prefer to get the paint on the roof first. This is normally the most difficult panel to spray, and you stand more chance of getting drips of paint on it from the gun, so take care. If your gun has a tendency to leak when tilted (and many do!), keep a rag held underneath the body of the gun, while you spray the horizontal sections.

When spraying the vertical panels, work your way around the car so that each section has a chance to dry before you reach it again on your next circuit of the vehicle. In any case, it is desirable to leave the paint a few minutes, at least, between coats, or the surface may sag.

ATP5.▲ This Capri was almost ready for the top coats, but this job is not one to be rushed. At this stage, give the bodywork a thorough inspection, to make sure that the entire surface is completely smooth.

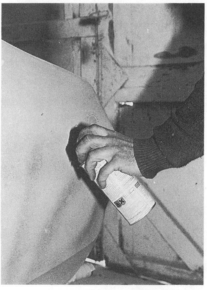

ATP3.► When the primer has hardened, go round the car with an aerosol can of contrasting coloured paint, and create your own 'custom' masterpiece! The aim is to produce a very light coating of paint over most of the surface of the primer.

ATP6.▼ The car now needs another application of the 'spirit wipe', followed by a tacky cloth or two, to get rid of all dust particles, before applying the top colour coats.

ATP4.► Leave the car for several hours (preferably overnight), then, using 600 grade 'wet or dry' paper, rub down the surface of the primer until all the aerosol paint disappears. When all traces of the aerosol paint have gone, even those in the tiny 'orange peel' pits of the surface, you will be sure it is smooth enough to apply the top coats. Use plenty of warm, soapy water to keep the paper lubricated and clean during this operation.

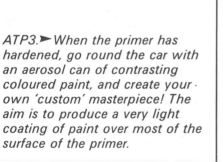

139

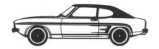

ATP7.►Again, where appropriate, paint the interior of the car, the insides of the doors and the underbonnet areas, before moving on to the exterior panels.

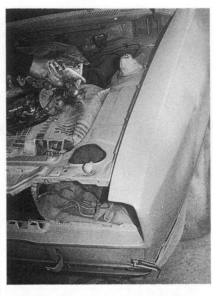

ATP10. ▲ Make sure that body ridges don't give the paint an 'excuse' to run; keep the gun moving evenly along the bodywork.

ATP8.►Three good coats will be sufficient for the interior of the car, but four or five are preferable for the exterior. To achieve a good gloss, the final coats can be thinned rather more than the early ones. You need to get the paint to the point of running, without it actually doing so, for a shiny finish! This is obviously easier on horizontal surfaces than vertical ones.

Make sure that the exposed 'corners' of panels receive adequate coverage, for it is here that subsequent polishing will quickly reduce paint depth!

ATP9.►It may take the first two coats to completely cover up the primer. Subsequent coats should then give the car its true colour. If in doubt, give the car an extra top coat or two.

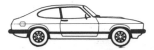

ATP11.➤ Large horizontal panels, such as the bonnet, require particular care to ensure that the paint coverage is even. Don't rush this job, and ensure that paint applied with each 'pass' of the gun overlaps that from the previous pass, before it is fully dry.

By now, the atmosphere in the workshop will be 'thick' with paint, as can be seen here. It is ESSENTIAL that a respiratory mask be worn.

ATP12.➤ Amidst the gathering paint mist, the roof of our project Mark II was given a glossy surface once again. To an experienced sprayer, there is no difficulty in achieving a smooth finish without blemishes. For the rest of us it is rather more difficult, but not impossible, provided care is taken. Make sure that the paint reservoir doesn't touch the surface.

The best thing to do, at the end of the spraying sessions, is to leave the car at least overnight, or for up to a week, if possible, for the paint to harden.

After the respray

Unless you are an experienced sprayer, to achieve a good gloss on the paintwork you will probably need to 'cut back' the top coats, using 1200 grade 'wet and dry' paper, used wet, followed by cutting compound, applied with a foam mop. These can be bought quite cheaply in car accessory shops, for fitting to an electric drill.

AR1.➤ You may be one of the lucky people who are able to produce a brilliant gloss 'straight from the spraygun'. However, if, like most people, you are not that lucky, you will have to work a bit harder for that deep shine.

Leave the car for about a week after spraying, for the paint to harden fully, then, using 1200 grade 'wet or dry' paper, used very wet, and with lots of soap, gently rub the paint surface down, one panel at a time, until all the 'nibs' of paint are removed, leaving a semi-matt finish. Don't rub too hard, especially on raised body mouldings, panel edges, etc., or you will eventually reach the primer coats!

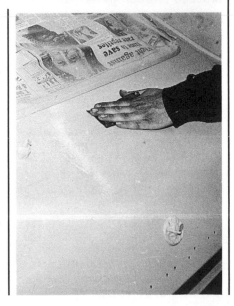

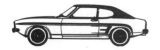

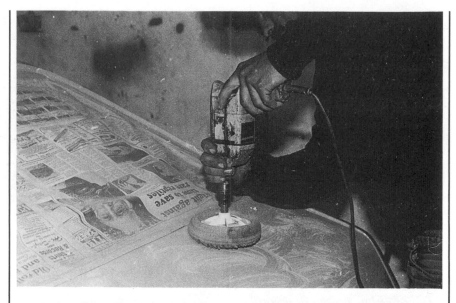

AR2.➤*Apply a little rubbing compound to a foam rubber 'cutting mop', which, for best results, should be slightly damp. The mop fits in an electric drill, and literally 'grinds' the paint back to a smooth surface, ready for polishing. The slower the drill speed, the better – apply a LITTLE water to the mop head every so often – unplug the drill first, of course. If you use the mop 'dry' you risk burning the paint surface, and the mop head! Always use the flat surface of the mop, not the edges, or, again 'burning' problems may result.*

AR3.➤*When you have tackled the whole car in this manner (it takes about a day to do it properly), follow up with a mild liquid cutting agent ('colour restorer' polishes can be used), and, finally, with a coat or two of wax polish, for a gleaming shine. Wipe off the residues after each stage, with a clean rag, as you proceed through these steps.*

AR5.▲ *When pulling the newspaper clear, take it easy, so that the outer rim of masking tape is not wrenched suddenly away from the paint – if it is, the paint may come with it!*

One of the most rewarding parts of a major restoration is seeing the car with all the masking paper removed, after it has been resprayed. It is best not to leave this job *too* long after the respray, so that the paint is still a little 'elastic', and a bit more forgiving when it comes to 'de-masking'. Nevertheless, great care is required when removing masking tape from the car, or the paint edges can be damaged.

AR4.➤*When de-masking windows, tackle the centre first, removing the newspaper but leaving the outer tape in place.*

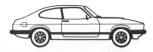

AR6.►*Pull the outer strip of tape away from the rubber seals at an angle, and don't rush the job. Take your time, and the tape should come away cleanly, leaving the paint where it should be, on the car!*

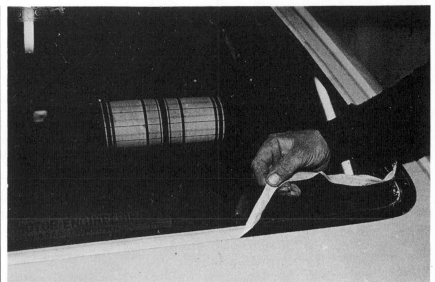

AR7. ▼*Our Capri now looked quite smart, but the wheels had yet to be cleaned, and it was still minus its lights, trims and various other fixtures and fittings.*

AR8.►*Even without its grille, the car looked far better than before the respray.*

AR9. ▼*Once the paintwork has been polished, the badges and other adornments can be re-fitted. This is far more fun than taking them off!*

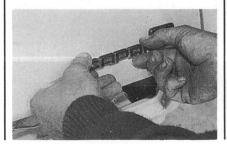

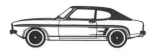

Gilding the lily

The overall effect of a car which has been restored depends, to a large extent, on the many items which, although small in themselves, are important as part of the whole vehicle. For example, a resprayed car will only look half decent if it has shabby wheels, scratched bumpers and bent number plates.

Dealing with the 'odds and ends' can be extremely time-consuming, but it is worth doing properly. The end result will be a vehicle which looks

smart, and which is 'tidy' in every respect. Whether you are intending to use the car as a 'concours' example or not, the satisfaction of having done the job properly means that you (and others) will get that much more pleasure from the vehicle.

Wheels and tyres

The appearance of wheels and tyres make all the difference to the overall look of any car, so it is worth spending some time on these items, especially if the car is fitted with what should be attractive alloy wheels

GL1.◀ Alloy wheels are difficult to keep clean. If normal cleaning fails to bring out surface pits, a little rubbing with fine (600 grade) wet or dry paper, used dry, can help. If your wheels fail to respond to cleaning at home, they will need to be tackled professionally.

GL2.▲ A coat of protective wheel lacqueur will help to preserve the wheels for the future. Mask the tyres to prevent the spray from reaching them.

The walls of the tyres can be cleaned with soap and water, followed by a wipe with one of the widely available rubber cleaners. it will restore that 'as new' look in seconds, and avoids the need for tyre paint.

Striping

Many Capris, including the 'S' models, had stylish stripes when new. To achieve the correct 'finished' look to the car, these must be re-instated following major bodywork repairs and/or a respray. To show what is involved, we illustrate here the fitting of a striping kit to our Mark II S Capri. We obtained the stripes from the Capri Owners' Club, who can supply kits for the various models.

GL3.◀ Work on re-instating the complicated stripes starts at the front wing.

This job requires a great deal of patience, and shouldn't be rushed. Lay the stripes (consisting of three strips, 'sandwiched' together) against the paintwork, while carefully pulling the lower backing strip away, as the stripe moves rearwards along the wing.

GL4.►Take great care to ensure that the stripe is perfectly level, as it is applied, or the results will look awful.

GL5.►When the stripe is in position as far back as the door (leave an extra half-inch or so protruding), very carefully pull the outer protective strip from the vehicle.

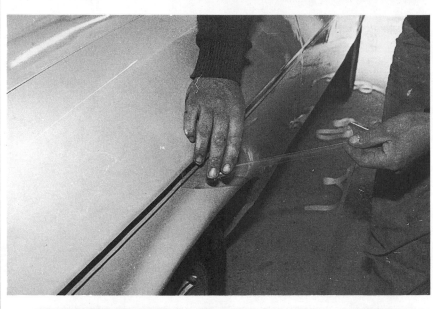

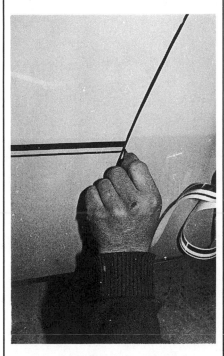

GL6.▲ Using a very sharp knife, trim the ends of the stripe, then tuck the protruding ends around the edge of the wing, and against the paintwork.

GL7.►Continue the stripe along the side of the car, across the door, and along the rear wing.

145

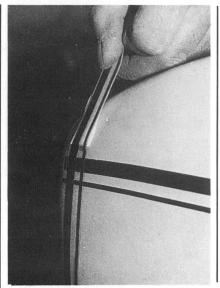

GL8. ◄ *With the top horizontal lines in place, the vertical stripes at the forward edge of the front wing need to be positioned. Start at the bottom, and bring the stripes up the wing, to overlap the horizontal lines.*

GL9. ► *Using the knife once more, trim away the unwanted sections of the lines, taking care not to cut through the paintwork in the process.*

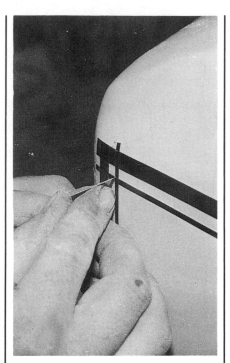

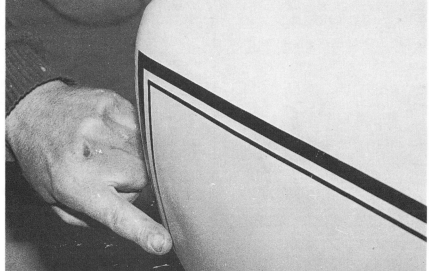

GL10. ◄ *Smooth the line against the wing, to release any air bubbles trapped.*

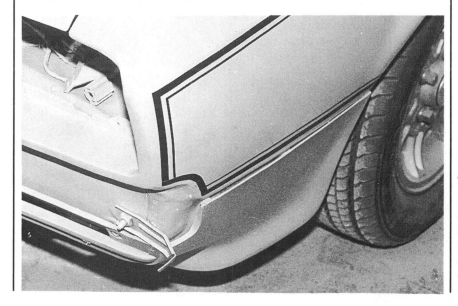

GL11. ◄ *It is quite tricky to get the radiused sections into position, but patience pays off. We found it necessary to 'relieve' the tape by making small 'vee' shaped knife cuts, to allow it to follow the tight bend at the lower forward corner of the wing. Before long the front wing should look like this, having added the lower stripes.*

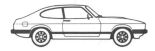

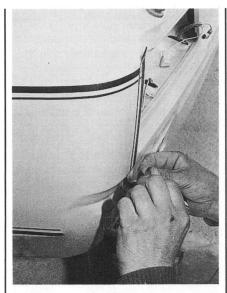

GL12.▲ *It is a little easier to add the stripes to the rear wing, but patience is still needed.*

GL13.► *There are still tricky sections to tackle, including the rear wheel arches. However, as the radius is gentle, and the stripe narrow in this vicinity, application is relatively straightforward. Try to keep the tape turning as it is applied, so that . . .*

Bumpers

Tatty bumpers make a car look scruffy, and the Capri is no exception. Whether chrome or black finish, the bumpers need to be looked at before they are refitted to the car, following major work.

GL15.◄ *The first job is to clean each bumper, inside and out. A wire brush is useful for removing rust and dirt from the rear of the bar.*

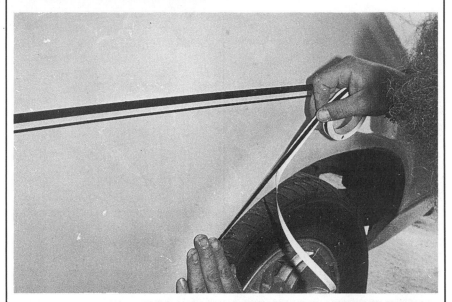

GL14.► *. . . the line follows a smooth path around the arch. You don't want a zig-zag line here!*

147

GL16. ▲ *Rub down the inner surface with coarse or medium wet or dry paper, then treat with a rust killer.*

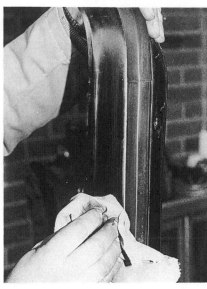

GL18. ▲ *The outer surface should be carefully cleaned, then rubbed down with 400, then 600 grade wet or dry paper, before finally being wiped with spirit wipe on a rag.*

GL17. ▼ *When the rust treatment has cured, apply two good coats of paint. We used a rust-resisting, hammered finish paint for the backs of the 'S' model bumpers.*

GL19. ▼ *An aerosol paint spray can then be used to bring back that 'as new' look. Make sure that any paint you use is compatible with the surface of the bumper, especially the plastic types used on Mark IIIs.*

Use warm soapy water and a soft sponge to clean all accumulated grime from a chrome bumper, before attempting to polish it. A proprietary chrome cleaner will clean even pitted rust from the surface; always apply a wax polish afterwards, and paint the backs of the bumpers with a silver anti-rust paint. This looks smart, as well as protecting the metal, and is not too far off the original silvery 'metal' finish.

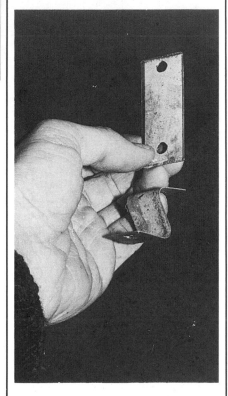

GL20. ▲ *It is very likely that the two brackets designed to hold the front number plate on will have all but rusted away. Indeed one of ours decided to break on the M6 motorway, leading to the number plate falling off.*

Fortunately replacement brackets are easy to fabricate from short lengths of steel. They can be painted with a black, rust-resisting paint, and then fitted in place of the originals. They will ensure that the number plate stays put for many years to come!

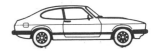

Rustproofing

If you are investing a great deal of time and money in restoring a car, it makes sense to protect the 'investment' by ensuring that it will be preserved well into the future. Therefore steps taken now to minimise the chances of attack by rust are well worth taking.

There are many ways in which you can discourage rust from forming on your Capri, and prevention is definitely easier and cheaper than the cure! Treating the inside of exposed chassis beams to two coats of anti-rust paint, during restoration work, the use of stone resistant coatings on the lower edges of the bodywork, and the sealing of bumpers from the rear, by painting them, are just three examples. It is also worthwhile using a seam sealant between newly welded panels, for example on sills and under-wing areas. The approach to rustproofing can vary a great deal, but the main aim is to prevent moisture and salt from coming into contact with bare metal, or rust will

quickly form, and eat the steel away!

You are at a disadvantage at the outset, with an older car, since rust will inevitably already be present over much of the underbody. The first step in any rustproofing operation on an old car is therefore to kill existing rust. This, again, can be tackled in a number of ways, but in all cases, start by grinding, scraping or brushing loose rust from the affected surfaces (WEAR GOGGLES). A chemical rust killer can then be applied. These vary in their contents and means of application, but, for best results, follow the instructions on the can TO THE LETTER. You then have a good chance of the product giving its best.

Having killed the rust, the metal needs to be protected. Some people like to spray the underside of the vehicle with old engine oil. This is certainly effective, if repeated, say, annually, but it is rather messy, and makes future maintenance under the car rather unpleasant.

Another approach is to paint the entire underbody with a rust-resistant paint, which will

prevent water from reaching the steel below it. Underbody seal also keeps out water. but is not normally chemically rust-resistant, it relies on total coverage to prevent water from attacking the metal.

Particularly popular these days are the wax-based solutions, which can be sprayed over the underbody, into box sections and 'chassis' members, and inside door panels, etc. Such waxes are cleaner than old engine oil, have a 'self-healing' effect if battered by flying stones, and are easy to apply.

Whatever method you decide upon, none are 'forever' treatments – check at least once a year that the *whole* underbody area is protected. Damaged areas of paint, wax or underbody seal should be re-treated immediately, or rust will soon take a hold on the exposed metal.

You can, of course, adopt a 'belt and braces' approach, first applying anti-rust paint, then a wax anti-rust fluid, or one of the new underbody sealing compounds which also contain wax.

Finally, hose down the underside of the car AT LEAST twice a year, to remove all mud and salt. This doesn't take long, and will prevent 'packs' of mud from being held against the steel. If left to accumulate – especially in under-wing areas– these seldom dry out, and actively encourage rust to start, and to spread.

R1.◄ Rust kills cars! When you think about the amount of work (and the cost!) necessary to rebuild a car which has been ravaged by corrosion, it makes sense to take steps to preserve your car before it needs major surgery of the type shown here. Provided your Capri is in sound condition at the moment, or has recently been restored, a little time and money spent now on rustproofing will save a great deal of bother later on.

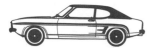

R2.►*If the underbody is kept clean – especially the well-known rust trap areas, rust is far less likely to develop. Frequent hosing will keep such sections clean, once the main deposits have been removed. If the car has not been cleaned underneath for some time, the first step is to use a blunt screwdriver, or similar probe, to hook out the accumulated mud and salt. We gathered a large bucketful of debris from just the front wings on this Mark II.*

R3.►*The enclosed sections anywhere on the bodywork can harbour dampness and dirt. Check all visible areas, like those encased by the leading edge of the bonnet, and treat as many as possible by physically de-rusting, chemically treating and re-painting, using the techniques described earlier in this chapter. Only when all such rust has been neutralised should further, preventive steps be taken.*

R4.◄*The use of a wax-based anti-rust spray treatment, such as the well-known Waxoyl, will help to preserve a car indefinitely, if it is properly treated. Start by treating all the under-bonnet framework, spraying the wax into the cavities until it emerges, using an extension probe, if necessary, to reach the hidden, inaccessible areas.*

R5.►*The front edges of Capri bonnets receive a great deal of salt spray from the road, and are particularly vunerable to rust attack. Make sure that the wax reaches all corners of the strengthening member here, as evidenced by seepage from the joints.*

R6. ►The 'chassis' sections below the car benefit from being sprayed inside with wax. There are numerous small access holes, through which an extension probe can be inserted, to cover the inside of each beam from end to end. Keep your eyes and hair, in particular, clear of the liquid, and also, of course, clothing and shoes. Place small, empty containers below the car, at the lowest point of each chassis member, to catch excess wax, which can then be re-used. Old newspapers can be placed below each side of the car, to absorb surplus wax.

Once the preservative has been applied, raise the car alternately at each end (on a jack or on car ramps), so that the wax runs along the length of each member, fully coating it.

R7. ►It is a good idea to apply the fluid through each access hole you can find, to ensure good coverage. For sections that have no apertures, small access holes can be drilled and then plugged on completion of the job.

It is important that the sills receive treatment, too.

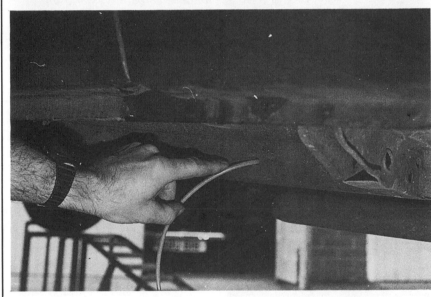

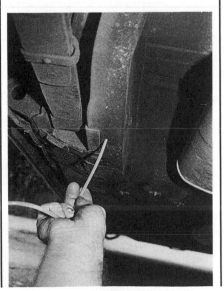

R8. ◄At the rear of the car, pay particular attention to the chassis sections adjacent to the rear spring supports. This will save a great deal of work and time in future years.

R9. ►Apply preservative to the transverse member above the rear axle, too. Once the inner surfaces are coated·with wax, they will find it difficult to gain access to water and air, so will be less inclined to rust.

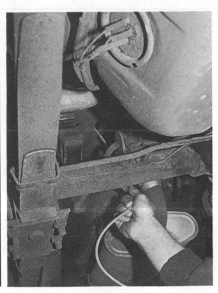

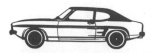

R10. ◄The doors are often overlooked, since owners can be reluctant to remove the trim panels. In fact, the panel need not be removed completely. If the rear lower corner is gently encouraged away from the door, using a wide bladed screwdriver, a narrow bore extension probe can be inserted into the door bottom. As the probe is withdrawn, the trigger can be operated, coating the lower surfaces of the door with steel-saving wax.

R11. ►For particularly narrow openings, such as around the tailgates on Mark II and III models, aerosol wax and oil mixtures are available. By using a narrow bore extension tube, the fluid can be sprayed into inaccessible areas. Open and shut the tailgate several times afterwards, to spread the wax before it semi-solidifies.

R12. ◄Before (or instead of) applying wax to the relatively flat underbody surfaces, the floor pan should be treated with two coats of a good quality anti-rust paint. Use a wire brush, initially, to clean dirt and light surface rust from the metal.

R13. ►Medium grit wet or dry paper can then be used in the next stage of surface preparation.

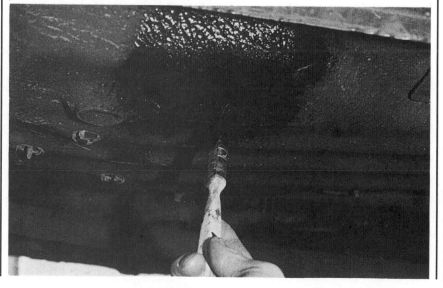

R14. ◄Finally, the entire underbody can be painted with two generous coats of anti-rust paint. We used Hammerite since it requires no primer, is easy to apply, and dries quickly. This will help to preserve the car for many years. Once the paint has fully cured, a wax based protector can be applied, if desired.

4 Engine compartment

The condition of the engine bay says a great deal about how you look after your car, for of course it is far more difficult to keep clean and tidy than most other parts of the vehicle. However, it is worth making the effort to spruce up the engine compartment, especially if you have carried out a lot of work on the car – a neat underbonnet area nicely rounds off the restoration.

There are also sound practical reasons why it is a good idea to keep the engine and its compartment clean – in particular, leaks of oil, or anti-freeze, can be spotted straight away, and dealt with before a major problem develops. Apart from that, an engine and its surroundings covered in filthy oil can smell awful when the motor gets warm.

Engine bay metalwork

The first step in the restoration of any underbonnet compartment is to evaluate and rectify any missing areas of metalwork. Capris are prone to rusting along the inner edges of the front wings, where they join the inner wings. If only minor damage is evident, plates can be riveted in position, and rust eradication/surface filling steps carried out as described in the 'Bodywork' chapter.

Where damage is considerable, and extends to the inner wings or bulkheads, rectification by welding in new metal is the only acceptable repair method. The techniques for such work are detailed in the 'Bodywork' chapter.

Start by making a detailed examination of the wings/inner wings and bulkhead areas, to evaluate exactly how much work needs to be done.

EBM1. ◄ The inner sections of the front wings on this Mark II Capri immediately spoiled the appearance of the engine bay every time the bonnet was opened. The first step is to find out how far the rust extends so that appropriate metal plates can be fabricated.

EBM2. ▲ *The dimensions of the repair patches can be transferred onto sheet steel, using a felt-tipped pen. For the wing edges, narrow strips of metal are usually required.*

EBM3. ▲ *Once cut to size, each strip can be offered up to the vehicle, and final trimming carried out. It is important to reproduce the profile of the downward-angled flange on the extreme inner edge of the original lip. This can be formed quite easily by clamping the repair strip between two lengths of angle iron, and using a hammer to bend the edge of the strip to shape. This technique was fully described in the 'Minor Bodywork Repairs' sections of the 'Bodywork' chapter.*

EBM4. ◄ *When finally shaped, the strip can be riveted in place on the car, prior to welding all around the edges where desired/necessary. The rivets will hold the metal firmly in position while welding takes place, if you are obliged to work on your own.*

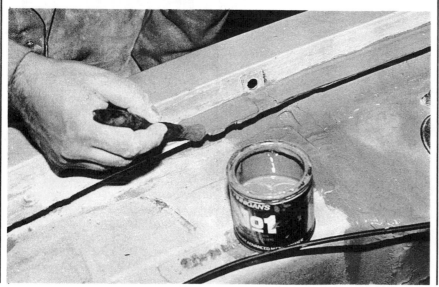

EBM5. ◄ *The repairs can be treated with an anti-rust primer, followed by final surface filling, where necessary, then primer and top coats. The restored flanges immediately make the engine bay look smarter.*

EBM6. ►*The area around the top of each MacPherson strut MUST be sound, for apart from visual appeal, the inner wings contribute to the overall strength of the car. Repair sections, like this one from LMC Panels, are readily available if rust does exist here. If plating the top of the inner wing, always make sure that the under-wing areas, and suspension mountings below this panel, are sound. If not, rectification by welding in new metal will be necessary, as described in the 'Front Wing (and Valance) Replacement' section of the Bodywork chapter.*

Fortunately the Capris do not seem to suffer quite so badly as other Fords in respect of rust at the tops of the inner wings. Nevertheless, check these areas thoroughly on your car.

When the metalwork in the engine bay has been restored, it can be prepared and resprayed in the same way as the exterior bodywork. Indeed the inner wing tops can easily be sprayed with the engine still fitted, and at the same time as the outer bodywork. However, for concours restoration, the engine must be removed, along with all ancillaries, wiring and so on. The engine bay should then be cleaned and de-greased, before spraying can take place. This work takes a long time, but the reward will be a spotless engine bay which makes maintenance easier, as well as looking good.

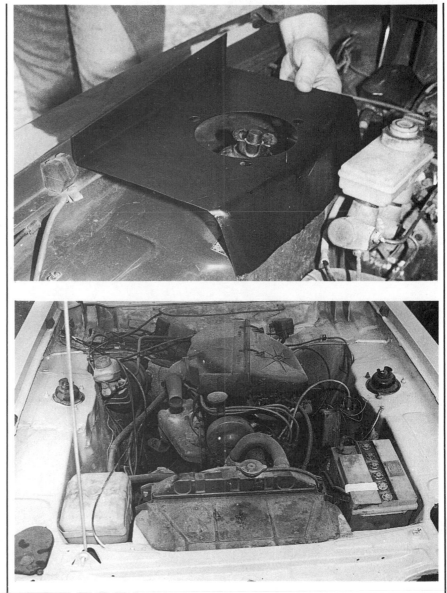

Tidy up!

It is not always possible, or even desirable, to remove an engine in order to tidy up the underbonnet area. Nevertheless there is plenty that can be done to improve the looks of an engine compartment, even with the unit still fitted. A little expenditure, and half a day or so of concentrated effort can work wonders.

TU1. ▲ *The inner wings of this Mark II 2.0S had been restored and painted, yet the power unit itself was rather grimy, and many of the engine ancillaries looked tatty.*

It is quite possible to clean an engine bay at home, using proprietary chemicals, applied by brush or aerosol. Paraffin could also be used (sparingly) to achieve the same result.

If you don't fancy getting your hands dirty, you may consider it worthwhile spending a few pounds on having the engine bay steam cleaned (protect electrical components first by wrapping them in plastic), or pressure-washed. We chose this option, which is a little kinder to the parts being cleaned, and less likely to remove paint. In addition, it will probably not leave such an oily mess on the driveway, which is often an important consideration. In any case, newspapers can be laid on the ground below the vehicle before you start, to prevent the drive from becoming oily.

Whichever method of cleaning you opt for, always cover any bare metal so exposed with paint or water dispellant spray, as soon as possible after the cleaning process has been

completed, or rust will soon set in.

We called in mobile vehicle cleaning experts 'Grimebusters' of Bournemouth, to tackle our Capri's engine bay. Their proprietor, Mark Hammond, explained that the chemicals used in his high pressure washing system are biodegradable, so will not harm animals or the environment, and should leave the driveway clean. We felt that while d-i-y is desirable in most cases, it was worth the few pounds it cost to take advantage of Mark's cleaning system, since it cleaned all the corners of the engine bay, left no mess, and

took only an hour or so from start to finish.

Manual cleaning of an engine bay is often a dirty job which can take a long time. The sequence of operations shown in the photographs would be similar if you prefer to carry out the work yourself.

TU2. ▼ With the front of the Capri raised on car ramps, the first job was to spray the de-greasant chemical onto the front cross-member. The cleaning agent was left for a few minutes to work through the accumulated grease.

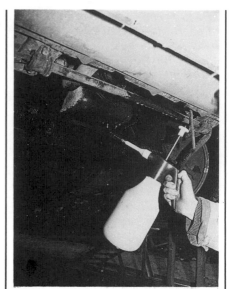

TU3. ▲ The sump and lower reaches of the engine bay are also best reached from below the vehicle; all greasy areas should be sprayed comprehensively, and the chemical left to act.

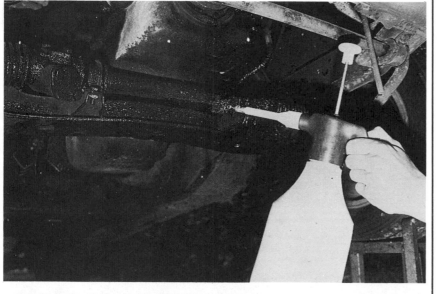

TU4. ▲ The underside of the engine, cross-member, steering rack and gearbox can all be sprayed with just the front of the car 'airborne'. These areas of the vehicle are usually the most greasy!

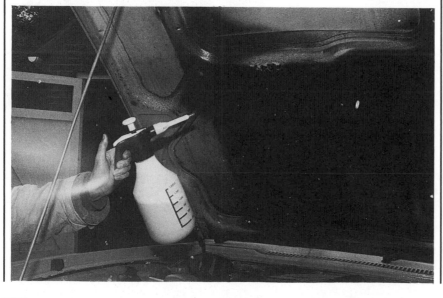

TU5. ◀ The same chemical is used to coat the walls of the engine bay, and the inside of the bonnet lid, since this is usually very grimy, as it was in the case of our Capri.

TU6.►The engine should be sprayed from all sides; Mark started on the nearside, and applied de-greasant to the whole of the unit, from top to bottom.

TU7.◄ The front of the engine is often particularly heavily coated in oily deposits; these should receive more than their fair share of chemical.

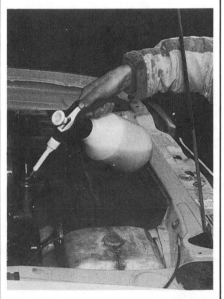

TU8.►To complete the cleaning process, the chemicals, together with the grime, are washed from all surfaces previously coated. The power washer applies water at high pressure, and transforms the appearance of the underbonnet area.

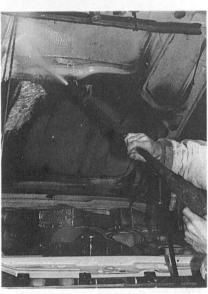

TU9.◄Once the engine compartment is clean, and has dried off, the various ancillary components within this area can be de-rusted (if necessary) and re-painted. We started by unscrewing the shield fitted in front of the radiator. This panel was devoid of paint and very rusty, on our car. Such items are noticeable as soon as the bonnet is lifted, and can ruin the appearance of an otherwise clean and tidy engine bay.

TU10.►With the panel removed, the first job is to scrape off all loose rust and paint.

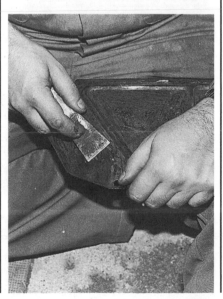

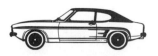

TU11. ▲ *A little cellulose thinners, applied with a rag, can then be used to rid the surface of unwanted 'islands' of old paint.*

TU12. ► *Next, the entire surface of the panel can be rubbed down, using fine wet or dry paper, used dry, to produce a uniform, smooth surface.*

TU13. *We applied black Hammerite paint to give an attractive finish which should also help to keep rust at bay in the future. We were more interested in longevity than pure originality. Alternatively, the panel can be sprayed with black paint, to restore it to 'original' condition.* ►

Similar procedures can be applied to all metal items within the engine bay, including the engine ancillaries, the radiator and so on. It is best – and essential if painting the engine itself – to use a high temperature paint designed for the job; apply two coats.

TU14. ► *The exhaust manifolds look superb if treated to a high temperature silvered finish, which 'bakes' on as the engine warms up. Although it is obviously preferable to paint such items when removed from the engine, they can be painted 'in situ', provided care is taken and the job is not rushed.*

Before leaving the engine bay, make sure that all the grommets and wiring are in good condition, replacing any such items which look perished. Examine each item bolted or screwed to the engine compartment walls, and replace any screws or bolts with rusty

heads. Use plated fasteners as replacements, to prevent rusting in the future.

For long term good looks, the regular application of a water dispellant spray, followed by a wipe with a clean rag, will give the engine, hoses and all ancillaries a shine, and protect them from the elements.

Finally, if seriously thinking of entering your car in concours competitions, it is vital that the engine bay (and indeed the entire vehicle) is 'as original', and attention to detail is vital. Take time and trouble over restoration, and this important area of the car will complement the rest of the vehicle.

5 Interior and trim

Whether you tackle work on the interior trim of your Capri before you put it on the road, or afterwards, on a 'running restoration' basis, it is an important part of the overall task of rebuilding a car. After all, it is the inside of your Capri which you will see when you are driving it, and by which the restoration is largely judged by your passengers.

It is appreciated that not everybody is good at upholstery work. In addition, unless you have an 'industrial' type, heavy duty sewing machine, the amount of work that you can do at home is limited anyway. For these reasons it is often better to tackle as much of the *initial* work as possible yourself, for example removing seats and perhaps stripping the damaged coverings, then welding up broken seat frames, etc., before taking the components to a professional vehicle upholsterer for the necessary material renewal, re-stitching and rebuilding.

Interior dismantling

You may not need to remove all the interior trim from your car, but, even if you do, there should be few problems. Taking the trim out is comparatively easy; putting it back again correctly takes rather longer, and requires patience. Take care if, for example, you intend to re-use door aperture sealing rubbers, for they will not stand a great deal of tugging. The same comment also applies to trim panels and most of the interior coverings; they need treating with respect if they are to survive and remain looking good.

Full details of stripping doors of their locks and window assemblies are included in the relevant *Haynes Owners Workshop Manual* relating to your particular Capri, so have not been repeated here. Indeed, given a little lubrication on an occasional basis, the moving components within the doors seldom need major attentions. The same cannot be said of the seats, however, which often show severe symptoms after a few years in service, and which frequently represent the worst aspect of a Capri's interior.

Seat renovation

The seats in Capris – and particularly the driver's seat – tend to suffer from wear after a few years. The seat facings become grubby, especially the cloth covered types, and can become 'brittle'. Probably worse even than this, for most people, is the gradual sinking feeling which takes place as the lower section of the seat collapses towards the floor. This problem becomes increasingly acute, and causes growing discomfort, unless remedial steps are taken.

It is very difficult, if not impossible, to obtain new seat assemblies, especially for the early Capris, and while those for the later cars can be obtained, they are usually extremely expensive to buy new. One alternative is to seek out a scrapped car with seats in good condition – probably the easiest and cheapest solution, if you are lucky enough to find a donor vehicle before anyone else does!

If this doesn't prove to be practical, a broken seat can usually be rebuilt. Rebuilding a car seat is one job which is difficult to tackle at home, unless you have heavy, industrial type sewing machinery. In addition, unless you are skilled at working with upholstery, or at least needlework, it is, with the best will in the world, quite likely that you will end up with a very unprofessional looking seat.

Therefore if the seats in your Capri are past their best, with sagging springs, broken frames and torn coverings, it would be better to enlist the help of a professional for the parts of the job you *cannot* do yourself. This usually includes making the new panels or replacement coverings, where necessary, having done basic preparation and repair work yourself, beforehand.

If you intend to 'have a go' yourself, bear in mind that spares for the seat frame assemblies are virtually unobtainable, although some improvisation is possible – for example the substitution of foam padding where metal springs once took the strain.

To illustrate the sort of preliminary work that most people can tackle at home on Capri seats, I talked to Mr. Peter Exley, of Poole, who has had many years of experience of rebuilding motor car interiors – particularly on Fords. He showed me how to dismantle Capri seats, in preparation for repair and, where necessary, re-covering. While there are some minor differences between models, the basic procedures are as illustrated, using our 'project' Mark II 2.0S driver's seat as an example.

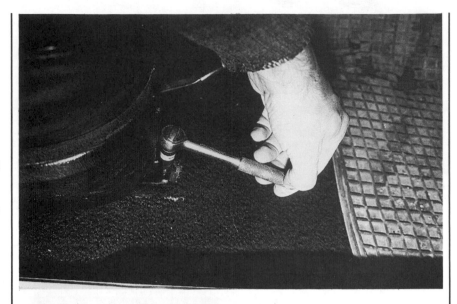

SR2. ▲ *Having made the decision, take the seat out of the car. By moving the seat as far back as it will go on its runners, the two forward mounting bolts are uncovered. These are best released using a socket spanner . . .*

SR3. ◄ *. . . as is the outermost mounting bolt at the rear, revealed when the seat is moved forward as far as it will go. However, the final bolt, adjacent to the transmission tunnel, is best tackled with a ring spanner.*

SR1. ► *The first step is to decide whether the seat is in bad enough condition to warrant a complete stripdown. In the case of this 2.0S, the decision was easy! The base of the seat had collapsed, and to enable normal driving to continue, a large piece of foam rubber had been wedged beneath the backrest, and under the seat, to provide some support.*

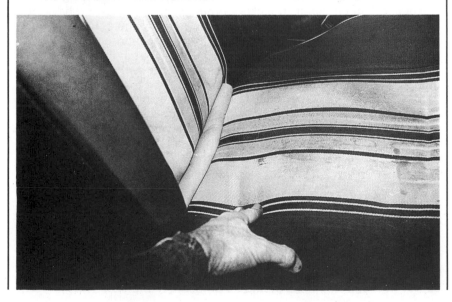

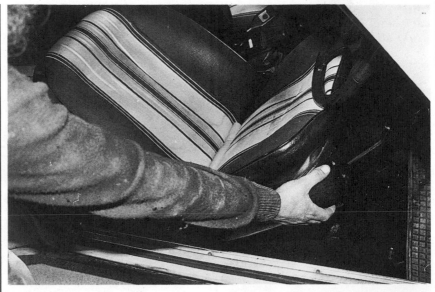

SR4.►*The seat can then be lifted out of the vehicle. Make sure that the runners don't catch the paintwork around the door as the seat is lifted out (and, later, back in again).*

Obviously this means that the car now lacks a driver's seat. As our two litre S was in daily use, we simply substituted the passenger seat for the driver's; although 'handed', they can be swapped.

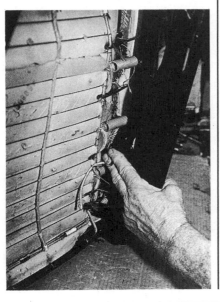

SR5.◄*With the seat on the bench, it can be given a proper examination. On this seat it was immediately evident that the support springs originally holding up the 'sprung' base had nearly all broken, causing the severe sinking feeling experienced when driving the car!*

SR6.►*Another common problem is separation of the piping at the outer edge of the backrest, and tears in the plastic in this area. Our seat showed typical symptoms. If damage is not too severe, repair panels can be 'let' into the side of the seat.*

SR7.◄*The first stage in dismantling the seat is to remove the side trim panels, in order to gain access to the main hinge bolts holding together the seat base and backrest.*

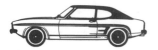

SR8.➤The two bolts (one at each side) are then released, using an 8mm Allen key.

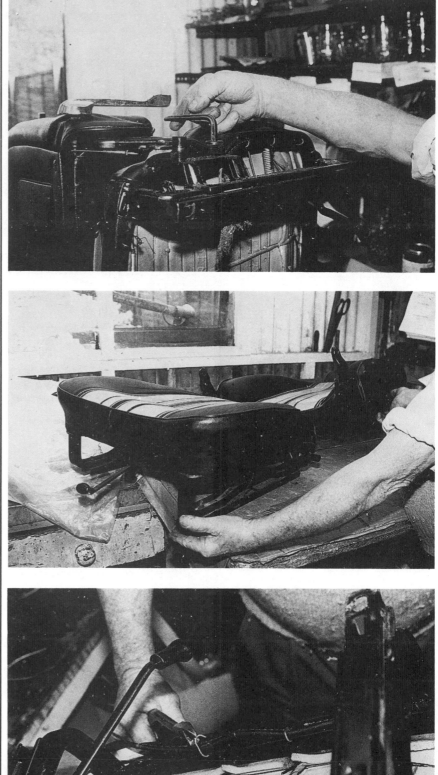

SR9.➤The two halves of the seat can now be separated, for dismantling individually. The seat is far easier to deal with when broken down into its component parts.

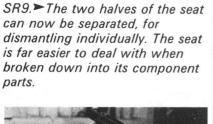

SR10.▲ Using a pair of side cutters, remove the 'hog rings' from around the perimeter of the base, taking care not to damage any material which may need to be re-used.

SR11.➤ Most of the hog rings can be removed without actually having to cut them, although you may find a few 'reluctant' ones. They normally twist out of the seat, if gently encouraged.

SR12.➤The seat covering can now be peeled back from the base. Don't rush the job, nor pull the seat covering too firmly, or it may tear.

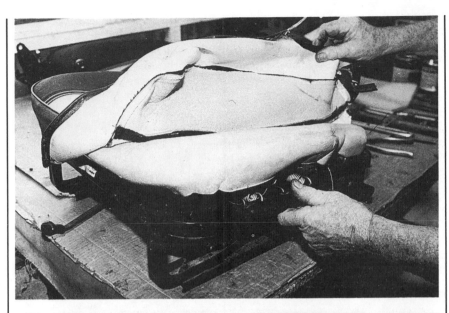

SR13.➤A common problem, now revealed, is sagging of the polyester foam, towards the back of the seat base. The foam sinks below the cross-bar at the back of the frame.

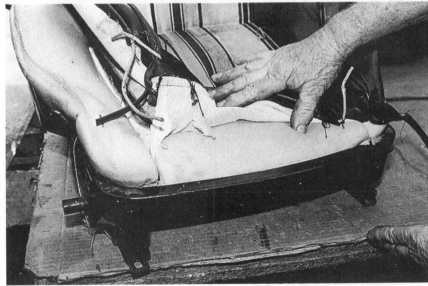

SR14.◄The main (central) section of foam can now be withdrawn from the seat base covering.

SR15.➤More hog rings to remove! This time, those securing the 'U' shaped wire which is inserted in a canvas pocket stitched to the underside of the cushion cover. The wire is in turn clipped to the springs of the cushion frame.

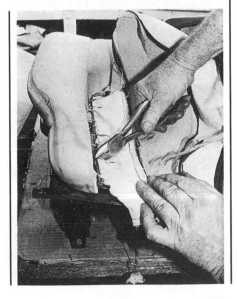

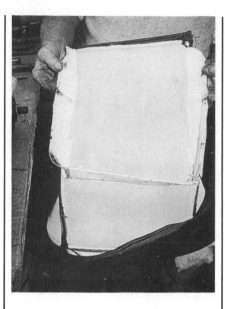

SR16.◄ The seat covering, with the 'U' shaped wire in its canvas pocket, can now be detached.

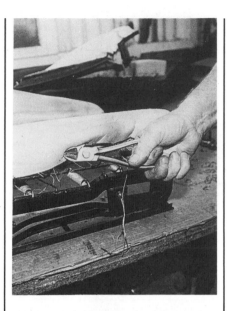

SR17.►Next to be removed is the side border cushion assembly. This will be found to be attached to the rim of the cushion frame with a few more hog rings.

SR18.◄ As the foam is taken off, the horrors lurking below become more easily visible – in the case of our seat, the support springs for the sprung frame had all (but one) broken.

SR19.►These are virtually impossible to obtain new, but the old ones must be removed from the frame before further remedial action can be taken. They are held to the frame with metal clips, which can usually be 'unwound' using a pair of grips or pliers. If all else fails, they can be (very carefully) cut off.

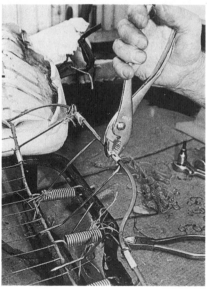

SR20.◄ This was the sole surviving support spring – if only one or two are broken on your seat, it may be worthwhile trying to obtain replacements from a seat taken from a scrapped car. The problem, of course, is finding another seat with intact springs.

SR21.▲ Leaving the seat base for a while, the next stage is to strip the backrest assembly. To start with, the backrest trim panel must be removed. This is held in place, at the bottom, by two plastic studs. DON'T attempt to remove them with pliers, or they will simply be cut in two. Far better to gently lever the backrest panel upwards, using a large, flat-bladed screwdriver, taking care not to damage the trim panel or the seat upholstery in the process.

SR22.▲ This is one of the studs, safely extracted. Put both studs in a safe place until it is time to re-assemble the seat.

SR23.▼ The trim panel can now be VERY CAREFULLY swivelled backwards and forwards, to free the hooked clips at each side, then lifted clear, and safely stored out of harm's way.

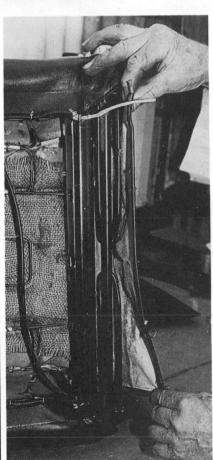

SR24.▲ The backrest is of similar basic construction to the seat base, and the stages of dismantling also follow the same lines. Release the hog rings from the lower return edge of the squab (backrest) cover, and inspect the unit for damage.

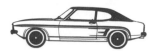

SR25. ►Next, disentangle the backrest control cable from the upholstery materials and springs.

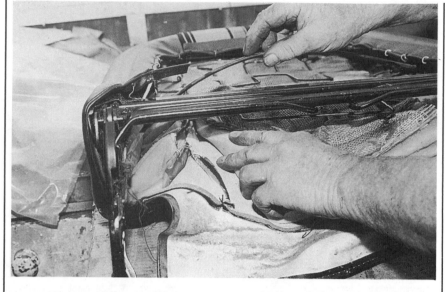

SR26. ►The trigger for the seat tilt mechanism is next to go. Take great care during this operation, to ensure that neither the trigger nor its plastic surround are damaged. Use a block of wood or chipboard, to lever against, and a large screwdriver, with which to prise the trigger off.

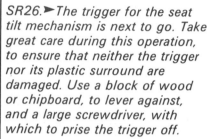

SR27. ▲The plastic surround can now be gently levered away from the seat. Again, take care not to damage it or the seat. We found that this one was already slightly cracked at one end, so it needed particularly careful handling, to avoid further damage.

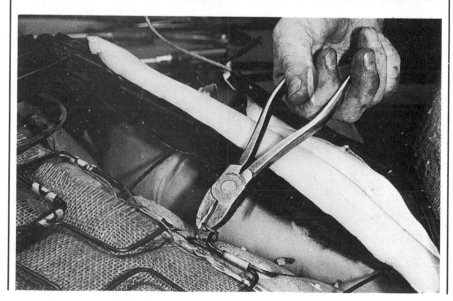

SR28. ►By now you should be very good at removing hog rings; to keep in practice there are more to be released; those which secure the 'base' assembly of the backrest.

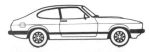

SR29.►*The backrest angle adjuster lever is removed by simply releasing the central Phillips retaining screw.*

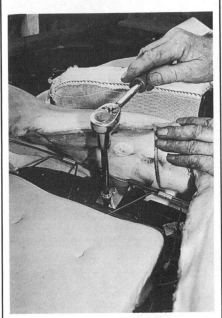

SR30. ▲*Peel back the foam padding, then release the two bolts securing the stem of the headrest, using a $^1/_2$ inch AF socket spanner.*

SR31.►*The headrest assembly can then be pulled from the top of the seat; there is no need to release the two screws beneath the base of the headrest assembly, unless you need to dismantle the headrest, too.*

SR32.►*The chrome cover plate that normally surrounds the headrest stem can now be removed after releasing the two Phillips retaining screws.*

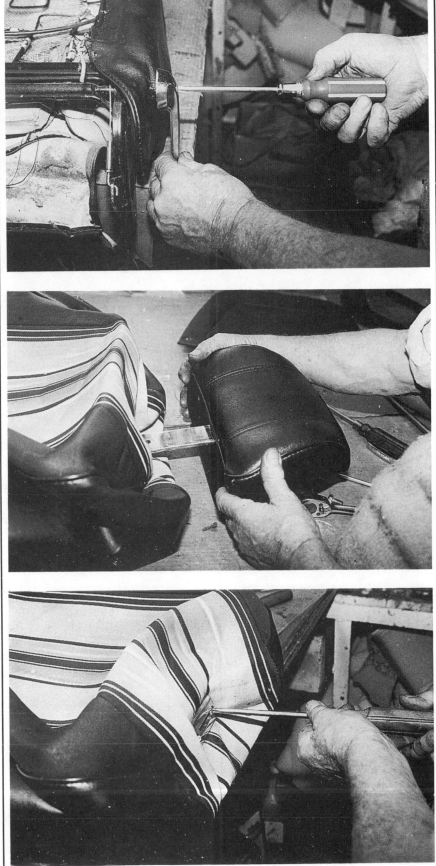

SR33. ►The backrest covering can now be separated from the frame, for a close examination to be made.

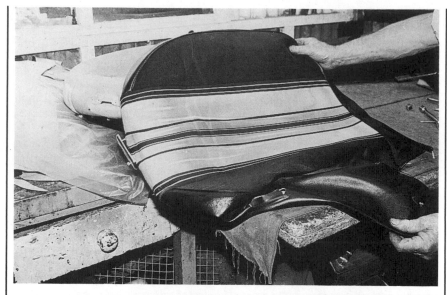

SR34. ►If damage is localised to just one section of the side border, as on our seat, it is unnecessary to remove completely the side border panel. Instead, mark the section requiring repair with a piece of chalk, allowing a reasonable margin of overlap beyond the damaged area, to enable a neat join to be made.

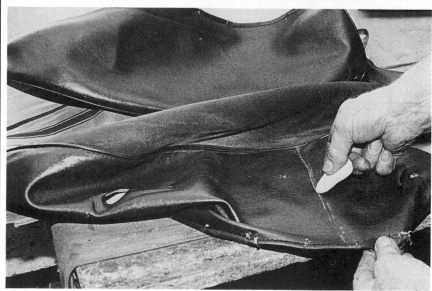

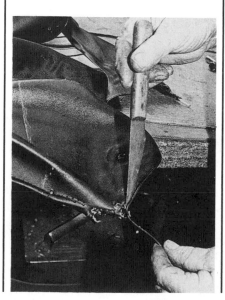

SR35. ◄ Using a sharp knife (and keeping your fingers well out of the way of its blade), cut the stitching securing the piping to the damaged section.

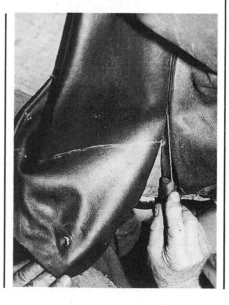

SR36. ►Make sure that the piping is freed to just above the marked area.

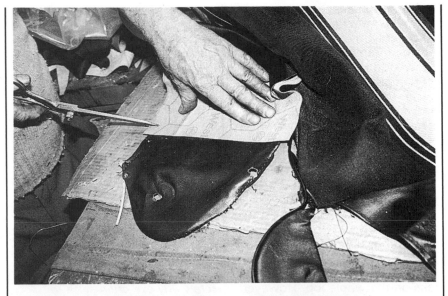

SR37. ►A length of new vinyl can then be offered up to the damaged panel, to assess the area required.

SR38. ►Lay the new material on top of the old; always allow for a fold approximately half an inch deep at the top of the repair panel. When sewn in position, this will give a neat, professional finish to the job.

Before sewing in the new section, it is a good idea to clean the seat coverings. It is far easier to clean them – especially cloth types – while they are off their frames. The coverings on this Capri seat responded very well to a short spell in the domestic washing machine.

SR39. ►Returning to the seat base, the main problem is usually finding replacement springs in good condition. An alternative is to do away altogether with the steel springs, and to fabricate a support, made from a strong material, as the basis for rebuilding the seat. To repair this Capri seat, Mr. Exley used part of another Ford – a section of the very strong canvas type hood material from a Mark II Consul convertible!

Slots need to be cut around the supports for the perimeter frame, so that the canvas can be laid flat onto the frame. When cutting out the material, allow a few inches of overlap all the way round, so that this can be securely glued/sewn in place.

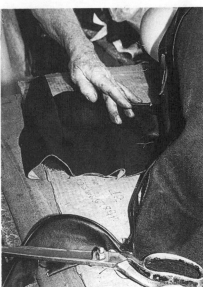

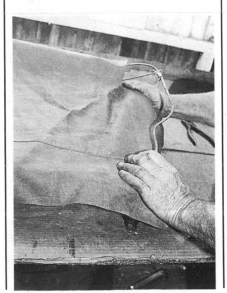

SR40. ▲ Tapered lengths of foam, like this, can be cut and shaped as necessary to provide the new side support lips. The foam should be wedged in position, to replace the broken support springs. The base foam can be renewed too, if necessary. Once the canvas has been secured in position, and the foam inserted, the seat can be rebuilt in the reverse order to that used for dismantling.

Obviously if the main seat frame is found to be cracked or broken, repairs by welding or brazing can be carried out while the

upholstery material is removed.

When the metal has cooled sufficiently, the frame can be treated to an anti-rust paint, and allowed to dry.

The seat, complete with its covers, damaged sections, frames and anchor clips, can then be transported to the upholsterer, for repairs to the cover material. It is best to ask the upholsterer to reassemble the seat, so that the material can be correctly tensioned and lined up on the frames.

Naturally it is a good idea to talk to your upholsterer before you start stripping the seat yourself; some may prefer only to take on the whole job. However, most will be quite happy for you to do the preliminary work, especially if they are very busy. It saves them time, and you money, of course. In addition, at least you will have the satisfaction of knowing that some of the work was your own.

With a bit of luck you may not need to strip the seats; sometimes there are just small blemishes on the surfaces of the material. Small tears in upholstery can be dealt with by using one of the special glues available, or, for slightly larger areas, patching kits can be bought. Often a small piece of 'spare' trim can be cut from overlapping edges underneath the seat, for example, to make good a small hole on the outside covering in a more visible area.

Interior dismantling

It won't always be necessary to completely strip a car of all its upholstery and trim, but this is the best course if, for example, you wish to paint the top surface of the floor, or if the entire interior is in poor condition. Fortunately this is generally straightforward on the Capri; the following notes may be of

assistance. Although there are minor variations between models, the techniques illustrated on a Mark II are typical.

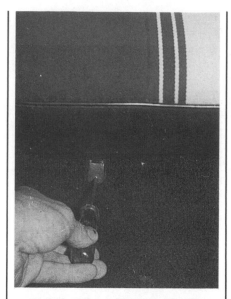

ID1.➤The rear seat base is held in position by Phillips screws at its lower edge; lift the base upwards and outwards to remove.

ID2.➤The kick plates along the inside, at the top of each sill, are secured by a row of Phillips screws. These often seize in position, so apply penetrating oil at intervals commencing several hours before you attempt to release them, and use a hefty screwdriver. An impact driver is ideal, but take care not to destroy the heads of the screws.

ID3. ▼ Always use the correct size of ring or socket spanner when releasing seat belt securing bolts. These have very shallow heads, and over-enthusiasm, or a spanner slightly too large, will round off the head of the bolt, rendering it extremely difficult to remove.

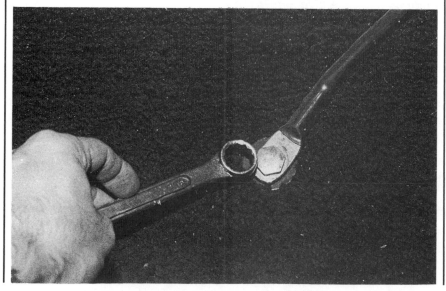

ID4.◀ It is a good idea to use an anti-seize, copper-based grease on the threads of the seat belt bolts, on re-assembly. Then, even when fully tightened, they will be relatively easy to release in the future, even years hence.

ID5.▶ The handbrake gaiter assembly is secured to the bodywork by means of Phillips screws. Save all the screws; put them into a marked container and store them safely until it is time for re-assembly.

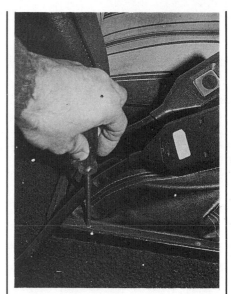

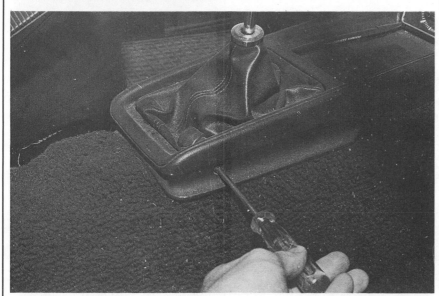

ID6.◀ Phillips screws also secure the gear lever surround/centre console (where fitted). Again, store the screws safely and in clearly marked containers.

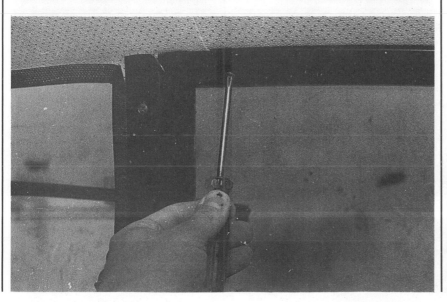

ID7.◀ Trim panels around the side windows, and down each side of the windscreen, are easily released by withdrawing their securing screws. If the panels are not to be repainted, wrap them in clean cloth and put them in a labelled cardboard box, out of harm's way, where they cannot get damaged.

171

ID8.◄To remove the window winder handle, prise the plastic trim strip away from the centre of the handle, then slide it away from the winder knob, to disengage it from the 'keyhole' slots in the handle.

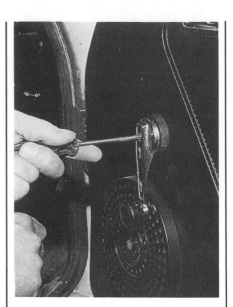

ID9.►A single Phillips screw secures the winder handle to the door. With the handle out of the way, the plastic bezel can be removed. Keep these parts safe – it is easy to lose such items during a long rebuild. On re-assembly, the handle should be re-fitted so that, with the window glass fully raised, the handle is pointing downwards.

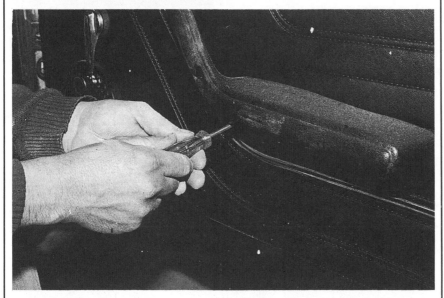

ID10.◄To remove the armrest, release the two Phillips screws from the underside. If you find that the armrest is also held by a locating peg, turn the rest through 90 degrees, and withdraw the peg shaft stud (upper fixing) from its location in the door panel. On re-fitting, position the spacer over the stud, and push the stud to secure it, before re-fitting the two screws.

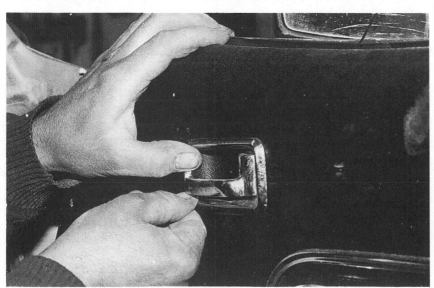

ID11.◄The interior door catch release surround can be tricky to remove. It should be slid forwards to disengage its locating lugs; slight pressure on the door trim panel, around the surround, helps. On some (early) cars, the surround is retained by a screw, which is accessible after prising the plastic trim from the chrome plate.

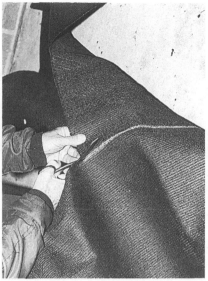

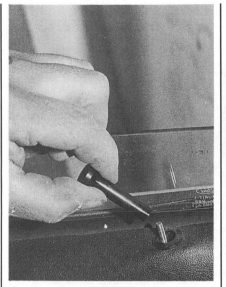

ID12. ▲ With the remainder of the 'door furniture' removed, the interior locking knob can be unscrewed from its shaft. The interior trim panel can now be very gently prised from the door, using a wide-bladed screwdriver. The position of each of the securing clips can be located by carefully feeling the surface of the panel, around its perimeter.

CF1. ▲ If you do decide to make your own carpets, try to buy good quality, rot-proof materials which will last for a very long time, and look good. Use the original carpets as templates, marking the correct points for cutting by using chalk or a felt-tipped marker. A sharp pair of scissors can be used to cut out the new sections. Take your time to ensure that the dimensions are accurate, for a perfect fit. If in doubt, cut the carpet slightly larger than necessary, trimming back as required after offering up the carpet to the car.

CF2. ▲ Use a waterproof adhesive to stick the carpet where necessary – for instance on vertical sections. The glue is easily spread, using an applicator designed for plastic body filler.

CF3. ▼ The use of good quality sound-proofing felt, cut to size and applied beneath the carpets, can help to reduce noise, especially on the less luxurious models.

Carpet fitting

If the carpets on your Capri are in poor condition, new 'pre-cut' sets can be purchased, from a range of suppliers. These should, in theory, be 'ready to fit', although, from experience, I know that the fit of some carpet sets is better than that of others, if dealing with non-original items.

If you wish, you can of course make your own carpets, by buying good quality carpet from a reputable upholstery supply company, then cutting out and fitting the various sections, using the originals as patterns.

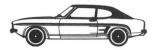

Interior clean-up

There is no excuse for having a car with a grubby interior, these days. Even very dirty upholstery can be cleaned using one of the many preparations currently available. There are products to clean (and polish, where applicable) all materials and surfaces. Regular valeting will keep the car looking smart inside, and enhance its value.

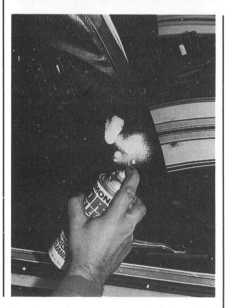

ICU1.►If the car is in daily use, the seats can be 'dry-cleaned', using an aerosol spray. The foam helps to lift the dirt, but can be wiped off, leaving the seat clean and dry.

ICU2.▼ The door trim panels can be restored to an 'as new' finish using a proprietary spray cleaner/polish. Apply in even coats, to cover the surface, then . . .

ICU3.▲ . . . use a soft cloth to wipe off and polish the surface. Quite spectacular results can be achieved.

ICU4.▼ The same approach applies to the oft-neglected plastic trim panels in the back of the car. After a few minutes and a little elbow grease, this area of your Capri can be transformed.

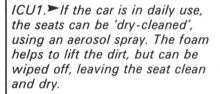

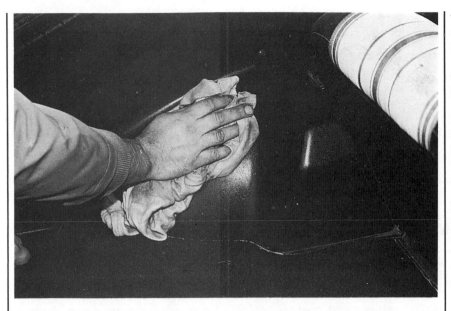

ICU5. ▲ *Always give such surfaces a final buffing with a dry cloth, to achieve the ultimate shine.*

Notes on headlinings

I have purposely left the headlining until last in this chapter, not because it isn't an important part of the interior of any car, but because it is a 'borderline' area when it comes to deciding whether to do the job yourself, or enlist the help of a professional.

Removing and re-fitting a headlining can be a traumatic experience, so, unless you are particularly keen, it is probably best left to an experienced upholsterer. However, if you are enthusiastic, the job can be done at home, but you should be aware that it is extremely difficult to get the lining back into the car and free from wrinkles. It is also far easier to tackle a headlining if the car is completely dismantled – with windows out and door trims off, and so on, since the lining tucks into the inner lips of the sealing rubbers/window trims.

The lining material can easily be torn when trying to remove it from the rubber/trims; a blunt screwdriver is useful for this, but even so, take care.

Unless you are particularly good at sewing, it would be best to let an experienced person make the new headlining, although it is *possible* to make your own from the appropriate material, using the original as a pattern.

Before fitting the new lining, ensure that felt or foam pads are placed between the 'listing' (support) rails which support the lining when in position, and the roof of the car. The padding will provide insulation between the roof and the rails, cutting down noise and holding the rails in place as the headlining is fitted. The hoop-shaped rails can easily invert themselves as the headlining is fitted to the car, necessitating a fresh start, so ensure that the rails are well secured during fitting.

Before installing the lining, it is a good idea to mark with a pencil the centre points of the headlining, and of the bodywork, at the front and back, and each side, to aid alignment. Provided the lining is then fitted 'squarely' in relation to these guide marks, the shaped lining should match perfectly with the curvature of the roof panel. This is particularly critical at the back of the car, where the roof dips sharply.

Secure the front and rear ends of the lining first, around the front and rear screens respectively, then work from the centre, outwards. Tap the seams of the lining at each side, where they fit above the doors, with the heel of the hand. This pulls the material across the car, keeping it taut.

As stated earlier, the job is not for the faint-hearted!

175

6 Modifications

Fords have always been candidates for modifications by their owners, either to make them go faster and handle better, or to make them look different, to stand out from similar models, or just to make them more comfortable.

The Capris, of course, are no exception, and there are almost limitless possibilities to the range of modifications you can make to your car.

Increasingly, as the cars get older, they get scarcer, and so the range of products available gradually shrinks. Therefore there are, naturally, more tuning and 'upgrading' parts available for the later Capris than there are, say, for the Mark Is. That doesn't mean to say that you cannot improve the performance, safety and comfort of the earlier cars, for there are many firms who do still cater for these models. It has to be said though that nowadays the emphasis on the earliest Capris is heading more towards 'originality', as the cars become more collectable.

Nevertheless there are many ways in which these Fords can be improved, without losing any of their character, and this is very good news if, for example, you use your car for everyday travel. In these circumstances the sacrifice of a little originality in return for improved performance, safety and comfort may be considered worthwhile. It all depends on how you, as an individual owner, view your car.

The subject of modifications to Capris would, of course, fill several books, let alone a single chapter. Therefore the aim here is to give an indication of the various possibilities, to 'whet the appetite'. There are many specialist volumes on, for example, the subjects of engine and 'chassis' tuning, which give full details of the various options. These are good investments, for it is well worthwhile researching the 'whys and wherefores' before parting with any money on parts which may be of limited benefit to you, or even be totally unsuitable for the type of motoring you do. Many of the specialist tuning firms will be only too pleased to talk about the likely effects of fitting various uprated components, and it is a good idea to talk to these experts before you start.

It also makes sense to talk to other owners who have attempted modifications (for better or worse) and benefit from their experience. There are, for example, many members of the Capri Owners' Club who have modified their vehicles, and the Club's excellent monthly magazine 'Capri Club International', formerly 'Capri News' contains regular in-depth studies of various aspects of uprating the cars.

It should go without saying that if you are considering boosting the power output of your car, you should think about ways of making it handle and stop safely too, so that improving the suspension and brakes will go hand in hand with the increase in power.

Insurance companies have traditionally taken a dim view of altering the vehicle manufacturers' standard specifications. However, they MUST be informed of any relevant changes to the car, or your insurance will be considered to be invalidated. This could have disastrous results, especially if you were to have an accident and damage someone else's property, or even kill someone.

It is worth finding out in advance how much extra premium will be required – you may have a nasty shock! While an insurance company may settle for just a modest increase if, for example, moving from 1300 cc to 1600 cc, the premium could get VERY expensive if say, uprating from 1300 cc to 2.8 or three-litres! You will almost certainly, in any case, need an 'Engineer's Report' on the car's condition, together with full details of all the alterations made.

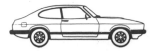

Power unit swaps

Before considering the various aspects of uprating a particular engine – which becomes increasingly expensive, the more power you attempt to wring out of a unit – it is worth looking at the possibility of an engine swap. This, in many cases, can prove to be a more practical and cost-effective alternative to modifying your existing engine. Of course there have been a wide variety of power units fitted to Capris over the years, and some swaps are easier than others.

It is worth bearing in mind that since Ford used engines of the same capacity in different models, it is quite possible to use the engine from, for example, a more powerful Escort, in your Capri. In addition, Ford produced engines of similar capacity, but in varying stages of tune. By buying carefully, you could, for example, gain as much as 20 bhp, simply by installing a 'GT' version of the engines already fitted to your car. A look at Appendix 3 – 'Specifications' – will show the ranges of engines and their respective power and torque outputs, as fitted to Capris, to give an idea of what is possible.

M1.►One of the easiest ways to gain more power is simply to change your engine for a larger – or simply more powerful – motor from the same range. Alternative power units can often be found in scrapped cars – either Capris or other Fords fitted with the same series of engines, giving a choice of possibilities. For example, the cross-flow engines fitted to early Capris can also be found in Cortinas and Escorts. The GT engine as found in this Cortina Mark II could be fitted to a Capri after simply changing the sump and oil pipes. If buying an engine which is still fitted in a vehicle, it is sometimes possible to hear it running before you buy it, which is obviously useful.

Of course, swapping engines often means that you will be buying secondhand. This can be okay, but there are risks, of course, especially when you cannot actually hear the engine running. This often applies in the case of breakers' yards, where the engine will already be out of the vehicle, in many cases.

Another possibility is that you may be able to buy the engine you need through advertisements in local newspapers. There may be someone living near you who is breaking a car, which perhaps has accident or severe rust damage, but which nevertheless has a good engine.

It is always sensible to examine the engine carefully before you buy. In particular, look at the state of the oil, the general condition of the unit (has it been blowing oil out all over the top of the engine, due to worn pistons/rings/cylinder bores, for example?) and inside the rocker cover. However, unless you can actually drive the car, or strip and examine the motor, neither of which options are usually practical, you will be taking some risk.

When you get the engine home, you can either fit it and 'try' it, which sometimes works out all right. Alternatively, you can at least take off the cylinder

head(s) and overhaul it (them), also removing the oil pump and the sump, to check the bearings and crankshaft, carrying out re-ringing and perhaps a rebore, if necessary.

If you do just fit the engine without any close inspection, don't hold your hopes too high – you may be disappointed. At the very least, in any case, you should use fresh engine oil and fit a new filter before you run the motor.

When fitting any 'non original' unit to your car, always try to obtain the ancillaries that belong with the engine, and fit the whole assembly. This includes the distributor and carburettor, both of which are matched to the engine size and type, and, if possible, the radiator. In addition, on GT types, try to obtain the correct manifolds/exhaust system for the engine, for best results.

Cross-flow

Probably the most straightforward swap is changing a cross-flow engine for that of a larger capacity – normally this means fitting a 1600 cc unit, complete with its ancillaries (carburettor, distributor, etc.) in place of the

1300 cc engine; the mountings are the same. While you may consider it to be better to use the gearbox designed for the 1600 cc engine, your existing gearbox, propeller shaft and rear axle can be retained, unless you specifically need higher gearing, in which case the differential could be changed – such decisions will really depend on the type of use to which the car will be put.

The oil pump, water pump and alternator from your 1300 cc engine can be used on the 1600 cc unit, if required, but the carburettor and distributor must be the items designed for the 1600 cc motor. To aid identification, it is worth noting that the 1600 cc engines are physically taller (by two inches) than their 1300 cc brethren. On the 1600 cc unit, if the water pump is bolted on, there is approximately 3/4 inch between the water pump and the cylinder head.

If you are considering buying a secondhand engine, you have a wide range of suitable 'donor' vehicles from which to choose, including, of course, the 1600 cc Capris, the Escort and the Mark III Cortina, all of which have the deep portion of the sump at the rear.

You could also use a 1600 cross-flow engine from a Cortina Mark II, in which case the sump will need to be changed, since the deep part of the sump on these cars is at the front, to suit the differing steering gear arrangements. To effect a swap from a Mark II Cortina, the sump from a 1600 Capri, Escort or Mark III Cortina engine will be required, along with the (differently positioned) oil pipes and dipstick, with its tube. When swapping the oil return pipe (carefully twist it out of the donor engine), take care not to push it into the new engine too far, or it will cut off the oilway. A hole will be needed in the cylinder block, to accommodate the new dipstick tube and dipstick; you will find a 'pilot' hole already, at the appropriate point. The redundant dipstick aperture should, of course, be securely plugged, to prevent oil and fumes from being forced out, all over the engine!

M2.◄ The 1600 cc cross-flow engine as fitted to the Cortina Mark II featured this straight oil pick-up pipe, to collect oil from the deeper part of the sump, at the front, whereas . . .

M3.◄ . . . on the Capri, Escort and Cortina Mark III versions of the engine, the sump has its deepest part at the rear, and employed a cranked pick-up pipe. This pipe, and the nearby oil return pipe, should be transferred to the Mark II Cortina unit, and the Capri-type sump fitted. The dipstick, too will need to be re-positioned.

The standard 1300 cc cross-flow engine can easily be swapped for a GT specification motor, from a Capri or Escort, to give a useful increase in power (typically around 12 bhp) and a small improvement in torque.

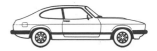

By fitting a standard 1600 cc cross-flow engine in place of a 1300 cc unit, you will gain between 7 and 13 bhp, depending on the dates of manufacture of the respective units, with even more impressive improvements (close on 30 per cent) in torque. Fuel consumption will remain around the same as for the 1300 cc motor, since the 1600 engine will not have to work so hard to propel the car along.

If considering fitting an engine from a Mark II Cortina, bear in mind that a 1600E power unit will give around 18 bhp more than the standard 1600 cc unit, and slightly improved torque, for little more outlay. The power units from Mark II 1600 Escort Sports or Ghias, and from cross-flow 1600 GT Capris and Mark III 1600GT Cortinas will give similar outputs.

In theory you could replace the 1300 cc unit with an 1100 cc motor, although this would give a very underpowered car, and you would gain very little, except perhaps a reduced insurance premium. However any gains here would be wiped out by the extra fuel needed to propel the big Capri bodywork along. The 1100 motor would be working far harder than it was designed to!

Pinto overhead cam units

It is a relatively straightforward swap to fit a two-litre overhead camshaft engine in place of a 1.6 litre unit, to give a 26 bhp boost, and an increase in torque of nearly 30 per cent. It is also a straight swap (apart from carburettor linkages, etc.) to fit a GT version of the 1.6 litre engine, instead of the standard unit, to gain 15–16 bhp and a small but useful torque increase.

The Pinto engines were, of course, used in many other Fords, other than the Capri, for example the Cortina Mark III, IV and V, the Sierra, and the Transit vans, so availability of parts and complete engines is good.

V4 and V6 Engines

The 2000 cc V4 engine used in the Capri was already in 'GT' guise, so you are not going to increase power by fitting the engine from say, a Corsair, a four cylinder Zephyr, or even a Transit into your Capri. However, these vehicles can be useful sources for a basic replacement motor, as they become increasingly rare. As with the cross-flow engines, fitting a unit from another model will necessitate a sump change, since the deep part of the sump is at the rear, on Capri engines, and at the front in the case of Corsairs and Zephyrs. The sump on the Transit is different again, so the correct Capri sump would need to be fitted. Swaps of oil pipes and dipsticks are also needed if fitting a V4 from another model.

These comments also apply to the V6 Essex engines, for the same reasons. A V6 engine can be fitted from a Zephyr Six, Zodiac or three litre Granada, but again variations in the position of the deepest part of the sump need to be taken into account.

It is important to match an engine and its ancillaries – by keeping them together – as far as possible – especially carburettors and distributors, to be sure that you will get the most from the 'new' unit.

Another engine swap which is feasible, if not necessarily desirable, is to fit a three-litre V6 engine into a Capri originally fitted with a V4 power unit. These days, the car will be more valuable if it has a V4 unit than a V6. Nevertheless, the six-cylinder unit can be fitted, if a Cortina Savage clutch plate is used (if you can find one). The engine cross-member needs to be

changed, and the gearbox cross-member must be altered. The propellor shaft from the three-litre car should be used, and, preferably, the gearbox (because it is far stronger than that made for the V4 engine), and the rear axle, to give more relaxed cruising from the higher overall gearing. In addition, the brakes on the axle from the V6 car are bigger. Change the front and rear springs also, to cope with the extra loads imposed on them.

Other swaps

Theoretically of course it is possible to switch engines of different types between vehicles, but generally speaking this is much harder work than fitting a unit of the same type. The problems you are likely to encounter are those of matching engine mounts, bell housings, propeller shafts, clutches, and gearboxes with the unit you are attempting to fit. For example, even if considering a fairly 'tame' conversion (perhaps between overhead cam engines and cross-flow units, or vice-versa) you will find that the engine mountings are different, the cross-member will need to be modified, the exhaust system must be altered, as must the coolant hoses and electrical wiring. In some cases the gear lever, too, may need to be re-located.

If you are not unduly worried by the thought of such problems, it pays, if obtaining the engine, say, from another type of Capri, to buy as many of the 'installation' components as possible from the donor car, since these can then be fitted to your own. These normally include the engine mountings, flywheel, gearbox/bell housing, propeller shaft, and radiator, where different from those items on your vehicle.

Be especially careful if trying to fit a motor such as a three-litre V6 into a body shell designed for a much less powerful unit. Frankly, it's not really a very good idea. Apart from the extra weight – the V6 engine weighs nearly twice as much as a cross-flow motor – the body shell and suspension on models designed for the more powerful engines were strengthened to cope with the additional power, and the faster cars had superior braking systems. It is important that relevant modifications are made to your basic vehicle, to cope with the extra power and weight of a larger engine.

Returning for a moment to the V4 engined cars, if you really need to change the engine for another unit, rather than using the V6 engine, an overhead camshaft two-litre 'Pinto' unit could be used instead. The original (V4 type) gearbox can be employed, provided it is fitted with the bell-housing from a cross-flow engine, and that the clutch designed for an overhead camshaft 1600GT is fitted. Alternatively, the stronger gearbox designed for the overhead camshaft engine can be installed, together with the propeller shaft for the ohc car.

I haven't so far mentioned the 2.8 litre V6 Cologne engine, which differs drastically from the V6 Essex unit. However, of course in recent years the Capri was factory-fitted with the 2.8 litre motor, and the conversion is possible to lesser-engined Capris, provided the engine mounts and gearbox for the 2.8 litre unit are also employed. However, the swap is not straightforward, and working out the revised locations for hoses, injection equipment and so on is a mammoth task. If you really want V6 power, it is far better, in most cases, to go for an Essex three-litre V6, which will give nearly as much power in return for much less work and, almost certainly, much less financial outlay as well.

Finally, if V6 power isn't enough, it is possible to fit a Rover V8 engine to a Ford gearbox (three-litre variety) by means of a commercially available adaptor plate, but such an installation obviously requires careful planning.

Tuning

The alternative to fitting a different engine is to improve the one you already have. Again, since you own a Ford, you are fortunate in that there are so many different tuning parts available specifically for uprating Ford engines. From carburettors to camshafts, cylinder heads to exhaust systems to turbochargers, there is an almost limitless supply of parts to make Fords move more quickly! The specialist magazines dealing with performance motoring carry advertisements in each issue from firms who can supply every imaginable tuning accessory. It is also worth enquiring of your local motor accessory shops, regarding tuning parts; many of the owners and managers are keen to help, and have a great deal of knowledge themselves about the equipment needed to uprate your car to different levels of performance/driveability.

With any engine, harnessing its potential performance is only possible if the 'breathing' is correct. Therefore the carburation, ports and manifolds need to be modified, if necessary, to smooth the gas flow, and to make the most of each cc of fuel mixture, as it passes through the engine.

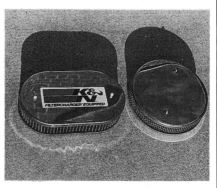

T1.▲ Standard air filters seldom allow the optimum quantity of air into the engine, and there are a wide range of different filters available for Fords, which not only work more efficiently, but which look smart, too.

T2.◄ A carefully designed exhaust manifold can make a world of difference to an engine, even without any other modifications. It is not being over-optimistic to expect a power increase of around 10 per cent by fitting a 4 into 2 into 1 manifold like this.

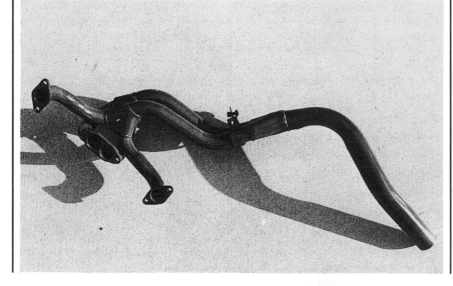

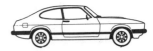

If you intend keeping your car for a long time, and particularly if you use it every day, it is worth spending some money to improve the performance. The fitting of a matched carburettor, cylinder head(s) and manifolding, for example, will normally improve the car's pulling power, acceleration AND fuel economy, for a properly tuned engine will make more efficient use of the fuel it burns.

Of course, further stages of tune are also possible, by fitting high performance camshafts and so on.

Plan ahead

It is always wise to think hard, before you start, about what you are trying to achieve by modifying your engine. Tuning engines is an art, and it is always helpful to talk to experts (and other owners) with experience from which you can benefit. Otherwise it is very easy to spend a lot of money on parts which may be of little real benefit for the sort of use you give your car. There are quite a few fast Fords on the road which would be ideal on a race track, but which are awful to drive in town traffic, where they spend most of their time! It is quite possible to 'over tune' an engine by going for maximum possible power, without considering other factors, such as low speed torque. As an example, rushing out and buying the 'wildest' camshaft you can find could give you a car with a lot of power at high revs, but no pull at low speeds, which can make it very difficult to drive in traffic.

If you are simply looking for a modest improvement in power and economy, without loss in flexibility, this can be achieved just by bolting on a modified manifold/exhaust system, and possibly a performance carburettor/air cleaner assembly. Useful gains can in fact sometimes be made simply by bolting on a carburettor and inlet manifold from a higher performance Ford fitted with the same basic engine, although it should be borne in mind that expert help may need to be sought on the subject of re-jetting, where required. This approach does have the advantage that minimal dismantling and/or linkage modifications are required. For example, the twin choke Weber carburettor fitted to the GT versions of the overhead cam 1.6 and 2.0 litre engines can be fitted, with its inlet manifold, to the 'standard' version of the 1600 cc engine, and a useful modification which could be made at the same time would be a conversion to manual choke operation, if appropriate.

A modified cylinder head(s) would be the next stage, with improved gas flow, and possibly larger valves. Beyond these relatively straightforward 'bolt on' items come camshaft changes and so on. The first few extra horsepower are fairly easy to attain, but further improvements need a lot more work, and, usually, a lot more money too.

In any event, before deciding to extract more power from your engine, it is sensible to ensure that it is in good shape to start with. Certainly, if it is already beginning to burn oil, and perhaps is low on compression, with a rattling camshaft, you should think carefully before buying tuning components. Trying to improve the motor's ailing performance by bolting on expensive goodies is only going to hasten its already imminent demise. Far better to spend some money now on overhauling the engine, then, when it has been fully run in, consider 'go faster' parts.

There are a multitude of firms who can help with advice and the necessary components for tuning your Capri, no matter which engine is fitted; the names and addresses of some of them appear in Appendix 6 – Clubs, Specialists and Books' – at the back of this book. While most of the firms listed will deal with all types of Ford engine, it is worth bearing in mind that some firms are particularly conversant with specific types. Examples include Burton Power Products (cross-flow, Pinto and Essex V6), Holbay Racing Engines (Pinto), Janspeed (cross-flow, Pinto, Essex and Cologne V6), Oselli Engine Services (cross-flow, Pinto, Essex V6), Power Engineering (supercharged V6s), Specialised Engines (cross-flow, Pinto, Essex and Cologne V6), Swaymar Engineering (Essex and Cologne V6), and Vulcan Engineering (cross-flow, Pinto, Essex and Cologne V6). For further lists of tuning firms, consult the specialist 'go faster' magazines.

In recent years an extra option has become more widely available – that of turbocharging – and several companies, including Turbo Technics and Janspeed, have developed the concept successfully for application in the Capri. As an example, 2.8i engines modified by Turbo Technics happily produce well over 200 bhp (and more). Their 200 bhp conversion also provides an extra 55 per cent of torque, at 500 rpm lower than for the standard engine! The conversion is not cheap, but it does transform the car, with appropriate suspension (bushes) and braking modifications. The top speed is raised to 140 mph or so, and 60 mph is passed in around $6^{1}/_{2}$ seconds, on the way!

Janspeed

As indicated at the outset, this book is a restoration guide, and not a tuning manual. Nevertheless it is useful to look at

the various options available when it comes to tuning an engine. There are, of course, many ways in which to achieve increases in power, and the approach to take will depend to an extent on the type and age of engine you have – for example, as a general rule, the more modern the design of engine, the more efficient it will be to start with. However, certain fundamentals apply to all engines, and a logical approach to gaining power is required. For general advice on what aspects to consider, I spoke to Simon Lee, of the well-respected and long-established tuning firm of Janspeed, in Salisbury.

Simon confirmed that more power will be obtained by increasing the gas flow through an engine, and first thoughts should be directed towards this, assuming that, as already mentioned, the engine is in A1 condition before you attempt any modifications. In 90 per cent of cases, modern carburettors and cylinder heads are found to be 'adequate' in terms of gas flow, and the first major gains can be obtained by dealing with the 'restrictive' exhaust manifolds normally found on production cars. After sorting out inadequacies of the exhaust manifolding, Simon advises a 'step by step' process of working through the power unit, improving the cylinder head, camshaft and carburation as required, to give the desired combination of power and torque.

In every case, for modern road traffic conditions, an adequate amount of torque, produced at reasonably low engine revs, is preferable to out and out power, produced at high revs. Driveability is an important factor, especially in a car used as daily transport.

Before going out and buying an assortment of tuning items which may or may not necessarily be matched items (and therefore may not work together to produce the best results), Simon advises buying all the items from one firm. They will be able to advise in advance the effects that each of their components will have, and will also have experience of how the parts work when used together, as a performance 'package'.

These are some of the normal tuning options for Janspeed customers wishing to uprate their Capri power units:

Cross-flow engines

It is interesting that, at the time of writing, the cross-flow engine is still by far the most popular Ford unit which Janspeed are called upon to supply parts for.

Janspeed estimate that by fitting a properly designed exhaust manifold system, to achieve optimum gas flow, power gains of up 16 per cent are achievable. Having sorted out the 'extraction' side of the engine, Janspeed then recommend various stages of cylinder head improvement. Their own 'Stage I' cylinder head modifications include gas-flowing of the head, which is polished and ported, with balanced combustion chambers, and the fitting of re-shaped standard valves. They feel that any alterations below this level amount to a compromise, and don't make the best of the available energy. Their Stage I modifications are, generally, aimed at achieving power improvements of 25 per cent – well worth having, for a relatively modest outlay.

Janspeed advise that the fitting of larger valves is not really worthwhile on its own, unless this is done in combination with gas-flowing.

Janspeed's Stage II cylinder heads feature larger inlet valves, but are otherwise as Stage I items, while their Stage III heads have larger inlet and exhaust valves.

It is perhaps worth mentioning here as a general point that head-skimming is not a good idea, on many Ford engines, including the cross-flow units. This is because the combustion chambers are formed within the piston crowns, and any reduction in clearance between the piston top and the cylinder head will result in violent contact between pistons and valves. This gives severe loss of compression (and valves and pistons!), rather than the desired increase in compression and power.

Pinto overhead camshaft engines

Janspeed find that the overhead camshaft Pinto engines – especially the two-litre unit – are more efficient in standard form than the cross-flow engines. Nevertheless, improvements are gained by the same general approach. Performance is first enhanced by fitting 'extractor' exhaust manifolds, followed by the fitting of twin-choke downdraught carburation, then by cylinder head work along the lines of that carried out on the cross-flow engines.

V6 Essex engines

Fairly hefty gains can be made by changing the exhaust manifolds and system on the three-litre V6 engines, depending on which model you have. The Mark I cars already have fairly efficient tubular exhaust manifolds, but also feature a single exhaust system. The fitting of a more efficient twin exhaust can give useful improvements in performance.

The Mark II and III engines have cast manifolds, which can

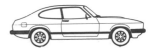

be replaced with tubular types, to advantage. They were also fitted with a twin exhaust system as standard, though, so power gains to be made by changing the system, while useful, are not quite so great. The engines on S models have tubular manifolds as original equipment, incidentally.

Typically, replacing the Essex engine's exhaust manifolds and system with the more efficient Janspeed items will give a welcome power increase of about 14 per cent.

RS2600 and 3100 engines can be uprated in the same way as the three-litre motors, and normally a large bore three-litre manifold will give good results.

2.8i engines

The fuel injection system actually limits the ultimate power output achievable from the 2.8 litre Cologne engine. However, Janspeed advise that a change of exhaust manifold and system will give 14 per cent more power. The next step is to carry out a Stage I

cylinder head conversion, which, combined with the exhaust modifications, will yield total gains of between 22 and 25 per cent.

For further improvements, Janspeed recommend turbocharging, in conjunction with the Bosch K Jetronic fuel injection system.

General notes

Janspeed can supply a suspension package appropriate to the power improvements gained from mechanical modifications, and also suggest the use of ventilated discs and four-pot callipers for the braking systems of highly tuned cars. They will be pleased to advise potential customers on specific proposed modifications, including turbocharging.

Although Janspeed no longer supply large quantities of tuning parts for the V4 engines, they will still be able to advise and help Capri owners who wish to uprate their engines.

Finally . . .

All the engines used in the Capris – including the powerful three litre and 2.8i engines – can be modified in the manner described, to give useful improvements in power and torque. If you are serious about making further gains, detailed investigation is required, to ensure that any money spent is money *well* spent.

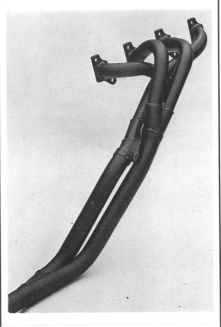

T3. ▲ *Janspeed's extractor exhaust manifolds give significant gains in engine efficiency – and hence performance. This one is destined to uprate an overhead camshaft Pinto engine.*

T4. ◄ *Performance can be improved by the fitting of different – or extra – carburettors. This is an inlet manifold made by Janspeed for the fitting of twin Weber carburettors.*

T5. ▲ *Single side draught Weber carburation can give useful improvements in power. This 40 DCOE unit is on a Pinto inlet manifold.*

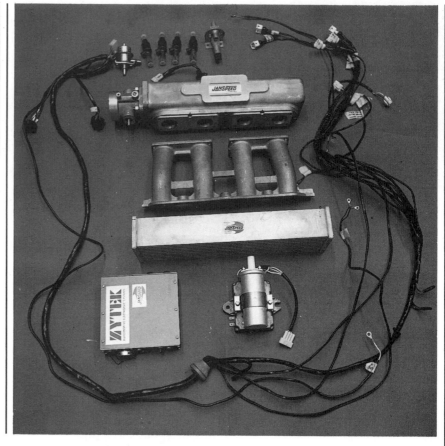

T6. ► *An alternative to carburettors is fuel injection – this is a Janspeed kit for a Pinto engine.*

T7. ▼ *The discreet 'Turbo' logos on the sides of this Capri mean what they say – this was the first Capri to be turbocharged by Janspeed, who can uprate V6 Essex or Cologne engines by adding turbos.*

T8. ▲ *Perhaps the ultimate in current turbo technology – the fitting by Janspeed of twin turbochargers to the 2.8 injection engine. This car is in fact an XR4i Sierra, but the work can equally be carried out to the same engine as fitted to a Capri.*

Other suggestions

No matter which Capri you drive, one of the easiest ways of improving power and economy (typically 10 per cent) is to fit a thermostatically controlled electric fan, in place of the engine-driven unit. This will allow quicker warm-up of the engine from cold, and, at all temperatures, will release several bhp which can be used to drive the wheels, instead of the engine cooling fan!

Electronic ignition can be fitted, more to reduce maintenance than to improve fuel consumption or performance, although in some cases marginal gains may be made, especially at high engine speeds.

There are additional, very interesting, if more expensive, modifications possible for increasing power, for example the twin cam conversion offered by Piper for the overhead camshaft

1.6 and 2.0 litre 'Pinto' engines. The kit, incorporating a fully modified cylinder head and aluminium cam carrier, plus all the necessary parts, is designed for d-i-y fitting – assuming that you have some experience of building engines.

Other possible alterations to your Capri engine include over-boring the cylinder block(s), lightening and balancing engine components, fitting higher-lift camshafts, and so on, all of which are outside the scope of this book. For further information on such 'wilder' modifications, consult the specialist tuning companies, and read the many books devoted to the modification of engines for power, torque and/or economy gains. Lists of books for further reading, and tuning specialists are included in Appendix 6, at the end of this book.

Gearboxes

If fitting a more powerful engine from the same range, it pays where possible to use the matching gearbox, with a new clutch assembly, if necessary, at the same time. At least then you will be sure that the gearbox is capable of handling the extra

power, rather than, for example, trying to mate a powerful engine with a gearbox designed for a lesser output. It will probably fit, and work for a while, but, if you use the extra power, it won't last very long. In addition, the ratios chosen for the gearboxes on the faster models are deliberately 'close', to match the performance characteristics of the engine; full details of the ratios used in each Capri gearbox are given in Appendix 3, at the back of this book.

It is possible to swap gearboxes about between different Ford models, and again, the range of permutations and combinations is vast. The best way of making sure that a particular gearbox will fit is i) to talk to other owners who have attempted the conversion you are planning, and ii) verification by physical inspection and measurement. Look particularly at the pattern of the bolts around the bell housing, and at the length and diameter of the first motion shaft, and the number of splines on this.

Among the many other options available when it comes to gearboxes are the Ford Rallye Sport (RS) components – these include close ratio gear sets for four speed 2.8is, and short gearchange kits for 1300 and 1600 models.

185

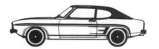

Five-speed Capris

An interesting conversion is to fit your Capri with five-speed transmission – this can be done and need not be difficult. The later (March 1983 on) 2.0 litre overhead camshaft engined cars (and 1.6 litre examples, first as an option, and then as standard) had five-speed gearboxes factory-fitted, as did the 2.8i, from January, 1983. The five-speed units slotted into the ohc cars were designated 'N' type, and originated from the Sierra. The five-speed gearbox fitted to the 2.8i was of Granada origin, with different ratios from five-speed units fitted to 1.6 and 2.0 litre Capris.

Fitting an 'overdrive' five-speed gearbox will give more relaxed cruising at speed, improved fuel consumption on longer journeys, and extended engine life.

OHC models

The easiest conversion is to fit an overhead camshaft engined Capri with the five-speed gearbox from a later example. Before you attempt the changeover, it is best to make sure that you obtain, beforehand, all the necessary parts from the donor vehicle, plus any additional new components required, as listed below.

The five-speed units are identical for 1.6 or 2.0 litre models, with the exception of variation in the speedometer drive gears. Depending on which vehicle you obtain your 'new' gearbox from, and the capacity of *your* engine, you may have to change the drive gears. If you are unsure of which engine/gearbox/rear axle is fitted to the prospective donor car, you can check by reference to the vehicle identification plate, and translate the relevant codes as explained in Appendix 5 of this book! Alternatively, or if you are buying a gearbox already taken out of a car, you can check the Finis numbers on the 'drive' and

'driven' gears. For a gearbox to suit a 1.6 litre car (axle ratio 3.778:1), the 'drive' gear should have Finis code no. 6095065; the 'driven' gear, Finis code no. 6011059 – this item should have 23 teeth. For a gearbox to suit a 2.0 litre car (axle ratio 3.444:1), the 'drive' gear should have Finis code no. 6095066; the 'driven' gear, Finis code no. 6011061 – with 24 teeth. So, if you buy a gearbox with the 'wrong' speedo drive gears to suit your car, simply buy the correct ones from your Ford dealer.

Before parting with your money for the gearbox, ensure that it *is* from a car with an overhead camshaft engine, and not a V6, in which case the bell housing has different bolt holes. Check by reference to your own car.

Use the propeller shaft, bell-housing, gear lever and speedometer drive cable from the donor Capri, together with the gearbox cross-member.

If your car is a two-litre model, you can use the clutch designed for the four-speed gearbox. However, if your car is a 1.6, you will need to buy a new clutch assembly. The new driven plate must have 23 splines, and cars before 1983 with VV carburettors, require a 7$\frac{1}{2}$ inch diameter item – Finis code no. 6107844 – while those prior to this date with Weber carburettors need an 8$\frac{1}{2}$ inch diameter driven plate – Finis code no. 1634820. Later cars already have a 23 spline clutch plate, which can be retained.

The first four gears in the new gearbox will have identical ratios to those in the four-speed, 1.6 or two-litre overhead camshaft Capris with 'H' type gearboxes (similar, but not quite the same as those in the 1.6 models with 'C' type transmissions – the ratios are given in Appendix 3 – 'Specifications'). However, the new top gear will give a step-down of 0.82:1, instead of the previous 1:1 top gear ratio.

2.8i

Fitting a four-speed 2.8i Capri with a five-speed gearbox is not a difficult operation, and the clutch and gearbox mountings for the four speed car can be used. The propeller shaft from the four speed set-up can also be used, although in fact it is 16 mm shorter than the 'correct' item; if you can obtain the longer propshaft with the gearbox, so much the better.

Three litre V6

If you intend to fit a five-speed gearbox to an Essex-engined V6 Capri, you will need to use the appropriate bell housing to link the power unit and transmission. This can be found in Granadas built between 1972 and 1974, and is identifiable by its part number, 72GB 7505 LA, which should be visible on the side of the unit. If you need to buy the bell housing from Ford, take around £100 with you and quote reference no. 1500914 to the parts man. (If you cannot obtain this bell housing, the existing one can be re-drilled to suit the new gearbox – take care when drilling!)

Assuming the use of the Granada bell housing, the first motion shaft of the gearbox will now be 14.7 mm too long for use in this application, and should be reduced in length by cutting or grinding, prior to fitting.

The gearbox cross-member also requires alteration; the four holes for the bodywork fixing bolts should be re-drilled 16 mm further forward in the cross-member.

After all this, the propeller shaft and the original three-litre cluth mechanism can be obtained, although for best results use a Capri 2.8i gear lever assembly, or an adapted RS 'quickshift' gearchange kit.

Finally, use the speedometer cable, circlip and white gear wheel from a Capri 2.8i, to give true speedo readings with the five-speed gearbox.

Incidentally, if you decide to

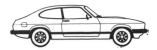

re-drill the existing bell housing, rather than obtaining the Granada item, you should use the propeller shaft from the five-speed 2.8i.

Caution . . .

If you are using a gearbox dating from prior to late 1986 in a car with a V6 engine, and drive it hard, you may find that excessive wear in the layshaft bearings will result. The later gearboxes were stronger in this respect. Firms such as Tickford and Turbo Technics can help with regard to improved lubrication for the bearings, and better layshaft alignment – desirable anyway, and essential on uprated engines.

Don't attempt to fit a five-speed gearbox from an overhead camshaft engined car, or a diesel model, into a V6 engined Capri – apart from the ratios being different, they will be unable to handle the extra power – at least, not in the long term.

Automatic?

Another interesting possibility is that of converting a 2.8i to automatic transmission, using a four-speed Granada auto box. Indeed such an option was commercially available when the Capri was still in production.

To fit the C3 Granada gearbox requires various alterations, including changing the pedal assemblies, shortening the propeller shaft, making a bracket to hold the gearchange unit, and the fitting of the automatic type console panel. Somar Transtec, of Gloucestershire, can help with such conversions, in three or four speed form.

Differential change

If you have changed the engine of your car for a more powerful unit, or even if you simply need to alter the overall gearing to take account of the vehicle's use, there are a wide variety of differential ratios to choose from. The various ratios used in the Capris are listed in Appendix 3 – 'Specifications', at the back of this book, and they allow for various compromises between acceleration, cruising speed, fuel economy and ultimate top speed.

Generally speaking, the higher the power of the engine, the higher the back axle ratio (and therefore the lower the number) can be. The higher the ratio, the slower the engine will need to turn for a given road speed. Therefore if you use your car a lot for high speed cruising,

and less for town work, a higher ratio differential will give you more relaxed driving, longer engine life and lower petrol consumption, even if you retain the original engine. On the other hand, if your vehicle is used almost entirely in town traffic, a high ratio differential will be a nuisance, calling for more gear changing than is necessary, and making the car less 'flexible'. A lower ratio differential will give improved acceleration and easier driving around town, but make the engine increasingly fussy as the speed rises, and will lower the ultimate maximum speed attainable.

Of course there are occasions when you can deliberately alter the characteristics of the car by fitting a more powerful engine and *not* changing the final drive ratio.

It is possible that you could be fitting a more powerful engine to cope with towing, or for carrying heavy loads, for example, and in either of those cases it may be preferable to leave the original ratio fitted, rather than 'uprating' the differential to a higher ratio unit.

The best compromise ratio for your vehicle really depends on what sort of motoring you normally do.

It should be borne in mind that changing the final drive ratio will alter the speedometer overall gearing, and hence the speedometer readings, unless the appropriate speedometer drive gear is also fitted, or the speedometer is recalibrated.

Two types of axle

DC1.◄ *Two types of rear axle were fitted to Capris – the 'Salisbury' (Type 'D'), with 'integral' differential unit, and the 'Timken' (Type 'J'), in which the final drive assembly is simply bolted to the front of the axle casing.*

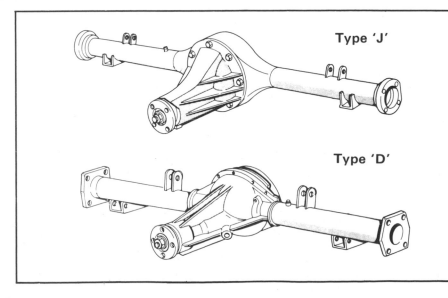

Type 'J'

Type 'D'

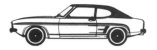

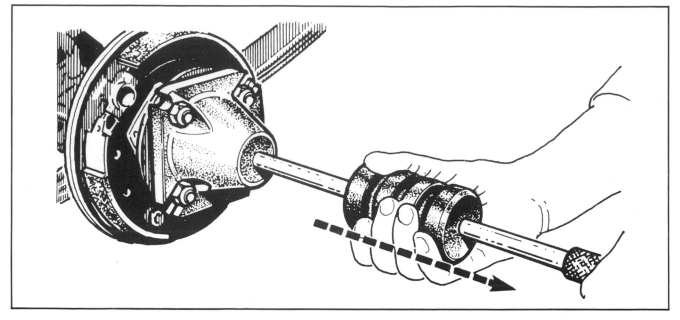

Timken Type

To change a differential on the Timken type axle is quite easy.

Before you start, make sure that you have a new differential case gasket and a supply of fresh axle oil.

If you are intending to fit a secondhand differential, the ratios fitted to the various Capris can be checked by reference to Appendix 3 – 'Specifications' – at the back of this book. Appendix 3 lists the ratios fitted to each model, together with the number of teeth on the crown wheel and pinion, for each version. The vehicle's identification plate should also be checked; the relevant axle ratio code can be translated by reference to Appendix 5 – 'Identify Your Car' – also at the end of this book.

If you are unsure which axle is fitted to a particular vehicle (perhaps the identification plate is missing, or the axle may have been changed at some time), you can double-check simply by counting the number of teeth on the crown wheel and pinion gear wheels, and compare the results with the list.

It is worth bearing in mind that Fords used common final drive ratios between models, and, if buying secondhand, you may find a suitable unit in another

Ford, if not in a Capri.

To change the differential assembly, the half shafts must first be released, having drained the axle oil (where a drain plug is provided). With the handbrake off, release the brake drums (each secured by a single screw), then take out the four bolts securing the bearing retaining plate to the backplate. The bolts can be released by using a socket spanner and extension bar, guided through the holes in the axle shaft flange.

The axle shafts can now be withdrawn from the casing, a few inches at each side, to clear the differential. The half shafts may be reluctant to move, in which case they can be 'encouraged' by the use of a slide hammer, which can be made from pieces of scrap found in the garage. The hammer consists of a steel plate (with holes spaced to fit at least two diametrically opposite wheel studs), to which is welded or bolted a length of steel rod, approximately half an inch in diameter, and about two feet long. Around this rod should be placed a heavy, cylindrical length of steel, around six inches long. At the other (outer) end of the tool should be fixed another, very strong, steel plate (either bolted or firmly welded).

DCT1. ▲ The hammer is attached to the hub by means of two (opposite) or all four wheel nuts. The sliding cylinder is then gripped and repeatedly struck against the outer plate, until the half shaft moves. Whatever you do, DON'T stand (or allow others, especially children, to stand) behind the slide hammer when operating it, in case the half shaft is suddenly released, or the slide hammer should break.

Alternatively, it is sometimes possible to remove the shafts by bolting an old road wheel onto the hub, and tapping the inside of the wheel on alternate sides, using a block of wood. Another option is to use two long bolts, passed through the end of the axle case and the backplate, at diametrically opposite points, to push the half shaft gently out of the axle.

On re-assembly, smear the outer surface of the bearing case with a little grease, to help prevent it from seizing in position in the future. Finally, tighten the bearing retainer plate bolts to the correct torque as specified in the *Haynes Owners Workshop Manual* relevant to your model.

DCT2. ►Two long bolts, with the same threads as the originals, can be used to push each half shaft out of the axle casing. Tighten the bolts evenly, a little at a time.

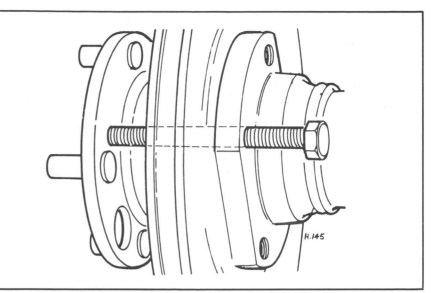

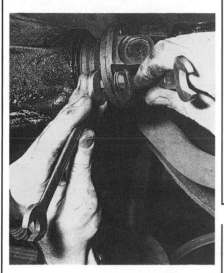

DCT3. ▲ With the half shafts clear, release the four bolts (or nuts and bolts) holding the propeller shaft to the front flange on the differential.

DCT4. ►The nuts around the perimeter of the differential casing are now released; take care that the final drive assembly doesn't drop as the last nuts are taken off. More often than not, however, it will need to be prised away from the axle casing.

DCT5. ►This is a new differential unit, and therefore spotlessly clean. If you are buying a secondhand unit, and removing it from a vehicle yourself, take a large plastic carrier bag with you, so that the assembly can be kept clean until it is fitted. Always check that there is no grit or dust in the 'works' immediately prior to fitting the unit.

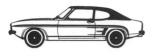

DCT6.▶Fit a new gasket to the axle casing, having cleaned the flange with a little cellulose thinners on a clean rag. Fit the new unit very carefully, then tighten the nuts to the torque setting as recommended in the appropriate Haynes Owners Workshop Manual covering your model. Re-fit the half shafts, again tightening the bearing retainer plate bolts to the correct torque, and finally re-fill the axle with fresh oil.

Salisbury type

If contemplating changing the final drive ratio of a car with a Salisbury type axle fitted, the differential unit must be withdrawn from the rear of the assembly. This can only be done after draining the unit, releasing the handbrake cable, extracting the half-shafts a few inches each side, removing the cover plate from the rear of the axle casing, and releasing the two 'U' shaped differential bearing caps. This work should be carried out in consultation with the appropriate *Haynes Owners Workshop Manual* for your model, and the appropriate torque settings strictly adhered to on re-assembly. Always fit a new gasket to the rear cover plate, and re-fill the axle with fresh oil, on completion.

Exhaust system

Modified exhaust manifolds and complete exhaust systems can be purchased for any of the Capris from 1969, giving, in many cases, quite drastic improvements in power and fuel consumption. By more efficiently purging the engine of exhaust gases, gas flow through the engine, and hence power, is increased.

An exhaust manifold made from smooth mild steel normally allows gases to escape rather better than through a cast manifold which is comparatively rough. Therefore a tubular steel manifold is a worthwhile investment. Generally speaking, for maximum power and torque, the pipework emerges from the engine on a one to one ratio between the number of cylinders and the number of pipes. Therefore, four branches will take gases from a four-cylinder engine, merging into twin pipes, and, finally, into the single exhaust outlet. If this is fed into a properly designed, relatively large bore exhaust system (such as a Peco – either standard large bore, or H.D.R. – 'Heavy Duty Rally''), further power will be released to the road wheels, which is, of course, where it needs to be. The amount of power so released will vary according to the system, of course. As an example, by fitting a Ford Rallye Sport high efficiency system to a three-litre Capri, another 8 bhp becomes available.

A problem which affects the heavy manifold/exhaust system on the three-litre cars is that of cracking of the exhaust manifold between exhaust ports two and three. This can be overcome by making a bracket which links the manifold with the bell housing, helping to take the weight, and to reduce excessive movement.

If you are intending to keep your Capri for a long time, a worthwhile modification is the fitting of a stainless steel exhaust system. These are available 'off the shelf' for the later cars, and even systems for the rarer models can be made using the original system as a pattern. Stainless steel systems are, of course, more expensive than standard items, but last indefinitely, and the investment is worthwhile, long-term.

Electrics

There are a wide range of electrical accessories which can be fitted to Ford Capris, ranging from driving lamps to electronic ignition systems.

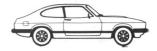

E1.➤ An electronic ignition system is useful for keeping the engine in tune for far longer than with a normal ignition system. On types where the contact points are used as 'triggers' for the system, the points will last a lot longer, and will not become burnt and pitted, as with a conventional system. On 'contactless' types, the physical limitations of the mechanical contact breaker are dispensed with, to give more accurate ignition timing, especially at speed.

Apart from other considerations, the fitting of an electronic ignition system means less time required in adjusting the points, and the inevitable consequent ignition timing alterations normally required. So going 'electronic' can save time and frustration in routine maintenance.

E2.➤ Auxiliary driving lamps are available, together with heavy duty mounting brackets, and they can make the front of the car look more imposing, apart from being a valuable driving aid at night.

The choice of useful electrical accessories is almost limitless, but one which is of particular interest on the hatchback Capris, for models not already so fitted, is the fitting of a rear screen wash/wipe system. This will help to keep the rear screen clean in all conditions, is not too expensive to buy, and is relatively straightforward to install.

Another useful modification, especially where extra electrical

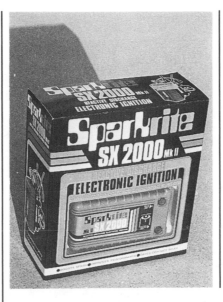

equipment has been fitted, is the conversion of an early dynamo-equipped Capri with an alternator from a later model. You will of course need an alternator – the Lucas ACR series units are readily available – plus the necessary mounting brackets and a new fan belt. These can be obtained through Ford dealers or, for example, the brackets can be purchased secondhand.

The first step during the actual fitting operation is to disconnect the vehicle's battery, then to remove the fan belt, dynamo and brackets, installing the new items and the alternator in their place – the belt should be

rather tighter than when using a dynamo – total belt deflection in the centre of the longest run should be approximately 1/2 inch.

When fitting an ACR alternator, which has its own, integral regulator, the original regulator box must be disconnected (pull off the connector block). The relatively thin cable which used to connect to the dynamo should be attached, at the 'engine' end, to the 'IND' terminal on the alternator. The other end of this cable (formerly connected to the 'F' terminal on the control box), should now be joined to the

dynamo (generator) warning lamp wire (originally connected to the 'WL' terminal on the control box).

The thick lead originally running between the 'D' terminal on the control box and the dynamo should now be joined to the '+' connectors on the alternator, and to the heavy duty lead originally linking the battery and the 'B' terminal on the control box.

These connections can effectively be made by bridging the connector block outlets. The lead originally connected to the 'E' terminal on the control box is earthed.

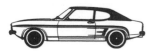

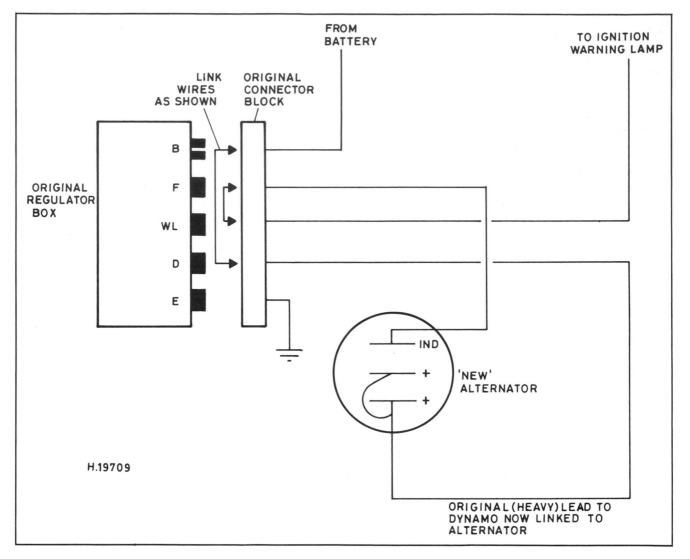

FROM
BATTERY

TO IGNITION
WARNING LAMP

LINK
WIRES
AS SHOWN

ORIGINAL
CONNECTOR
BLOCK

ORIGINAL
REGULATOR
BOX

B

F

WL

D

E

IND

+

+

'NEW'
ALTERNATOR

H.19709

ORIGINAL(HEAVY)LEAD TO
DYNAMO NOW LINKED TO
ALTERNATOR

E3. ▲ Fitting a Lucas ACR alternator is relatively straightforward, requiring wiring changes as illustrated.

Useful yet relatively straightforward modifications which can be carried out to the lighting circuits include the fitting of a 'lights on' warning device, and improving the efficiency of the headlamps. For example, the four headlamp system on the 2.8i can fairly easily be converted to 100 watt operation, using Cibie lamp units and twin relays.

Bodywork

Bodywork modifications can be made to any of the Capris, to improve the car's looks, to gain aerodynamic efficiency or even to disguise rusty wings!

Before going into the various options available, one word of caution regarding the early cars; the more the bodywork is modified, the more difficult it would be to revert the vehicle to 'standard' if you ever wanted to sell it as a 'collector's car', for example. While this may not matter if you intend to keep the vehicle anyway, it may be worth thinking about. The value of a car which has modified bodywork will, generally (with the

exception of the higher quality styling 'kits' available) be lower than that of an 'original' vehicle.

Bodywork kits

The already low-slung styling of the Capri lends itself to further modification by the addition of add-on panels, to make the appearance sleeker still. Many such panels – often in the form of kits – have been available over the years, and there are a number of styles on offer at a wide range of prices. Materials vary, too, from glass fibre to ABS – deformable plastic. Many styling kits have the additional benefit of

improving the car's aerodynamics; however, always check on this point with the manufacturers. One word of warning is necessary on this aspect; by fitting un-matched body components, or even individual items, the car's aerodynamics may be upset, especially at speed, causing possible instability, so ALWAYS check with the suppliers/makers about the possible effects of what you are intending to fit, before you buy.

These days, the majority of complete kits are designed for the Mark II and III cars, although individual panels – and in some cases full kits – are still available for the Mark Is.

To give you an idea of the variety of styling packages (and panels) on offer, kits available to date have included those by Richard Grant Accessories, KAT Designs, Individual Products Ltd., Cartel Cars and Conversions, Ford's own Rallye Sport Accessories, Auto Motiv Body Styling, and so on and so on.

It is worth mentioning that a wide range of RS bodywork components are still available from Ford RS dealers. These include the wide and all-embracing 'X-Pack' wheel arches. These look spectacular, but fitting them is rather involved, and takes a long time. They also require the use of 7 1/2 inch wide wheels.

Aerodynamically efficient front and rear spoilers are also available.

Richard Grant Accessories

It is, of course, impossible to show the fitting of all the various kits on offer, in one book. Therefore most of the general techniques required are shown by reference to the fitting of a popular and relatively inexpensive bodywork kit, suitable for Mark II or Mark III Capris. The 'Lazer' kit illustrated is by Richard Grant Accessories, and has been praised for its ease of fitting, and its durability. The step by step photographs were taken at the premises of JGS Customising – telephone (0525) 220360 – and

depict the kit being fitted to a Mark III Laser model. The procedures are very similar when fitting the kit to a Mark II Capri, except that in this case a different, one-piece front spoiler is employed, in place of the three-piece item used on the Mark III cars.

It is always handy to have at least one extra pair of hands available when fitting a kit such as this; it makes life far easier when trying to check alignment, and when holding the various panels in place.

It makes sense to ensure that the bodywork is spotlessly clean before you attempt to fit a styling kit, and it is a good idea to apply a coat of wax polish to the areas of paintwork which will be hidden by the new panels, to discourage rust from forming.

BK1. ▼ *Styling kits are made by Richard Grant for all Mark II and Mark III Capris; individual panels can be purchased for the Mark I cars. Shown here is a Mark II, with the one-piece front spoiler.*

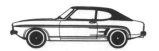

BK2. ▲This is a 2.8i fitted with the three-piece front spoiler and side skirts . . .

BK3. ➤ . . . complemented by the rear valance which fits neatly below the original bumper.

BK4. ➤The 'Lazer' kit for a Mark III Capri consists of these components; it is a good idea to offer them all up to the vehicle before you start work in earnest, to establish the relative positions of all the panels when fitted. They are attached to the car by a combination of blind rivets and double-sided adhesive tape.

　　The panels can be painted before fitting to the car, or afterwards, in which case masking will be necessary. Since a 'two pack' paint **(which is poisonous if inhaled)** is recommended for the panels, it is best to get them painted professionally.

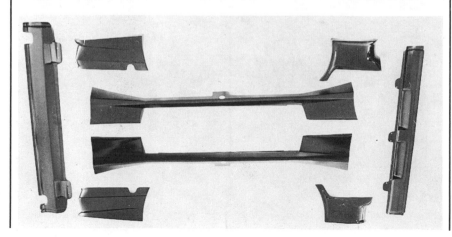

Plastic drive rivets can be used as an alternative to steel or aluminium blind rivets. The plastic rivets are inserted into holes drilled in the panel and the bodywork, and the centre of the rivet is then tapped with a hammer. This spreads the rivet, making it grip the panel. Don't hit the rivet too hard, or its shoulder will break! It is worth bearing in mind that metal rivets will pull the steel panels of the vehicle and the ABS sections of the body styling kit together more effectively than plastic rivets.

It is a good idea to prime and paint the inner surface of each hole drilled in the car's bodywork, using a fine paintbrush. Allow the paint to dry, before attaching the rivets for the panels. This will help to avoid corrosion problems in the future.

When fitting rivets, use washers to spread the load around the panel; if joining two ABS panels, use an extra washer, behind the panels, for the same reason.

Always check the alignment of the panels at each end, and all along their length, BEFORE drilling the bodywork and attaching the rivets!

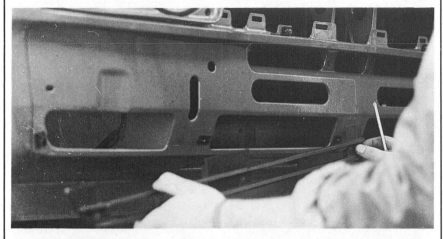

BK5.◄ The front bumper can be completely removed, as on this car, for easy access, but in fact you need only take off the two end caps. The next step is to unscrew and remove the two (lower) black plastic grilles below the bumper.

BK6.◄ The centre section of the new front spoiler can now be attached to the car, using the retaining screws from the black plastic grilles, re-fitted on top of the spoiler.

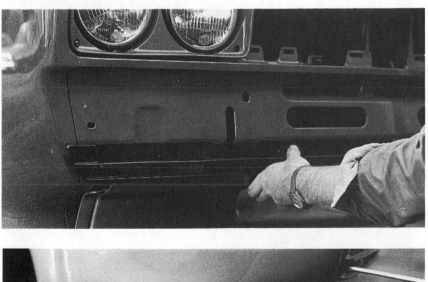

BK7.◄ The front corner sections of the spoiler assembly can now be added, making sure that they sit flush around the wheel arches. With the sections held in this position (with the aid of an assistant, 'G' clamps or self-grip wrenches) they can be secured at their upper forward edges by the retaining screws for the lower grilles.

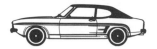

BK8.►After checking that the rear flange of each corner section is still aligned with the front section of each wheel arch, the outer flange of the arches should be drilled, and the panels riveted in place.

BK9.►The corner sections must now be joined to the centre panel of the front spoiler assembly. Once more, drill the panels . . .

BK10.▼ . . . and fix them firmly together, using three rivets at each end (two horizontal, one vertical).

    Finally, at the front, the support stay (supplied in the kit) should be fitted between the forward edge of the spoiler and the steel valance on the car.

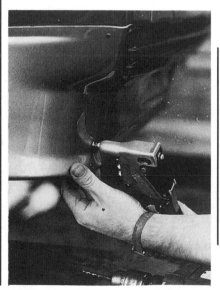

BK11.◄ Next, fit the side skirt (sill) sections of the kit, having first carried out a 'trial fit'. Open the door and attach the double-sided tape to the step panel of the door sill. Now, with the side skirt section securely held in position at each end (against both fore and aft wheel arches), 'feed' the inner edge of the skirt under the draught excluder rubber, while releasing the protective covering from the top of the double-sided tape. Press the new panel downwards along its length, onto the sticky tape, as the protective cover is removed.

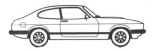

BK12. ▲ *Now, still with the panel held firmly at each end, check that it fits perfectly around the door. If all is well, drill a single hole in the lower rear edge of the door shut panel, and secure the side skirt in this position, with another rivet.*

An additional complication, on late Capris fitted with body side mouldings, is that the skirts must 'lip' beneath the mouldings. This can be achieved, in warm conditions, by very carefully easing the mouldings away from the bodywork with the aid of a screwdriver. A less risky alternative is to release the mouldings by slackening their retainers, to allow the side skirts to be fitted. The moulding on the front wing can be released from behind the panel, while to get at the mouldings on the rear quarter panels, the interior trim has to be removed. The Lazer skirts are clamped in place when the mouldings are re-tightened to the bodywork.

If you have an earlier car, without side mouldings, the new side skirts can be fitted flush and sealed to the body with a silicone sealer, or the later mouldings can be purchased and fitted to your car. The Ford part numbers are:

offside-front section, 1577577; door section, 1577579; rear section, 1577581; nearside-front section, 1577578; door section, 1577580; rear section, 1577582.

BK13. ▲ *With the front wheels turned on full lock towards the side of the vehicle that you are working on, secure the front end of the skirt panel with a rivet.*

BK14. ◀ *The rear wheel will have to be removed to allow sufficient clearance for the electric drill and the rivet gun, when securing the rear end of the panel to the forward section of the rear arch flange.*

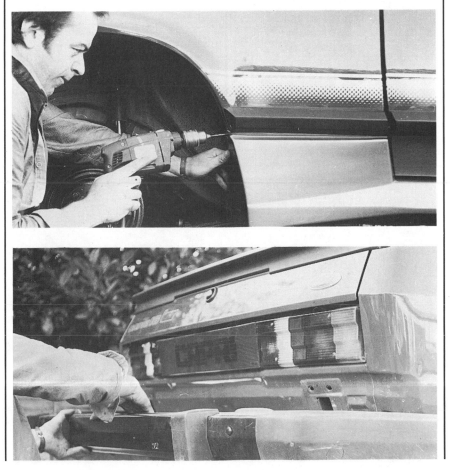

BK15. ◀ *The final stage is to fit the rear spoiler assembly, and the first step towards this is removal of the rear bumper, as described in the 'Initial Work' section of Chapter 3 – 'Bodywork'.*

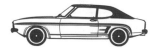

BK16. ►Attach the centre section of the rear spoiler assembly to the vehicle, initially through the original bumper fixing points, and using similar-sized nuts and bolts. The corner sections of the spoiler should now be carefully positioned, drilled, and riveted together, and to the vehicle, at the rear lower corner of each wheel arch. Offer up the bumper at each stage, to ensure that the panels fit together perfectly.

Drill the bodywork and rivet the centre panel to it, then remove the nuts and bolts, so that the bumper can be replaced. Refit the rear bumper, after sealing the joints between the rear spoiler and the bodywork, using a flexible silicone sealing compound.

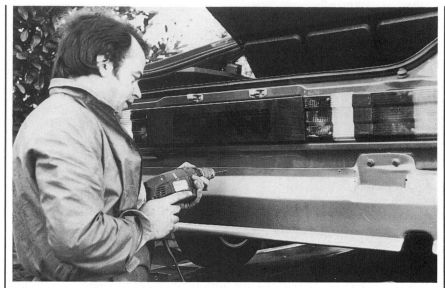

BK18. ◄ The final job is to re-fit the front bumper.

BK19. ▼ Stand back and admire! The car now looks sleeker and even lower than with the standard bodywork, from any angle.

BK17. ▼ Apply the same sealant to the front spoiler, and to the edges of the side skirts, to give a weatherproof finish.

Other bodywork modifications

It is quite likely that the fitting of a rear spoiler to the tailgate of a Mark II or III Capri will lead to the rear door gradually sinking, instead of staying fully open. This can be extremely annoying, not to mention painful, if it hits you on the head. An easy way to overcome such problems is to fit the tailgate support rams from a Sierra XR4, which are much stronger (and cheaper), and can easily be changed for the original Capri items. Sierra studs are required, in place of the Capri screws. The part numbers are: support struts – (two of) 1618864; studs – (four of) 1615064.

The wiring for the heated rear screen, and for the tailgate wash/wipe (if fitted) will need to be extended and re-routed, but otherwise the job is straightforward.

Another attractive modification which can be made to any Capri is the fitting of a vinyl roof. Ripspeed, of Edmonton, North London, supply kits for this purpose.

Other, more major bodywork alterations include conversion to an attractive convertible (as carried out originally by Crayfords, and, more recently, by Paul A. de Rome, Coachwork Conversions, Blackpool), and building your Capri into a kit car, such as the JBA Javelin, based on Mark II or III cars.

Last, but not least, the Capri Owners' Club often arrange special offers on a range of bodywork accessories, including, for example, X-Pack body styling packages, Mark I, II and III striping kits, and headlamp louvres. Their excellent magazine, *Capri Club International* regularly includes full, step-by-step details of bodywork modifications of all descriptions.

Wheels and tyres

The choice of alternative wheels and tyres for your Capri is extremely wide. It pays to buy good quality items, of course, and it is essential that, when fitted, the new wheels and tyres do not hit the suspension, brake pipes or suspension/steering components under full lock or 'rough road' conditions. Before parting with your cash, survey the market and talk to other owners (perhaps fellow club members) and to the wheel suppliers – they will be able to advise you on specific fitting problems.

If fitting wide wheels, the widest you can go to with standard bodywork is 7J items, (7½ inch rims might *just* fit), with appropriate tyres. The choice of tyres is a complex one, and is dependent on the use to which you put the car, and whether, for example, you prefer ultimate wet grip to extremely long life, and so on and so on. The choice is usually a compromise between competing parameters! Again, talk to other owners, and to the wheel suppliers, who will have a good idea of which tyres will best suit their wheels.

WAT1. ▲ Wheels and wheel spacers are available in a variety of types. If fitting wheel spacers, ALWAYS ask the advice of the suppliers, since extra load will be placed on the wheel bearings, proportional to the increase in the distance between the wheel and the hub.

WAT2. ◄ It is useful if you are able to 'offer up' to the vehicle a wheel of the type you intend to buy. You can then be sure that the pitch circle diameter (the diameter of an imaginary circle drawn through the centres of the hub studs) of the wheel matches that of the studs on your car. You will also be able to establish whether the wheel is likely to protrude beyond the bodywork.

You may find it difficult if you are trying to obtain original type road wheels for one of the rarer early Capris – for example the RS3100. The originals were four spoke, cast alloy items, with polished rims and spokes, and are almost impossible to find today. An alternative is to fit later wheels which are similar, if not identical. For example, in this case, you could fit 6 x 13 inch RS alloy wheels. If these are

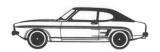

polished and have their insets and the rear of the spokes painted in black gloss, they will look close to, if not the same as, the originals.

Suspension

Uprated springs and shock absorbers can make a great deal of difference to the handling of your car. Revised springing and firmer shock absorbers will usually improve cornering, at the expense of ride comfort, so talk to the supplier before you buy, and explain what you are aiming for. It is also important to realise that, as with engine tuning, it is easy to spend a great deal of money and still not achieve the results you desire; always talk to other owners who may have attempted the modifications you are contemplating. It is especially important with the Capri only to make changes as part of a balanced package including springs, shock absorbers and anti-roll bars, since otherwise the car may exhibit poor handling and a rough ride.

It is also important to appreciate that there is a great deal of difference in weight between the smaller engined Capris and the V6 powered cars, and that the suspension requirements are therefore different for each type.

If you have a larger, heavier engine fitted to your Capri, you may be obliged to fit heavy duty front springs, to cope with the extra weight. If you use your Ford for carrying heavy loads, and particularly if it is used for towing, spring assisters or auxiliary springs can be fitted, to preserve the original suspension, and to help prevent the vehicle from riding too low at the rear. Alternatively, heavy duty rear springs could be substituted, as direct replacements for the originals.

S1. ▲ There are an enormous variety of uprated shock absorbers and springs available for improving roadholding. Most normally affect ride quality to some extent, and the result is therefore usually a compromise. Talk to your supplier about the type of use the car receives, and he will be able to advise you on the best units to fit for that particular application.

It is possible to use suspension parts from other Capris, or even other Ford models – for example the struts from an Escort RS2000 can be fitted, provided the discs and hubs are also used.

The suspension from a 2.8i Capri can be fitted to other Mark II or Mark III Capris, provided that the spring and shock absorber rates, to which the Capri is particularly sensitive, are revised. For example, if you have a Pinto engined car, the shock absorbers from a two-litre S (after 1983) would provide a good ride/handling compromise.

As with engine tuning, it is impossible in just a section of one chapter to give a full description of all the options available, when it comes to tuning Capri suspension. Some extremely informative features have appeared on the subject in

Capri Club International (formerly Capri News), the magazine of the Capri Owners' Club – in particular two articles by Steve Saxty (December 1985 and November 1987 issues). There are also detailed analyses of Capri 'chassis tuning' which appear from time to time in the specialist 'performance motoring' magazines, as well as several books devoted to the subject of general chassis tuning. It is best to read as much as possible about the subject, and, as indicated at the start of this section, to talk to owners who have already modified their cars. You will then be in a good position to spend money wisely on modifications which will improve your suspension.

Brakes

Your brakes will almost certainly need to be improved if you have uprated the power output from your own engine, or have fitted a more powerful unit. This can be quite easy, if expensive. For example, if you have simply fitted a larger engine from a more powerful model, swapping your existing braking system for one as employed on the faster model (and overhauling it as a matter of

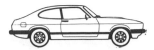

course before fitting) is one answer.

There are other options, of course, such as, for example, on the 2.8i, where fitting four piston calipers and a rear disc conversion is an expensive but effective means of improving the braking. Incidentally, standard 2.8i ventilated front discs will not fit the struts on three-litre V6 cars; either the strut assemblies will have to be changed, or an (expensive) Rallye Sport vented disc kit fitted.

Another useful modification, which can be applied to three-litre and other models, is to fit a more powerful brake servo unit. Contrary to popular belief, a servo does *not* improve braking efficiency, but simply reduces the pedal pressure required to slow the car. It is a useful aid, but not an improver of the braking efficiency of the car, in itself. The same applies to the fitting of harder 'competition' type brake pads and linings. These will probably be more resistant to 'fade' than ordinary types, when under prolonged or hard use, but the brake effort required may well be *increased*. In addition, wear on the discs and drums may be more rapid. Again, the use of such items, in isolation, will not help very much, but will be more useful as part of a properly planned, co-ordinated braking system re-vamping.

On the subject of servos, the unit from a three-litre Granada can be made to fit a three-litre Capri, with advantage. All that is required is to extend the operating rod, elongate the mounting holes, and slightly reshape the inner wing, to accommodate the larger vacuum tank.

Always take care when swapping brake assemblies from one model to another. For instance, you may find that if you attempt to fit larger brakes from a more powerful car in another model range, they may not physically fit onto your vehicle.

With brakes, more than any

other of the vehicle's systems, modifications must be made VERY carefully, and with due regard to all the possibilities. Talk to the club(s) and to as many people as possible who have tried similar conversions – you will then learn about many of the possible snags.

Finally, if in doubt about uprating brakes to this extent, don't attempt it yourself. Take the car to a tuning specialist with experience in this field. Far better to pay to have the job done, than to risk lives with inadequate/ unsafe brakes.

Interior

The interior of any car can be improved in terms of its fixtures and fittings. One of the easiest ways to do this on a base model Capri, or lower trim specification versions, is to replace some or all of the interior fittings with those from a more luxurious model. Items such as seats and trim panels are fairly easy to change, and, with the exception of some early models, are still fairly easy to find in breakers' yards, or on offer for sale by other enthusiasts.

The facia and steering wheel can be improved by fitting those from more 'upmarket' models, or 'aftermarket' accessory items. Burr walnut dashboards are available, if required.

The complete interior 'package' can be transferred from one model to another, if desired. For example, the trim from Mark III cars (including 2.8is) can be installed in Mark IIs without too many problems. This can give a wide range of options for sources of panels, and for upgrading.

A problem for some Capri drivers is that the seat belts are mounted a long way back at each side of the vehicle, due to the use of such wide doors. An interesting idea to overcome this problem is to fit the seat belts from a Vauxhall Astra GTE. The

belts are then brought further forwards. The parts required (two of each) are: no. 90046083 – seat belt arm; 90046084 – belt head; 90046085 – belt insert; 90046869 – spacer; 90288049 – spring. The original spacer is removed, and these components fitted.

Another worthwhile modification, for those who like to get the best from audio system speakers fitted to the rear shelf, would be the addition of an acoustic rear parcel shelf (for Mark II and III cars), such as the one made by Auto Acoustics, of Byfleet, Surrey (address given in Appendix 6 – 'Clubs, Specialists and Books' – at the back of this book).

The special acoustic, waterproof shelf should also rid the car of annoying rattles from behind the rear seats!

Instruments

Driving can be made more enjoyable by having a set of instruments to keep one up to date with what is happening under the bonnet. Supplementary instruments can be fitted to the non-sports models, and among the dials generally available, tachometer, coolant temperature, oil pressure, vacuum, voltmeter and ammeter gauges are probably the most useful. If you are enthusiastic, it is also possible to obtain oil temperature gauges, ambient temperature indicators, and so on. It all depends just how much information you need.

Another instrument I find particularly useful is an 'Icelert'; this is fitted to the outside of the car, and, when the temperature dips, a light flashes as it approaches freezing point. The intensity of the flashing increases as the temperature drops still further, and the warning lamp stays on continuously when the temperature is below freezing. If travelling long distances in winter

201

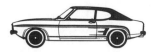

it can give early warning of a temperature change between areas, also of changing weather conditions, and especially the possibility of ice on the road.

There are other instruments one can fit, of varying degrees of usefulness. I must confess to once having fitted an aeroplane's altimeter to my car, which was not perhaps the most essential of instruments, but nevertheless very entertaining when crossing the Alps, and when visiting the Lake District and Scottish Highlands. It had the dual role of acting as a barometer, as the pressure changed, provided you knew what height you were at!

11.➤ Sets of four gauges, complete with a neat mounting bracket, all the necessary sender units, and full instructions for fitting, can be bought at reasonable prices from most motor accessory shops. A tachometer (rev counter) is rather more expensive, but nevertheless useful. It could help to prolong your engine life, as could the other instruments, provided that you take notice of what they are trying to tell you!

Security

It is a sad fact that if you restore a vehicle to a high standard, it can increasingly become a target for car thieves. It seems that the Capri is particularly prone to the attentions of 'joyriders', as well as those with more serious criminal intent in mind.

Although the vehicles stolen are sometimes recovered, they are usually damaged, if not wrecked, by the thieves, so it pays to secure your car as well as you can.

The fairly basic door locks fitted as standard equipment can

be replaced or supplemented by the use of extra, high security locks, such as those made by Safeways Security Products.

Capris with separate door locks (only) can have the original types replaced by the much more sophisticated Ford/Chubb designed Granada Scorpio/Transit van items, which are far more secure. These locks are fitted with disc-type tumblers which make them more difficult to pick. The locks are available at reasonable prices from Ford dealers.

'Accessory' vehicle security locks which can be incorporated into the existing lock positions

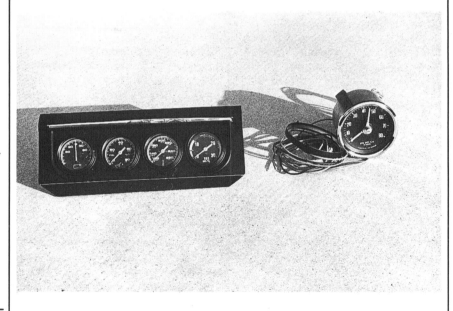

(where separate from the door handles) are made by a number of firms, including ERA and Hykee. Security locks are also sold by Advance Alarms Ltd., of London.

It is also possible to fit extra locks to the bonnet and boot/tailgate, and to equip the car with a comprehensive alarm system and ignition immobiliser, to supplement other anti-theft measures. Alarm systems range from the inexpensive and basic to the sophisticated ultrasonic types. Most motor accessory shops stock a wide range of alarm systems.

Cheap anti-theft deterrents

include the use of a steering wheel/control pedal immobiliser, such as the 'Krooklok', and window etching. The windows and screen are permanently marked with the registration number of your vehicle, so that changing the car's identity is far more difficult. Since to do this a thief would be obliged to change all the vehicle's glass, this would be a deterrent to all but the most determined of thieves.

It is worth fitting a homemade deflector plate within each of the car's passenger doors, over the top of the locking mechanism, so that it makes life more difficult for a would-be

thief endeavouring to illicitly open the doors from above.

If you are planning to leave your car unattended in one place for any length of time, it is worth buying a wheel clamp, which physically prevents the vehicle from being moved (at least not when on its wheels).

Hopefully, of course, your car will not be stolen, but, if it is, the results can be horrifying. I have been involved with recovering several 'classic' cars which have been stolen and dumped, and the wicked way in which some of them have deliberately been torn apart by the vandals who stole them is

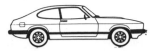

sickening. In many cases, there is little left to salvage or rebuild. Take care of your Ford.

General

As stated at the start of this chapter, it is impossible to list all the possible modifications which can be made to Capris.

In many cases, ingenuity and common sense will suggest ways and means of improving your car, often with very little outlay.

It is often possible to fit parts from other Fords, where required, since many Fords use the same basic components, and a trip round a breaker's yard will usually yield all sorts of interchangeable parts, and ideas for useful modifications. At the same time, there is no reason why parts from other makes of vehicle cannot be used successfully.

With a little careful thought and time spent in experimentation, a great deal of pleasure can be derived from improving your Capri; in most cases this can be done without altering its basic character.

APPENDICES

1 Workshop procedures and safety first

Professional motor mechanics are trained in safe working procedures. However enthusiastic you may be about getting on with the job in hand, do take the time to ensure that your safety is not put at risk. A moment's lack of attention can result in an accident, as can failure to observe certain elementary precautions.

There will always be new ways of having accidents, and the following points do not pretend to be a comprehensive list of all dangers; they are intended rather to make you aware of the risks and to encourage a safety-conscious approach to all work you carry out on your vehicle.

Essential DOs and DON'Ts

DON'T rely on a single jack when working underneath the vehicle. Always use reliable additional means of support, such as axle stands, securely placed under a part of the vehicle that you know will not give way.

DON'T attempt to loosen or tighten high-torque nuts (e.g. wheel hub nuts) while the vehicle is on a jack; it may be pulled off.

DON'T start the engine without first ascertaining that the transmission is in neutral (or 'Park' where applicable) and the parking brake applied.

DON'T suddenly remove the filler cap from a hot cooling system – let it cool down first, cover the cap with a cloth and release the pressure gradually first, or you may get scalded by escaping coolant.

DON'T attempt to drain oil until you are sure it has cooled sufficiently to avoid scalding you.

DON'T grasp any part of the engine, exhaust or catalytic converter without first ascertaining that it is sufficiently cool to avoid burning you.

DON'T inhale brake lining dust – it is injurious to health.

DON'T allow any spilt oil or grease to remain on the floor – wipe it up straight away, before someone slips on it.

DON'T use ill-fitting spanners or other tools which may slip and cause injury.

DON'T attempt to lift a heavy component which may be beyond your capability – get assistance.

DON'T rush to finish a job, or take unverified short cuts.

DON'T allow children or animals in or around an unattended vehicle.

DO wear eye protection when using power tools such as drill, sander, bench grinder etc, and when working under the vehicle.

DO use a barrier cream on your hands prior to undertaking dirty jobs – it will protect your skin from infection as well as making the dirt easier to remove afterwards; but make sure your hands aren't left slippery.

DO keep loose clothing (cuffs, tie etc) and long hair well out of the way of moving mechanical parts.

DO remove rings, wrist watch etc, before working on the vehicle – especially the electrical system.

DO ensure that any lifting tackle used has a safe working load rating adequate for the job.

DO keep your work area tidy – it is only too easy to fall over articles left lying around.

DO get someone to check periodically that all is well, when working alone on the vehicle.

DO carry out work in a logical sequence and check that everything is correctly assembled and tightened afterwards.

DO remember that your vehicle's safety affects that of yourself and others. If in doubt on any point, get specialist advice.

IF, in spite of following these precautions, you are unfortunate enough to injure yourself, seek medical attention as soon as possible.

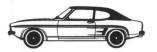

Fire

Remember at all times that petrol (gasoline) is highly flammable. Never smoke, or have any kind of naked flame around, when working on the vehicle. But the risk does not end there – a spark caused by an electrical short-circuit, by two metal surfaces contacting each other, or even by static electricity built up in your body under certain conditions can ignite petrol vapour, which in a confined space is highly explosive.

Always disconnect the battery earth (ground) terminal before working on any part of the fuel system, and never risk spilling fuel on to a hot engine or exhaust.

It is recommended that a fire extinguisher of a type suitable for fuel and electrical fires is kept handy in the garage or workplace at all times. Never try to extinguish a fuel or electrical fire with water.

Fumes

Certain fumes are highly toxic and can quickly cause unconsciousness and even death if inhaled to any extent. Petrol (gasoline) vapour comes into this category, as do the vapours from certain solvents such as trichlorethylene. Any draining or pouring of such volatile fluids should be done in a well ventilated area.

When using cleaning fluids and solvents, read the instructions carefully. Never use any materials from unmarked containers – they may give off poisonous vapours.

Never run the engine of a motor vehicle in an enclosed space such as a garage. Exhaust fumes contain carbon monoxide which is extremely poisonous; if you need to run the engine,

always do so in the open air or at least have the rear of the vehicle outside the workplace.

If you are fortunate enough to have the use of an inspection pit, never drain or pour petrol, and never run the engine, while the vehicle is standing over it; the fumes, being heavier than air, will concentrate in the pit with possibly lethal results.

The battery

Never cause a spark, or allow a naked light, near the vehicle battery. It will normally be giving off a certain amount of hydrogen gas, which is highly explosive.

Always disconnect the battery earth (ground) terminal before working on the fuel or electrical systems.

If possible, loosen the filler plugs or cover when charging the battery from an external source. Do not charge at an excessive rate or the battery may burst.

Take care when topping up and when carrying the battery. The acid electrolyte, even when diluted, is very corrosive and should not be allowed to contact the eyes or skin.

If you ever need to prepare electrolyte yourself, always add the acid slowly to the water, and never the other way round. Protect against splashes by wearing rubber gloves and goggles.

Mains electricity

When using an electric power tool, inspection light etc, which works from the mains, always ensure that the appliance is correctly connected to its plug and that, where necessary, it is properly earthed (grounded). DO NOT use such appliances in

damp conditions and, again, beware of creating a spark or applying excessive heat in the vicinity of fuel or fuel vapour.

Ignition HT voltage

A severe electric shock can result from touching certain parts of the ignition system, such as the HT leads, when the engine is running or being cranked, particularly if components are damp or the insulation is defective. Where an electronic ignition system is fitted, the HT voltage is much higher and could prove fatal.

Compressed gas cylinders

There are serious hazards associated with the storage and handling of gas cylinders and fittings, and standard precautions should be strictly observed in dealing with them. Ensure that cylinders are stored in safe conditions, properly maintained and always handled with special care and make constant efforts to eliminate the possibilities of leakage, fire and explosion.

The cylinder gases that are commonly used are oxygen, acetylene and liquid petroleum gas (LPG). Safety requirements for all three gases are: Cylinders must be stored in a fire resistant, dry and well ventilated space, away from any source of heat or ignition and protected from ice, snow or direct sunlight. Valves of cylinders in store must always be kept uppermost and closed, even when the cylinder is empty. Cylinders should be handled with care and only by personnel who are reliable, adequately informed and fully aware of all associated hazards. Damaged or leaking cylinders should be immediately taken

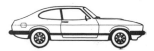

outside into the open air, and the supplier should be notified. No one should approach a gas cylinder store with a naked light or cigarette. Care should be taken to avoid striking or dropping cylinders, or knocking them together. Cylinders should never be used as rollers.

One cylinder should never be filled from another.

Every care must be taken to avoid accidental damage to cylinder valves.

Valves must be operated without haste, never fully opened hard back against the back stop (so that other users know the valve is open) and never wrenched shut but turned just securely enough to stop the gas. Before removing or loosening any outlet connections, caps or plugs, a check should be made that the valves are closed.

When changing cylinders, close all valves and appliance taps, and extinguish naked flames, including pilot jets, before disconnecting them.

When reconnecting ensure that all connections and washers are clean and in good condition and do not overtighten them.

Immediately a cylinder becomes empty, close its valve.

Safety requirements for acetylene: Cylinders must always be stored and used in the upright position. If a cylinder becomes heated accidentally or becomes hot because of excessive backfiring, immediately shut the valve, detach the regulator, take the cylinder out of doors well away from the building, immerse it in or continuously spray it with water, open the valve and allow the gas to escape until the cylinder is empty.

Safety requirements for oxygen: No oil or grease should be used on valves or fittings. Cylinders with convex bases should be used in a stand or held securely to a wall.

Safety requirements for LPG: The store must be kept free of combustible material, corrosive material and cylinders of oxygen.

Dangerous liquids and gases

Because of flammable gas given off by batteries when on charge, care should be taken to avoid sparking by switching off the power supply before charger leads are connected or disconnected. Battery terminals should be shielded, since a battery contains energy and a spark can be caused by any conductor which touches its terminals or exposed connecting straps.

When internal combustion engines are operated inside buildings the exhaust fumes must be properly discharged to the open air. Petroleum spirit or mixture must be contained in metal cans which should be kept in a store. In any area where battery charging or the testing of fuel injection systems is carried out there must be good ventilation and no sources of ignition. Inspection pits often present serious hazards. They should be of adequate length to allow safe access and exit while a car is in position. If there is an inspection pit, petrol may enter it. Since petrol vapour is heavier than air it will remain there and be a hazard if there is any source of ignition. All sources of ignition must therefore be excluded. Always take the greatest care when preparing for welding any part of the vehicle, and particularly when the petrol tank and fuel lines are still attached. NEVER weld, braze or apply heat to, or anywhere near, a petrol tank.

Even a tank which has long been empty will contain explosive petrol fumes, so take very great care. It is always best to remove the fuel tank and petrol lines when welding; if a spark reaches the fuel within a pipe, fire will travel to the tank very quickly!

Don't take any chances; if in doubt, completely remove any parts of the fuel system near to where you are welding.

Cellulose thinners should be treated with great respect. Keep the lids on all cans, and keep the cans well away from heat and naked lights – the vapour will ignite readily. Avoid excessive skin contact, and keep away from eyes.

The same general comments apply to refinishing paints. In addition, make sure that the paints you are using do not contain isocyanates, or are otherwise poisonous. If they do (certain 'etching' primers and synthetic finishes are typical examples), you will need special breathing apparatus. Even when spraying cellulose, you should wear the correct protective mask and goggles specified for the product. Most paint companies supply printed sheets giving health and safety information about their products, readily available at your paint suppliers. Don't take any chances – if in doubt, ask for such information, or contact the paint suppliers direct.

Finally, keep naked flames well away from paint vapour – DEFINITELY NO SMOKING!

Work with plastics

Many plastic materials are used these days in connection with bodywork repair, in particular. Many of the polymers, resins, adhesives, and materials acting as catalysts and accelerators, are toxic. They can produce poisonous fumes, skin irritation, and risk of fire or explosion. Avoid skin contact where possible, and wear gloves.

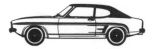

Jacks and axle stands

Particular care should be taken when working underneath a vehicle; lifting jacks are for raising vehicles ONLY. They should never be used as supports for the vehicle while working on it. Axle stands should be used to keep the car airborne while you are below it – use a jack to lift the car, slide the axle stands underneath a firm part of the vehicle's structure, and lower the car back onto the stands. Double-check that the car is securely mounted, before venturing underneath.

If possible, buy four axle stands; they are more versatile than just two. Strong, cheap, adjustable stands can be obtained readily from motor accessory shops.

For jobs where the wheels can remain on the car, drive-on ramps can be very useful, and provided you have an assistant to guide you on and off the ramps safely, are secure. If you are rich enough, there are even 'wind-up' ramps – the car is driven onto the ramps, and then elevated by winding the ramps up – very useful devices.

Make sure that the wheels are chocked securely, or the handbrake applied, BEFORE jacking the car. Bear in mind, though, that jacking the rear wheels of your Ford will, of course, render the handbrake ineffective! Wedges cut (at 45 degrees) from timber, approximately 4 ins x 4 ins, or larger, make ideal chocks. Take care when jacking if the car is in gear, or the handbrake on – sometimes the jack may tip.

My advice is to forget the Ford jack supplied with the car, as far as restoration work is concerned. It is really designed for wheel-changing purposes only. Far better to invest in a bottle or scissor jack, or preferably, a trolley jack. These are now inexpensive, and are quick and easy to operate.

MAKE SURE, WHEN USING ANY JACK, THAT THE CAR IS ON *LEVEL* GROUND.

The best places to jack and support your Ford are under the front cross-member, at each side and either under the rear axle, again at each side, or, if working on the rear suspension, under the main 'chassis' rails towards the rear of the car – make sure that these are SOLID before you jack!

Workshop safety – General hints

1) Always have a fire extinguisher within arm's length when working on the fuel system, or when welding/brazing – either under the car, or under the bonnet.

2) Never use a naked flame near a battery or the car's fuel tank.

3) Keep inspection lamps clear of fuel.

4) If removing the fuel tank and piping from the car, store these items well away from places where you may be welding. The same applies to cans of thinners, paraffin, etc.

5) If you use petrol to clean components, BAN all naked flames from the area. Preferably use paraffin or kerosene for cleaning operations. White spirit may also be used.

6) NO SMOKING during any work on your vehicle – it could be bad for your health in more ways than one!

If you should have a fire, DON'T PANIC! Direct your fire extinguisher at the base of the fire. If you still cannot halt the fire, clear all people and animals from the immediate vicinity, and telephone for the fire brigade (999) straight away. Briefly give any helpful details regarding the nature of the fire, especially if welding gases or petrol, for example, are involved.

7) Take great care when working on a car with the engine running; keep spanners, etc. and fingers away from high tension cables, and from moving parts, such as the cooling fan. Never wear a tie, chains, or rings, when working.

8) When cutting metal, mind your fingers. Only use sharp tools, and use the correct one for the job. Wear thick protective gloves designed for the purpose.

Clear away all swarf and excess metal from the working area to a proper receptacle as you go – don't let it build up. Sharp edges could damage you, or another person, or an unsuspecting child or animal. Clearly mark any dustbins, etc. containing sharp metal.

9) Keep your working area CLEAN AND TIDY. Put your tools away after each working session, wiping them clean if necessary, and sweep up the floor around and under the vehicle. Dust and accumulated paper, etc. can cause a fire hazard, and make working on or under the car uncomfortable. If it gets to the stage during a work session where you cannot find anything, stop and have a 'clear up' – for safety as well as for avoiding frustration!

10) Make sure that, when working with electricity, the cables, switches and the tools themselves are sound. Keep cables free from entanglement, and ALWAYS unplug tools immediately after use. Double check that no power tools are plugged in, after each working session. Keep such tools under lock and key if children are liable to enter the working area when you are not around.

All this may be obvious, but accidents happen all the time, and it would be sad if your restoration project turned out to ruin your life, or that of someone else, simply through lack of care.

2 Tools and working facilities

Introduction

A selection of good tools is a fundamental requirement for anyone contemplating the maintenance and repair of a motor vehicle. For the owner who does not possess any, their purchase will prove a considerable expense, offsetting some of the savings made by doing-it-yourself. However, provided that the tools purchased are of good quality, they will last for many years and prove an extremely worthwhile investment.

To help the average owner to decide which tools are needed to carry out the various tasks detailed in this manual, we have compiled three lists of tools under the following headings: Maintenance and minor repair, Repair and overhaul, and Special. The newcomer to practical mechanics should start off with the 'Maintenance and minor repair' tool kit and confine himself to the simpler jobs around the vehicle. Then, as his confidence and experience grows, he can undertake more difficult tasks, buying extra tools as, and when, they are needed. In this way a 'Maintenance and minor repair' tool kit can be built up into a 'Repair and overhaul' tool kit over a considerable period of time without any major cash outlays. The experienced do-it-yourselfer will have a tool kit good enough for most repairs and overhaul procedures and will add tools from the 'Special' category when he feels the expense is justified by the amount of use these tools will be put to.

Maintenance and minor repair tool kit

The tools given in this list should really be considered as a minimum requirement if routine maintenance, servicing and minor repair operations are to be undertaken.

Ideally purchase sets of open-ended and ring spanners, covering similar size ranges. That way, you will have the correct tools for loosening nuts from bolts having the same head size, for example, since you will have at least two spanners of the same size.

Alternatively, a set of combination spanners (ring one end, open-ended the other), give the advantages of both types of spanner. Although more expensive than open-ended spanners, combination spanners can often help you out in tight situations, by gripping the nut better than an open-ender.

Combination spanners – 3/8, 7/16, 1/2, 9/16, 5/8, 11/16, 3/4, 13/16, 7/8, 15/16 in. AF.

Combination spanners – 8, 9, 10, 11, 12, 13, 14, 15, 17, 19 mm.

Adjustable spanner – 9 inch
Engine sump/gearbox/rear axle drain plug key (where applicable)
Spark plug spanner (with rubber insert)
Spark plug gap adjustment tool
Set of feeler gauges
Brake adjuster spanner (where applicable)
Brake bleed nipple spanner
Screwdriver – 4 in. long x 1/4 in. dia. (plain)
Screwdriver – 4 in. long x 1/4 in. dia. (crosshead)
Combination pliers – 6 inch
Hacksaw, junior
Tyre pump
Tyre pressure gauge
Grease gun (where applicable)
Oil can
Fine emery cloth (1 sheet)
Wire brush (small)
Funnel (medium size)

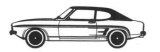

Repair and overhaul tool kit

These tools are virtually essential for anyone undertaking any major repairs to a motor vehicle, and are additional to those given in the Basic list. Included in this list is a comprehensive set of sockets. Although these are expensive they will be found invaluable as they are so versatile – particularly if various drives are included in the set. We recommend the $1/2$ square-drive type, as this can be used with most proprietary torque wrenches. If you cannot afford a socket set, even bought piecemeal, then inexpensive tubular box spanners are a useful alternative.

The tools in this list will occasionally need to be supplemented by tools from the Special list.

Sockets (or box spanners) to cover range in previous list
Reversible ratchet drive (for use with sockets)
Extension piece, 10 inch (for use with sockets)
Universal joint (for use with sockets)
Torque wrench (for use with sockets)
'Mole' wrench – 8 inch
Ball pein hammer
Soft-faced hammer, plastic or rubber
Screwdriver – 6 in. long x $5/16$ in. dia (plain)
Screwdriver – 2 in. long x $5/16$ in. square (plain)
Screwdriver – $1^1/2$ in. long x $1/4$ in. dia. (crosshead)
Screwdriver – 3 in. long x $1/8$ in. dia. (electrician's)
Pliers – electrician's side cutters
Pliers – needle noses
Pliers – circlip (internal and external)
Cold chisel – $1/2$ inch
Scriber (this can be made by grinding the end of a broken hacksaw blade)

Scraper (This can be made by flattening and sharpening one end of a piece of copper pipe)
Centre punch
Pin punch
Hacksaw
Valve grinding tool
Steel rule/straightedge
Allen keys
Selection of files
Wire brush (large)
Axle stands
Jack (strong scissor or hydraulic type)

Special tools

The tools in this list are those which are not used regularly, are expensive to buy, or which need to be used in accordance with their manufacturer's instructions. Unless relatively difficult mechanical jobs are undertaken frequently, it will not be economic to buy many of these tools. Where this is the case, you could consider clubbing together with friends (or a motorists' club) to make a joint purchase, or borrowing the tools against a deposit from a local garage or tool hire specialist.

The following list contains only those tools and instruments freely available to the public, and not those special tools produced by the vehicle manufacturer specially for its dealer network.

Valve spring compressor
Piston ring compressor
Ball joint separator
Universal hub/bearing puller
Impact screwdriver
Micrometer and/or vernier gauge
Carburettor flow balancing device (where applicable)
Dial gauge
Stroboscopic timing light
Dwell angle meter/tachometer
Universal electrical multi-meter
Cylinder compression gauge
Lifting tackle
Trolley jack

Light with extension lead
Rivet gun

Buying tools

Tool factors can be a good source of implements, due to the extensive ranges which they normally stock. On the other hand, accessory shops usually offer excellent quality goods, often at discount prices, so it pays to shop around.

The old maxim "Buy the best tools you can afford" is a good general rule to go by, since cheap tools are seldom good value, especially in the long run. Conversely, it isn't always true that the MOST expensive tools are best. There are plenty of good tools available at reasonable prices, and the shop manager or proprietor will usually be very helpful in giving advice on the best tools for particular jobs.

Care and maintenance of tools

Having purchased a reasonable tool kit, it is necessary to keep the tools in a clean and serviceable condition. After use, always wipe off any dirt, grease and metal particles using a clean, dry cloth, before putting the tools away. Never leave them lying around after they have been used. A simple tool rack on the garage or workshop wall, for items such as screwdrivers and pliers is a good idea. Store all normal spanners and sockets in a metal box. Any measuring instruments, gauges, meters etc., must be carefully stored where they cannot be damaged or become rusty.

Take a little care when the tools are used. Hammer heads inevitably become marked and

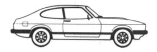

screwdrivers lose the keen edge on their blades from time-to-time. A little timely attention with emery cloth or a file will soon restore items like this to a good serviceable finish.

twist drills, is virtually essential for fitting accessories such as wing mirrors and reversing lights.

Last, but not least, always

keep a supply of old newspapers and clean, lint-free rags available, and try to keep any working areas as clean as possible.

Working facilities

Not to be forgotten when discussing tools, is the workshop itself. If anything more than routine maintenance is to be carried out, some form of suitable working area becomes essential.

It is appreciated that many an owner mechanic is forced by circumstance to remove an engine or similar item, without the benefit of a garage or workshop. Having done this, any repairs should always be done under the cover of a roof, if feasible.

Wherever possible, any dismantling should be done on a clean flat workbench or table at a suitable working height.

Any workbench needs a vice: one with a jaw opening of 4 in. (100mm) is suitable for most jobs. As mentioned previously, some clean, dry storage space is also required for tools, as well as the lubricants, cleaning fluids, touch-up paints and so on which soon become necessary.

Another item which may be required, and which has a much more general usage, is an electric drill with a chuck capacity of at least $5/16$ in. (8mm). This, together with a good range of

Spanner jaw gap comparison table

AF size	Actual size	Nearest metric size	Metric size in ins.
4BA	0.248in.	7mm.	0.276in.
2BA	0.320in.	8mm.	0.315in.
$7/16$in.	0.440in.	11mm.	0.413in.
$1/2$in.	0.500in.	13mm.	0.510in.
$9/16$in.	0.560in.	14mm.	0.550in.
$5/8$in.	0.630in.	16mm.	0.630in.
$11/16$in.	0.690in.	18mm.	0.710in.
$3/4$in.	0.760in.	19mm.	0.750in.
$13/16$in.	0.820in.	21mm.	0.830in.
$7/8$in.	0.880in.	22mm.	0.870in.
$15/16$in.	0.940in.	24mm.	0.945in.
1in.	1.000in.	26mm.	1.020in.

Whitworth size	Actual size	Nearest AF size	AF Actual size
$3/16$in.	0.450in.	$7/16$in.	0.440in.
$1/4$in.	0.530in.	$1/2$in.	0.500in.
$5/16$in.	0.604in.	$9/16$in	0.560in.
$3/8$in.	0.720in.	$11/16$in.	0.690in.
$7/16$in.	0.830in.	$13/16$in.	0.820in.
$1/2$in.	0.930in.	$7/8$in.	0.880in.
$9/16$in.	1.020in.	1in.	1.010in.

Whitworth size	Actual size	Nearest Metric size	Metric size in ins
$3/16$in.	0.450in.	12mm.	0.470in.
$1/4$in.	0.530in.	14mm.	0.550in.
$5/16$in.	0.604in.	15mm.	0.590in.
$3/8$in.	0.720in.	18mm.	0.710in.
$7/16$in.	0.830in.	21mm.	0.830in.
$1/2$in.	0.930in.	24mm.	0.945in.
$9/16$in.	1.020in.	26mm.	1.020in.

③ Specifications

Engines

Note: Units used in this section have been standardised to provide ready comparison between models.

Capri I/II/III 1300

Type	Four cylinder, in-line, overhead valve (pushrod), cross-flow cylinder head
Capacity	1298 cc (79.21 cu.in.)
Bore	80.98 mm (3.188 in.)
Stroke	62.99 mm (2.480 in.)
Compression ratio	HC – 9.0:1
	LC – 8.0:1
	GT – 9.2:1
Max. power (net)	HC – until September, 1970 – 52 bhp @ 5,000 rpm
	HC – September, 1970 on – 57 bhp @ 5,000 rpm
	HC – April, 1979 – 60 bhp @ 5,000 rpm
	LC – until September, 1970 on – 49 bhp @ 5,000 rpm
	LC – September, 1970 on – 54 bhp @ 5,000 rpm
	GT – until September, 1970 – 64 bhp @ 6,000 rpm
	GT – September, 1970 on – 72 bhp @ 6,000 rpm
Max. torque (net)	HC – until September, 1970 – 67 lb.ft. (9.26 kg.m.) @ 2,500 rpm
	HC – September, 1970 on – 71.5 lb.ft. (9.88 kg.m.) @ 2,500 rpm
	LC – until September, 1970 – 63 lb.ft. (8.71 kg.m.) @ 2,500 rpm
	LC – September, 1970 on – 68 lb.ft. (9.40 kg.m.) @ 2,500 rpm
	GT – 70 lb.ft. (9.68 kg.m.) @ 4,300 rpm
Compression pressure at cranking speed	HC/GT – 168 psi
	LC – 157 psi

Capri I 1600 (and U.S.A. specification Capri I 1600, 1970 – 72)

Type	Four cylinder, in-line, overhead valve (pushrod), cross-flow cylinder head
Capacity	1599 cc (97.58 cu.in.)
Bore	80.98 mm (3.188 in.)
Stroke	77.62 mm (3.056 in.)
Compression ratio	HC/GT – 9.0:1
	LC/U.S.A. spec. – 8.0:1
Max. power (net)	HC – until September, 1970 – 64 bhp @ 5,000 rpm
	LC – until September, 1970 – 62.5 bhp @ 5,000 rpm
	GT – 82 bhp @ 5,400 rpm
	HC – September, 1970 on – 68 bhp @ 5,000 rpm
	LC – September, 1970 on – 66.5 bhp @ 5,000 rpm
	GT – September, 1970 on – 86 bhp @ 5,000 rpm
Max. torque (net)	HC – 91.5 lb.ft. (12.58 kg.m.) @ 2,500 rpm
	LC – 87 lb.ft. (12.03 kg.m.) @ 2,500 rpm
	GT – 96 lb.ft. (13.27 kg.m.) @ 3,600 rpm
Compression pressure at cranking speed	HC/GT – 188 psi
	LC – 170 psi

Capri 2000GT (V4)

Type	Four cylinder, V formation, overhead valve (pushrod)
Capacity	1996 cc (121.80 cu.in.)
Bore	93.67 mm (3.688 in.)
Stroke	72.42 mm (2.851 in.)
Compression ratio	9.0:1
Max. power (net)	92 bhp @ 5,250 rpm
Max. torque (net)	104 lb.ft. (14.38 kg.m.) @ 4,000 rpm
Compression pressure at cranking speed	160 psi

Capri I/II/III 3000 (V6)

Type	Six cylinder, V formation, overhead valve (pushrod)
Capacity	2994 cc (182.70 cu.in.)
Bore	93.67 mm (3.688 in.)
Stroke	72.42 mm (2.851 in.)
Compression ratio	8.9:1
Max. power (net)	Until October, 1971 – 128 bhp @ 4,750 rpm
	October, 1971 on – 138 bhp @ 4,750 rpm
Max. torque (net)	192.5 lb.ft. (26.61 kg.m.) @ 4,000 rpm
	Capri II – 173 lb.ft. (23.92 kg.m.) @ 3,000 rpm
Compression pressure at cranking speed	160 to 180 psi

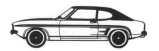

Capri I 1600 'Facelift'/Capri II/III 1600

Type	Four cylinder, in-line, overhead camshaft
Capacity	1593 cc (97.21 cu.in.)
Bore	87.65 mm (3.451 in.)
Stroke	66.00 mm (2.598 in.)
Compression ratio	Standard – HC – 9.2:1
	LC – 8.2:1
Max. power (net)	Standard – Until April, 1979 – 72 bhp @ 5,500 rpm
	Standard – April 1979 on – 73 bhp @ 5,500 rpm
	LC – 68 bhp @ 5,300 rpm
	GT/'S' – Until April 1979 – 88 bhp @ 5,700 rpm
	'S' – April 1979 on – 91 bhp @ 5,700 rpm
Max. torque (net)	Standard – 86.8 lb.ft. (12.0 kg.m.) @ 2,700 rpm
	LC – 83.4 lb.ft. (11.53 kg.m.) @ 2,800 rpm
	GT/'S' – 92 lb.ft. (12.72 kg.m.) @ 4,000 rpm
Compression pressure at cranking speed	HC/GT – until 1979 model – 142 to 170 psi
	HC/GT – 1979 on – 156 to 184 psi
	LC – 128 to 157 psi

Capri RS 2600

Type	Six cylinder, V formation, overhead valve (pushrod)
Capacity	2637 cc (160.92 cu.in.)
Bore	90.00 mm (3.543 in.)
Stroke	69.00 mm (2.717 in.)
Compression ratio	10.5:1
Max. power (net)	150 bhp @ 5,700 rpm
Max. torque (net)	159 lb.ft. (21.98 kg.m.) @ 4,000 rpm

Capri RS 3100

Type	Six cylinder, V formation, overhead valve (pushrod)
Capacity	3091 cc (188.62 cu.in.)
Bore	95.19 mm (3.748 in.)
Stroke	72.40 mm (2.850 in.)
Compression ratio	9.0:1
Max. power (net)	148 bhp @ 5,000 rpm
Max. torque (net)	187 lb.ft. (25.85 kg.m.) @ 3,000 rpm

Capri II/III 2000 (and U.S.A. specification Capri I 2000, 1970 – 75)

Type	Four cylinder, in-line, overhead camshaft
Capacity	1993 cc (121.62 cu.in.)
Bore	90.82 mm (3.576 in.)

Stroke	76.95 mm (3.030 in.)
Compression ratio	9.2:1, (9.0:1, U.S.A., to 1971; 8.2:1, U.S.A., 1972 on)
Max. power (net)	98 bhp @ 5,500 rpm
	April, 1979 on – 101 bhp @ 5,500 rpm
Max. torque (net)	111 lb.ft. (15.35 kg.m.) @ 3,500 rpm
	April, 1979 on – 113 lb.ft. (15.62 kg.m.)
Compression pressure at cranking speed	Until 1979 model – 142 to 170 psi
	1979 on – 156 to 184 psi

Capri 'X' Pack 3 litre

Type	Six cylinder, V formation, overhead valve (pushrod)
Capacity	2994 cc (182.70 cu.in.)
Bore	93.67 mm (3.688 in.)
Stroke	72.42 mm (2.851 in.)
Max. power (net)	175 bhp @ 5,000 rpm
Max. torque (net)	194 lb.ft. (26.82 kg.m.) @ 4,000 rpm

Capri 2.8i

Type	Six cylinder, V formation, overhead valve (pushrod)
Capacity	2792 cc (170.38 cu.in.)
Bore	93.02 mm (3.662 in.)
Stroke	68.50 mm (2.697 in.)
Compression ratio	9.2:1
Max. power (net)	Standard – 160 bhp @ 5,700 rpm
	Aston Martin Tickford – 205 bhp @ 5,000+ rpm
	Zakspeed Turbo – 188 bhp @ 5,500 rpm
	Turbo Technics – 200 bhp @ 5,700 rpm
Max. torque (net)	Standard – 152 lb.ft. (21.01 kg.m.) @ 4,000+ rpm
	Aston Martin Tickford – 260 lb.ft. (35.95 kg.m.) @ 3,500 rpm
	Zakspeed Turbo – 206 lb.ft. (28.48 kg.m.) @ 4,000 rpm
	Turbo Technics – 252 lb.ft. (34.84 kg.m.) @ 3,800 rpm
Compression pressure at cranking speed	167 to 181 psi

Abbreviated data re. U.S.A. specification engines, not covered under other units already detailed:

U.S.A. Capri I 2.6, 1972–73

Type	Six cylinder, V formation, overhead valve (pushrod)
Capacity	2600 cc (158.67 cu.in.)
Bore	90.04 mm (3.545 in.)
Stroke	66.80 mm (2.630 in.)
Compression ratio	8.2:1
Max. power (net)	107 bhp @ 5,700 rpm
Max. torque (net)	130 lb.ft. (17.97 kg.m.) @ 3,400 rpm

U.S.A. Mercury Capri II 2.3, 1975 on

Type	Four cylinder, in-line, overhead camshaft
Capacity	2300 cc (140.35 cu.in.)
Bore	96.01 mm (3.780 in.)
Stroke	79.40 mm (3.126 in.)
Compression ratio	8.4:1
Max. power (net)	88 bhp @ 5,000 rpm
Max. torque (net)	116 lb.ft. (16.04 kg.m.) @ 2,600 rpm

U.S.A Mercury Capri II 2.8, 1975 on

Type	Six cylinder, V formation, overhead valve (pushrod)
Capacity	2792 cc (170.38 cu.in.)
Bore	93.02 mm (3.662 in.)
Stroke	68.50 mm (2.697 in.)
Compression ratio	8.2:1
Max. power (net)	105 bhp @ 4,600 rpm
Max. torque (net)	140 lb.ft. (19.36 kg.m.) @ 3,200 rpm

Abbreviated data re. German specification engines, not covered under other units detailed:

Capri I 1300, 1969 on

Type	Four cylinder, V formation, overhead valve (pushrod)
Capacity	1288 cc (78.60 cu.in.)
Bore	84.00 mm (3.307 in.)
Stroke	58.86 mm (2.317 in.)
Compression ratio	8.2:1
Max. power (net)	50 bhp @ 5,000 rpm
Max. torque (net)	69 lb.ft. (9.5 kg.m.) @ 2,500 rpm

Capri I 1500, 1969 on

Type	Four cylinder, V formation, overhead valve (pushrod)
Capacity	1488 cc (90.80 cu.in.)
Bore	90.00 mm (3.543 in.)
Stroke	58.86 mm (2.317 in.)
Compression ratio	Until September, 1970 – 8.0:1
	September, 1970 on – 9.0:1
Max. power (net)	Until September, 1970 – 60 bhp @ 4,800 rpm
	September, 1970 on – 65 bhp @ 5,000 rpm
Max. torque (net)	82 lb.ft. (11.40 kg.m.) @ 2,400 rpm

Capri I 1700GT, 1969 on

Type	Four cylinder, V formation, overhead valve (pushrod)
Capacity	1688 cc (103.01 cu.in.)
Bore	90.00 mm (3.543 in.)
Stroke	66.80 mm (2.630 in.)
Compression ratio	9.0:1
Max. power (net)	75 bhp @ 5,000 rpm
Max. torque (net)	94 lb.ft. (13.00 kg.m.) @ 2,500 rpm

Capri I 2000, 1969 on

Type	Six cylinder, V formation, overhead valve (pushrod)
Capacity	1999 cc (121.99 cu.in.)
Bore	84.00 mm (3.307 in.)
Stroke	60.14 mm (2.368 in.)
Compression ratio	Standard – 8.0:1 (Until September, 1970 only) 2000R/GT – 9.0:1
Max. power (net)	Standard – 85 bhp @ 5,000 rpm (Until September, 1970 only) 2000R/GT – 90 bhp @ 5,000 rpm
Max. torque (net)	Standard – 109 lb.ft. (15.07 kg.m.) @ 3,000 rpm (Until September, 1970 only) 2000R/GT – 114 lb.ft. (15.76 kg.m.) @ 3,000 rpm

Capri I/II 2300GT/Ghia, 1969 on

Type	Six cylinder, V formation, overhead valve (pushrod)
Capacity	2294 cc
Bore	90.00 mm (3.543 in.)
Stroke	60.14 mm (2.368 in.)
Compression ratio	9.0:1
Max. power (net)	Until April, 1980 – 108 bhp @ 5,100 rpm [Autumn, 1969 on, until Autumn, 1970, 125 bhp @ 5,600 rpm version available] April, 1980 on – 114 bhp @ 5,300 rpm
Max. torque (net)	Until April, 1980 – 134 lb.ft. (18.53 kg.m.) @ 3,000 rpm [135 lb.ft. (18.66 kg.m.) from 125 bhp version] April, 1980 on – 130 lb.ft. (17.97 kg.m.) @ 3,000 rpm

Capri I 2600GT, Autumn 1970 on

Type	Six cylinder, V formation, overhead valve (pushrod)
Capacity	2520 cc (153.78 cu.in.)
Bore	90.00 mm (3.543 in.)
Stroke	66.80 mm (2.630 in.)
Compression ratio	9.0:1
Max. power (net)	125 bhp @ 5,300 rpm
Max. torque (net)	148 lb.ft. (20.46 kg.m.) @ 3,500 rpm

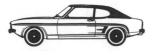

Capri I/Capri II 1300, 1973 on

Type	Four cylinder, in-line, overhead camshaft
Capacity	1293 cc (78.90 cu.in.)
Bore	79.00 mm (3.110 in.)
Stroke	66.00 mm (2.598 in.)
Compression ratio	8.0:1
Max. power (net)	55 bhp @ 5,500 rpm
Max. torque (net)	66 lb.ft. (9.19 kg.m.) @ 3,000 rpm

Capri II 2000, 1976 on

Type	Six cylinder, V formation, overhead valve (pushrod)
Capacity	1999 cc (121.99 cu.in.)
Bore	84.00 mm (3.307 in.)
Stroke	60.14 mm (2.368 in.)
Compression ratio	8.75:1
Max. power (net)	90 bhp @ 5,000 rpm
Max. torque (net)	110 lb.ft. (15.21 kg.m.) @ 3,000 rpm

Transmissions

Gearbox ratios

(All models have four speed, all synchromesh gearboxes, unless otherwise stated).

	I 1300/1600	I 1600GT/ 2000GT	I 1600 OHC	I/II 2000/2.6 /2.8 (U.S.A.)	I 3000 V6
Reverse	3.963:1	3.324:1	3.324:1	3.660:1	3.346:1
First	3.543:1	2.972:1	2.972:1	3.650:1	3.163:1
Second	2.396:1	2.010:1	2.010:1	1.968:1	2.214:1
Third	1.412:1	1.397:1	1.397:1	1.368:1	1.412:1
Top	1.000:1	1.000:1	1.000:1	1.000:1	1.000:1

	I/II/III 3000 V6, 1973 on, RS2600, RS3100, 'X' Pack and four-speed 2.8i	Automatic (Borg-Warner 35) (inc. U.S.A.)	Automatic (C4 type – USA Capri II 2000/2.8)	Automatic (C3 type – 'Bordeaux') (inc. U.S.A.)
Reverse	3.346:1	2.094:1	2.20:1	2.111:1
First	3.163:1	2.393:1	2.46:1	2.474:1
Second	1.942:1	1.450:1	1.46:1	1.474:1
Third	1.412:1	–	–	–
Top	1.000:1	1.000:1	1.00:1	1.000:1

	II/III 1.3	II/III 1.6/ 1.6GT ('C' Type)	II/III 1.6/ 1.6GT/2.0/ U.S.A. 2.3/ 3.0 ('H' Type)	III Five-speed 1.6/2.0 'N' (Sierra) Type	Five-speed 2.8i
Reverse	3.324:1	3.324:1	3.660:1	3.660:1	3.346:1
First	3.580:1	3.580:1	3.650:1	3.650:1	3.163:1
Second	2.010:1	2.010:1	1.968:1	1.968:1	1.942:1
Third	1.397:1	1.397:1	1.368:1	1.368:1	1.412:1
Fourth	–	–	–	1.000:1	1.000:1
Top	1.000:1	1.000:1	1.000:1	0.816:1	0.825:1

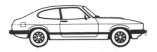

Rear axle ratios
(All models have semi-floating, banjo casing axle with hypoid final drive)

I/II/III 1300	4.125:1, (4.444:1, 3.889:1 ['Economy'] and 3.778:1 optional)
I 1600	3.900:1 (4.125:1 optional)
I 1600GT	3.778:1
I 1600 Automatic	3.889:1
I 2000GT	3.444:1
I 2000GT, 1973 on	3.545:1
I 3000GT/RS 2600	3.222:1
I 3000GT/E/RS 2600, 1971 on	3.091:1
I 1600 OHC	3.778:1
I 2000 OHC (U.S.A.) – Jan. to Dec. 1971	3.889:1
– Oct. 1971 to Mid 1974	3.444:1
I 2600 V6 (U.S.A.) – Oct. 1971 to Sept. 1973	3.222:1
I 2800 V6 (U.S.A.) – Sept. 1973 to Mid. 1974	3.222:1
II/III 1.6 OHC – Timken axle (Type 'J')	3.778:1
II/III 1.6 OHC – Salisbury axle (Type 'D')	3.750:1
II 2.0 OHC/U.S.A. Capri II 2.0/2.3 – Salisbury axle (Type 'D')	3.444:1
II/III 3.0/U.S.A. Capri II 2.8 V6 (except California)	3.091:1
U.S.A. Capri II 2.8 V6 (California only)	3.222:1
2.8i	3.091:1

Pinion/crown wheel, number of teeth	
	4.125:1 – 8/33
	4.444:1 – 9/40
	3.900:1 – 10/39
	3.778:1 – 9/34
	3.889:1 – 9/35
	3.444:1 – 9/31
	3.545:1 – 11/39
	3.222:1 – 9/29
	3.091:1 – 11/34
	3.750:1 – 8/30

Fuel system

Notes:
1. Unless otherwise stated, the fuel pumps on all models are of the mechanical, diaphragm types.
2. All the carburettors are downdraught types.
3. Unless otherwise stated, years shown indicate 'model years', normally starting from the previous autumn.
4. 'Sonic idle' (by-pass) type carburettors were introduced from the 1976 model year onwards.
5. 'Tamperproof' carburettors were introduced from the 1977 model year onwards.

Carburettored models

	Mk I 1300	1300GT	Mk II/II 1300
Make	Ford	Weber	Ford
Type	Single choke	Twin choke	Single choke
Model	C7AH-B (early)	32 DFE (early)	Until 1976: 711W-9510-RC
	711W-JA (later)	32 DGV (later)	761F-9510-AA
			71HF-9510-KDA
			1976-79 761F-9510-KBA/KTA
			771F-9510-KBA/KTA

	Mk III 1300 **Nov. 1979 on**	**1600 OHV**	**1600GT OHV**
Make	Ford	Ford	Weber
Type	Variable venturi	Single choke	Twin choke
Model		Manual choke: C9CH-E (early) 711V-VA (later) Automatic choke: C9CH-F (early) 711W-BNA (later)	32 DFM-2 (early) 32/36 DGV/DGAV (711F-FB/BA/GB later)

	1600 OHC	**1600 OHC** **Nov. 1979 on**	**1600GT OHC**
Make	Ford	Ford	Weber
Type	Single choke	Variable venturi	Twin choke
Model	Until 1976: 71HF/73 HF-9510-KDA (manual transmission) 71HF-9510-KFA (automatic transmission) 1976 on: 75HF-9510-KEA/KKA (manual transmission) 75HF-9510-KDA (automatic transmission) 1977 on: 77HF-9510-KBA/KCA (manual transmission) 77HF-9510-KDA (automatic transmission)		Until 1976: 73HF-9510-GA/HA/JA/KA 1976 on: 76HF-9510-JA/JB (manual transmission) 76HF-9510-KA/KB (automatic transmission) 1977 on: 77HF-9510-JA (manual transmission) 77HF-9510-KA (automatic transmission)

	V4 2000GT	**2000 OHC**	**U.S.A. 2.3 OHC**
Make	Weber	Weber	Ford
Type	Twin choke	Twin choke	Twin choke
Model	32/36 DFV (2724E-9510-H) (manual choke) 32/36 DFAV (692F-9510-BA) (automatic choke)	Until 1976: 74HF-9510-CA (manual transmission) 74HF-9510-DA (automatic transmission) 1976 on: 76HF-9510-AA/AB/ BA/BB 1977 on: 77HF-9510-CA (manual transmission) 77HF-9510-DA (automatic transmission)	5200 2V

	U.S.A. 2.6 V6	**U.S.A. 2.8 V6**	**3000 V6**
Make	Weber	Ford/Holley-Weber	Weber
Type	Twin choke	Twin choke	Twin choke
Model	2V	2150 2V	Until Oct. 1971: 40 DFAV Oct. 1971 on: 38 DGAS 7A/07A (722F-9510-JA/LA) 1974: 38 DGAS (722F-9510-JA) 1975: 38 DGAS (742F-9510-DA) 1976: 38 DGAS (762F-9510-EA) 1977 on: 38 DGAS (772F-9510-EA)

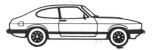

	RS3100	X Pack
Make	Weber	(Triple) Weber
Type	Twin choke	Twin choke
Model	38 EGAS	42 DCNF

Fuel-injected models

	RS2600	2.8i
Injection system make	Kugelfischer/Weslake	Bosch-K-Jetronic
Injection system type	Mechanical	Electronic

Ignition system

Notes:
1. Equivalent types and grades of spark plugs by other manufacturers may be fitted.
2. Bosch distributors are identifiable by their red caps, whereas Motorcraft units have black caps.
3. Electronic ignition was fitted to all U.S.A. models from 1975.

	Spark plug type	Plug gap	Contact points gap	Firing order
Capri: Mk I 1300	Autolite/Motorcraft AG22A	0.023 in.	0.025 in.	1–2–4–3
Mk II/III 1300	Motorcraft AG22/ Champion N4 or Motorcraft AGR22/Champion RN9Y (Engine code J3, AGR12)	0.025 in.	0.025 tin.	1–2–4–3
1600 OHV	Autolite/Motorcraft AG22A	0.023 in.	0.025 in.	1–2–4–3
1600 OHC	Autolite/Motorcraft BF22 or BRF 22 (BF32, 1600 LC)	0.025 in.	0.025 in. (Motorcraft distributor) or 0.016 to 0.020 in. (Bosch distributor)	1–3–4–2
Late Capri III 1600 OHC	Motorcraft BF22X	0.030 in.	0.016 to 0.020 in.	1–3–4–2
V4 2000 GT	Autolite/Motorcraft AG22/Champion N4 or Motorcraft AGR22/Champion RN9Y	0.023 to 0.025 in.	0.025 in.	1–3–4–2
2000 OHC	Motorcraft BF32 or BRF32	0.025 in.	0.025 in. (Motorcraft distributor) or 0.016 to 0.020 in. (Bosch distributor)	1–3–4–2
Late Capri III 2000 OHC	Motorcraft BF32X	0.030 in.	0.016 to 0.020 in.	1–3–4–2
U.S.A. 2.3 OHC	Refer to engine decal	Refer to engine decal	Breakerless ignition	1–3–4–2
U.S.A. 2.8 V6	Refer to engine decal	Refer to engine decal	Breakerless ignition	1–4–2–5–3–6
Mk I 3000 V6	Autolite/ Motorcraft AG32/Champion N5	0.023 in.	0.025 in.	1–4–2–5–3–6

| Mk II/III 3000 V6 | Motorcraft AGR22/Champion N9Y | 0.025 in. | 0.025 in. (Motorcraft distributor) or 0.012 to 0.018 in. (Bosch distributor) | 1–4–2–5–3–6 |
| **2.8i** | Motorcraft Super AGR22 | 0.025 in. | Breakerless ignition | 1–4–2–5–3–6 |

Steering

All models have rack and pinion steering; some have power-assistance by Hobourn-Eaton roller pump.

Turning circle: approximately 32 feet, between kerbs.

Suspension

| **Front** | MacPherson struts, with coil springs, integral shock absorbers and anti-roll bar, plus track control arms. Negative camber geometry on RS models. |
| **Rear** | Semi-elliptical leaf springs, with telescopic shock absorbers and radius arms (cars up to September, 1972) or anti-roll bar (September, 1972 on). Aston Martin Tickford models feature 'A' frame rear axle location. Gas-filled shock absorbers used on RS 2600, RS 3100, X Pack cars, and Capri 'S'. From 'Mark III' models, gas-filled rear shock absorbers fitted to all except basic models. |

Brakes

Notes:
1. All cars fitted with front discs, and rear drums, except where indicated.
2. Dual line systems fitted to export Mark I cars and all later models.
3. Vacuum servo unit fitted to some Mark I 1300cc and 1600cc cars, and all other models.

	Mk I 1300 (and some 1300GT/1600 models)	Mk II/III 1300	Mk I 1300GT, 1600, 1600GT	1600 OHC, 2000 OHC and U.S.A. 2.3 OHC
Front discs	9.59 in.	9.5 in.	9.625 in.	9.625 in.
Rear drums	8 x 1.5 in.	8 x 1.5 in.	9 x 1.75 in.	9 x 1.75 in.

	V4 2000GT	Mk I 3000 V6 and U.S.A. 2.6 V6	Mk II/III 3000 V6 and U.S.A. 2.8 V6	RS2600 and RS3100
Front discs	9.625 in.	9.625 in.	9.7 in.	9.75 in. (vented)
Rear drums	9 x 1.75 in.	9 x 2.25 in.	9 x 2.25 in.	9 x 2.25 in.

	X Pack	2.8i	Tickford
Front discs	10.3 in. (vented)	9.6 in.	9.6 in.
Rear drums	9 x 2.25 in.	9 x 2.25 in.	
Rear discs			10.43 in.

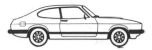

Wheels and tyres

All wheels are pressed steel types, except where indicated.

1300/1600 OHV
Wheels	4¹/₂ x 13 in., or 5 x 13 in.
Tyres	6.00 x 13, 165SR 13, or 185/70HR 13

V4 2000GT
Wheels	4¹/₂ x 13 in. or 5 x 13 in.
Tyres	165SR 13

1600/2000 OHC
Wheels	5 x 13 in., 5¹/₂ x 13 in., 6 x 13 in., or 5¹/₂ x 13 in. cast aluminium (Ghia)
Tyres	165SR 13, 185/70SR 13 or 185/70HR 13

3000 V6 and U.S.A. 2600/2800 V6
Wheels	5 x 13 in.
Tyres	185/70HR 13

RS 2600/RS 3100
Wheels	6 x 13 in. alloy
Tyres	195/70HR 13

X Pack
Wheels	7¹/₂ x 13 in. alloy
Tyres	205/60VR 13

2.8i
Wheels	7 x 13 in. alloy
Tyres	205/60VR 13 (50 Series low profile on Capri 280)

Electrics

1. All Capris have 12 volt, negative earth electrical systems.
2. Battery capacities quoted are for standard fittings; higher capacity batteries may be fitted.

1300/1600 OHV
Battery capacity	Standard, 38 amp/hr.; Cold climate, 57 amp/hr.
Dynamo output	Standard, Lucas C40, 22 amps; Cold climate, Lucas C40 L, 25 amps
(Optional) Alternator output	Lucas 15 ACR, 28 amps; 17 ACR, 35 amps Bosch G1, 28 amps; K1, 35 amps or 55 amps Femsa, 32 amps

V4 2000 GT
Battery capacity	Standard, 38 amp/hr.; Cold climate, 54 amp/hr.
Dynamo output	Standard, Lucas C40, 22 amps; Cold climate, Lucas C40L, 25 amps.

Mk I 1600 OHC
Battery capacity	Standard, 38 amp/hr.; Cold climate, 57 amp/hr.; Cold climate heavy duty, 66 amp/hr.
Alternator output	Lucas 15 ACR, 28 amps Bosch K1, 35 amps

Mk II/III 1600 OHC/2000 OHC
Battery capacity	1600 – 38 amps 1600GT, 2000 – 44 amps 1600 automatic – 44 or 55 amps 1600GT automatic, 2000 automatic, 55 amps U.S.A. Capri II, manual – 55 amps U.S.A. Capri II, automatic – 66 amps
Alternator output	Lucas 15 ACR, 28 amps; 17 ACR, 35 amps Femsa, 32 amps

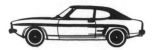

Mk I 3000 V6

Battery capacity	Standard, 44 amp/hr.; Cold climate, 55 amp/hr.; Cold climate heavy duty, 66 amp/hr.
Alternator output	Lucas 15 ACR, 28 amps; 17 ACR, 35 amps

Mk II/III 3000 V6/U.S.A. 2600/2800 V6

Battery capacity	3000 manual, 44 amps or 55 amps
	3000 automatic, 55 amps or 66 amps
	U.S.A. Capri, 66 amps
Alternator output	Lucas 15 ACR, 28 amps; 17 ACR, 35 amps
	Bosch G1, 28 amps; L1, 35 amps; K1, 55 amps
	Femsa, 32 amps

2.8i

Battery capacity	44 or 55 amps
Alternator output	45 amps (Lucas or Bosch)

Performance

These figures give an *approximate* guide to the sort of performance to expect from a particular model. It is impossible to list figures for *every* example of Capri produced, and allowance should therefore be made for minor variations in engine specification, gearbox and differential ratios, and so on, all of which affect acceleration, maximum speed and fuel consumption figures. The figures quoted represent *true* speeds, as opposed to those recorded by the vehicles' speedometers, since these are almost invariably optimistic. It is therefore quite possible, for example, that your car will reach an *indicated* 60 mph more quickly than these figures suggest, but it is also probable that at this speed, the speedo will be recording up to around 4 mph too fast! However, it is impossible to generalise, as each instrument varies.

	0-60 mph (seconds)	Max. speed (mph)	Overall mpg (approx.)
1300	20	85 (89 from Sept. '70)	28-30
1300GT	16$\frac{1}{2}$	95 (99 from Sept. '70)	28-30
1600 OHV	16	90 (96 from Sept. '70)	28-30
1600GT OHV	13$\frac{1}{2}$	100- (105 from Sept. '70)	28-30
V4 2000GT	11-	105+	25-28
2300GT V6	10	110	20-25
2600GT V6	10-	110+	·20
3000 V6	9$\frac{1}{2}$ (8+ from Oct. '71)	114 (120 from Oct. '71)	20-25 (21-25 from Oct. '71)
3000 V6 Auto	11.4 (9.4 from Oct. '71)	110 (118 from Oct. '71)	20-23 (21-24 from Oct. '71)
Weslake 3000GT	8-	120	20+
RS 2600	8-	125-	20
RS 3100	8-	125-	20
1600 OHC	14-	95	30
1600GT OHC	11.4	106	30
2000 OHC	11-	105	25-28
2.8i	8-	131	23-26
Tickford Capri	6$\frac{1}{2}$	140-	20+
Turbo Technics 2.8i	6$\frac{1}{2}$	143	20+

Dimensions

	Length	Width	Height
Capri I	14 ft. 1$\frac{1}{2}$ in.	5 ft. 4$\frac{1}{2}$ in.	4 ft. 5 in.
Capri II	14 ft. 3 in.	5 ft. 7 in.	4 ft. 5$\frac{1}{2}$ in.
Capri III	14 ft. 4 in.	5 ft. 7 in.	4 ft. 4 in.

4 Production modifications

Production modifications

Full details of the changes made through the production life of the Capri are included in the 'Heritage' Chapter, 1. However the main production 'landmarks' for the car are summarised here, for easy reference:

November 1968   Capri production started at Halewood, Liverpool.

January 1969   Capri debut at Brussels Motor Show.

February 1969   Introduction to U.K. public. All models featured new, fastback bodywork. Mechanical components based around those of existing Ford models. Engines used for U.K. models were 1.3 and 1.6 litre cross-flow 'Kent' units, in 'standard' or 'GT' form, or V4 two-litre motor. Range of option packs available – 'X', 'L', and 'R' designations, available in various combinations to suit the buyer.
German Capri range had V4 power units, in 1300, 1500, 1700 and 2000 cc versions. Rear wheel drive via four-speed gearbox and live rear axle.

May 1969   German 2.3 litre V6 GT announced; 108 bhp.

September 1969   3000GT Capri announced for U.K., with strengthened version of three-litre V6 'Essex' engine as used in Mark IV Zephyr/ Zodiac models, and developing 128 bhp. Fastest production Ford built in Britain.
Standard fittings include wide wheels with high speed radial tyres, high performance exhaust system and alternator.

October 1969   125 bhp version of German 2.3 litre V6 introduced.

March 1970   3000E – the 'ultimate' Capri – introduced at Geneva Motor Show, with 'XLR GT' pack as standard. Very high specification included full instrumentation, opening rear side windows, push-button radio, and so on.
'Pre production' German RS2600 on display at Geneva Show, with 2.6 litre, fuel-injected V6 engine giving 150 bhp, plus modified suspension and running gear. Glass fibre doors, bonnet and bootlid, for lightness.

April 1970   275,000 Capris built so far. From this month, the car was imported to the United States – the 'Federal' Capri, with differing frontal treatment (for example, four circular headlights, within rectangular surrounds), heavier bumpers and so on. First imports had British 1.6 litre cross-flow 'Kent' engines. Debut at the New York Motor Show. Eventually, over half a million Capris were to be sold in the U.S.A.

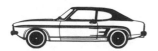

September 1970	Approximately 400,000 Capris sold to date worldwide. Ford of Germany introduced 2600GT, with 125 bhp V6 engine, with same power as 2300GT, but with more torque. Changes announced for 1971 model year cars, including uprating of the 'Kent' engines by porting, valve timing and carburettor jet revisions. Vacuum servo and radial tyres now standard on 1600 models and 1300GT.
September 1971	RS 2600 production starts. First production Capri Special announced, based on V4 2000GT. 1,200 produced, all in 'Vista Orange' and with many extra fittings as standard.
October 1971	'Caprice' – convertible Capri by Crayfords of Kent – shown at Earls Court Motor Show. V6 engines gain more power through modifications to the cylinder heads and manifolding, camshaft and carburettor jetting. Gear ratios revised to make maximum use of the extra 10 bhp so released, and final drive ratio raised. Front brakes on three-litre models now better cooled, and larger servo fitted. In addition, rear suspension softened, and viscous fan fitted to automatics. RS2600 modifications included softening of the suspension, and raising the ride height. Ventilated disc brakes were now employed. New alloy wheels were fitted, plus quarter bumpers, front and rear.
May 1972	By the end of this month nearly three quarters of a million Capris had been produced.
June 1972	Limited run of high specification 1600GT, 2000GT and 3000GT models produced, all with 'power bulge' type bonnets previously only used on three-litre cars.
September 1972	'Facelift' Capris introduced, with 151 specification changes. Major suspension changes were made, with one piece rear anti-roll bar replacing previous twin radius arm set-up. Ride softened all round, but suspension designed to stiffen progressively and give more control on rough surfaces. All Capris now had the 'power bulge' bonnet, more powerful, rectangular headlights (except three-litre GXLs, which had four circular, halogen units), front indicators fitted into the bumper, larger rear lamps, better seats with increased (rear seat) legroom, and revised interior design. 'Pinto' based overhead camshaft 1600 cc engine, as used in the Mark III Cortina, and in 'standard' or 'GT' form, replaced previous 1600 cc cross-flow 'Kent' power unit. All three-litre Capris now had viscous fan, and manual versions had slicker top-opening German Ford gearbox. Automatic transmission optional on all except 1300 cc cars. Range 'streamlined' to L, XL and GT models, plus three-litre GXL versions, with various options.
August 1973	The millionth Capri – an RS2600 – was built.
December 1973	RS 3100 production started at Halewood. Based on 3000GT, with front airdam and rear spoiler, front quarter bumpers, quadruple headlamps, and running gear similar to the (revised) RS2600. V6, 3,091 cc engine giving 148 bhp and nearly 125 mph. RS2600 production finishes.
February 1974	Capri II introduced, with crisper lines and hatchback bodywork, with fold-forward rear seats. New model slightly wider, longer and heavier than first Capris. Mechanical changes included improved brakes, the fitting of alternators as standard equipment, and softening of the suspension. Two-litre models now had the overhead camshaft 'Pinto' engine. British Capri range designations were L, XL and GT, plus the luxury Ghia, available in two-litre or three-litre form only, and with a long list of standard equipment, including a split folding rear seat backrest. Ford's C3 ('Bordeaux') automatic transmission system was optional. The German line-up started with four-cylinder, 1300 cc models, and ran to the 2300 cc V6 GT/Ghia, plus their top of the range three-litre, featuring the British V6 'Essex' engine.

226

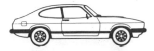

March 1975	Midnight Black Capri S debut at Geneva Motor Show. 1.6 litre or 2.3 litre V6 engines, for European buyers.
June 1975	'J.P.S.' Capri S available in U.K., with 1.6, 2.0 or 3.0 litre power units, uprated suspension, and black and gold paintwork and trim.
October 1975	Unlimited mileage, 12 month warranty introduced. Base model 1300 announced, with black trimmings, non-folding rear seat backrest, etc. Equipment level improved on 1300L and 1600L, and new GL models, with extra fittings, replaced previous XL cars. S models replaced earlier GT versions. Ghias now featured a remote control door mirror Three-litre Ghia and S models now had power steering.
February 1976	'Kent' engines revised, and 'Sonic Idle' carburettor fitted to 1300 cc and 1600 cc Capris, to improve fuel consumption. 'Bordeaux' automatic transmission and tinted glass available on all except 1300 cc models.
May 1976	Low compression versions of German 1.3 and 1.6 litre engine available. New, 90 bhp two-litre German V6 engine introduced.
October 1976	Halewood Capri production ceased, after 337,491 cars had been built. All Capris now built in West Germany.
November 1976	Minor changes made to S models, including fitting front airdam and rear spoiler, to improve stability.
August 1977	Production of the 'Federal' Capri for the U.S.A. ceased in Cologne. A total of 513,449 Capris were sold in the United States.
March 1978	'Capri III' announced, with new, more aerodynamic styling. Grille, bonnet lip, and bumpers were redesigned, and front airdam and (on S versions) rear spoiler were standard fittings. Large rear lamp clusters incorporated foglamps on GL/Ghia models. Deep body side mouldings on L, GL and Ghia versions. Lifting parcel shelf on GL, S and Ghia cars. Interiors modified on all models, with new colours. Engines retuned to give improved economy/emission levels. Gas-filled shock absorbers now on all but 1300 cc Capris. Major services now every 12,000 miles.
April 1979	Viscous coupled cooling fans fitted across the range, giving modest power increases. Automatic chokes fitted to 1.6 litre cars; lower profile tyres used on 2.0 litre models. Brake fluid warning light now standard on all Capris. Rear fog lamps fitted on L cars; head restraints, passenger door mirror, remote control driver's door mirror and headlamp washers now formed part of the GL specification. S models now gained integral rear fog lamps as fitted to GL and Ghia versions, plus a driver's door mirror, and improved soundproofing for the bonnet and rear quarter panels. Ghias had stereo cassette player/mono radio as standard equipment.
May 1979	Two 'Series X' Capris with modified V6 three-litre motor, developing 175 bhp, and extensive bodywork modifications, available for motoring press at International Test Day, Donington.
March 1980	'Limited Edition' 1600 Capri – the GT4 – available, based on 1600L but with special seats, silver sports wheels and extra instrumentation, including tachometer, oil pressure gauge and ammeter.
October 1980	5½ inch wheels standard on GL cars, optional on L models. 6 inch steel wheels with 185 tyres optional on GL cars and Ghias, and standard on S versions.

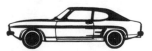

January 1981 S models now featured Recaro seats as standard fittings plus revised interior trim.
LS designation introduced, with 73 bhp, 1.6 litre engine, replacing 1.6S model. 1.6LS had single venturi carburettor. Centre console, clock, sports wheels, tailgate spoiler and S type suspension all standard fittings on LS.
Detachable rear parcel shelves now fitted to all Capris. Two and three litre Ghia Capris now had metallic paintwork, rear seat belts and stereo system.

March 1981 Capri 2.8i introduced, with bodywork based on that of Ghia three-litre, but powered by 160 bhp, 2.8 litre V6 Granada engine, with Bosch K-Jetronic fuel injection.
Specification included seven-inch alloy wheels with low profile tyres, ventilated front brake discs, power steering, lowered and uprated suspension with gas-filled shock absorbers, plus thicker anti-roll bars, tilt and slide sun roof, stereo system, door mirrors, rear spoiler, and Recaro seats. Maximum speed 130 mph plus.
Three-litre Capris now discontinued.
'Special Edition' Cameo and Calypso Capris introduced. Budget priced Cameo based on 1.3L/1.6L, but minus rear parcel shelf, clock, radio and centre console. Calypso based on 1.6LS, but with high specification, including two tone paintwork, tinted glass, head restraints, tailgate wash/wipe system, and full carpeting throughout, including luggage compartment.

July 1981 German Zakspeed 2.8 litre Capri on sale, with wide wheel arches, plus accentuated front airdam and rear spoiler. Turbocharged V6 engine, giving 188 bhp.

October 1981 Ford's 'Econolight' fuel-saving system optional on Capris.

May 1982 'Special Edition' Cabaret introduced, based on 1.6L but with two-litre engine optional. Features included decorative body flashes, sun roof, rear spoiler, GL type 5^1/$_2$ inch sports wheels, fabric LS style seats, Ghia door trims, a centre console and full instrumentation.

October 1982 Prototype Aston Martin Tickford Capri, based on 2.8i, shown at NEC Motor Show, Birmingham. Extensive bodywork modifications, with extra glass fibre reinforced panels, and opulent interior, with red leather, walnut facings and Wilton carpets, plus electrically operated windows and an automatic burglar alarm system included in the 'standard' specification. Mechanical changes included the use of a Japanese IHI turbocharger (helping total engine power output to 205 bhp), AFT digital electronic ignition, improved gearbox lubrication, a limited slip differential, rear disc brakes, and 'A' frame rear axle location. Maximum speed nearly 140 mph.

December 1982 Capri led sales of sporting coupes in Britain, accounting for 1^1/$_4$ per cent of total car market.

January 1983 2.8i specification improved, with the use of a five-speed 'overdrive' gearbox.
Cabaret II introduced, similar in concept to earlier Cabaret, and based on the 1.6 or 2.0L models. Recaro reclining seats with head restraints, revised interior trim, centre armrest, stereo system with electric aerial, opening rear side windows, tinted glass, locking fuel cap, 'torch' key and 185/70 tyres all standard.

March 1983 Capri range 'rationalised' to comprise only 1.6LS, 2.0S and 2.8i models; L,GL and Ghia versions discontinued.
LS now had a sun roof, uprated S type suspension, tailgate wash/wipe system, a remote control driver's door mirror, improved seats and new trim. Four-speed gearbox retained on this model.
S gained Sierra type five-speed gearbox, plus sun roof and new trim, similar to that in 2.8i, incorporating Escort XR3i sports seats. Uprated suspension and opening rear side windows standard.
2.8i continued unchanged.

September 1983 Electronic stereo systems fitted to all Capris.
Ford 'formally' put Tickford Capri on sale.

June 1984   'Special Edition' Laser models introduced, in 1.6 or 2.0 litre form, to fill the gap between LS and S models. The Lasers featured colour-coded grilles, headlamp surrounds and mirrors, plus a remote control driver's door mirror, four spoke alloy wheels with 185/70 tyres, new cloth upholstery, leather gear lever knob, comprehensive instrumentation, and four speaker stereo system, with electric aerial.

October 1984   Capri range reduced to just Laser models and new 2.8 'Injection Special'. Features of this new Capri included leather interior trim panels, rear seat belts, a limited slip differential unit, and seven inch RS spoked alloy wheels.
Six year anti-corrosion warranty offered by Ford.
Changes made to ignition and cooling systems of Tickford Capri. Production of this model now three cars per week. Motor Show announcement that Capri was to continue through 1985.

November 1984   Production of left-hand drive Capris ceased.

January 1986   Further refinements made to Tickford Capri, including the use of a new, integrated remote control central locking system, a redesigned facia, pearlescent paintwork and new badging.

June 1986   Ford-approved 200 bhp, 143 mph Turbo Technics Capri became available through Ford dealers. This model based on 2.8 Injection, but with Garrett turbocharger, plus uprated suspension bushes and brake pads.

December 1986   Last production Capri built, at the end of a run of 1,038 'Special Edition' Capri 280 models. Features of this model included 'Brooklands Green' metallic paintwork, Raven (Connolly) leather upholstery, leather trimmed steering wheel and gear lever knob, Recaro front seats, and 50 series low profile tyres on alloy wheels.
Capris built totalled 1,886,647 during a production life of 18 years.

March 1987   The final Capri model – the 280 – went on sale.

5 Identify your car

It is always useful to be able to identify your car in terms of the engine fitted, bodywork, paint colours, trim and so on, or at least be able to find out what the original specifications were for your vehicle, in these respects.

Fortunately, Ford Capris carry a detailed vehicle identification plate, found under the bonnet, on the driver's side of the engine bay (U.S.A. model Capris have an additional identification number stamped on a metal plate, located just inside the windscreen, on the driver's side.)

The identification plate helps make Fords easier to identify than most other makes of vehicle, *provided* you are able to translate the various codes employed.

While the exact details

shown on each plate have altered over the years, the following translations of the codes (not including German market models) should help to identify the type of Capri you are dealing with.

As far as the author is aware, the complete information to enable you to do this has not been published previously in one volume.

Capri I (until September, 1972):

IYC1.▼ The identification plate can tell you a great deal about the car, and will contain information as laid out on this plate. The relevant code translations are shown below.

Drive:
British Capris to August, 1970:
1 = right-hand drive
2 = left-hand drive
British Capris from August, 1970, and German Capris from December, 1968:
1 = left-hand drive
2 = right-hand drive

Eng (i.e. Engine):
S or J2 = 1300 cc high compression
T or J1 = 1300 cc low compression
U or L2 = 1600 cc high compression
W or L1 = 1600 cc low compression
R or J3 = 1300 cc GT
X or L3 = 1600 cc GT
N = 2000 cc
H = 3000 cc

Trans (i.e. transmission):
5 = floor change, manual
7 = floor change, automatic

Axle:
A = 3.545:1 (3.444:1, to August, 1970) (Z = heavy duty, 3.545:1, from August, 1970)
B = 3.778:1 (W = heavy duty)
C = 3.889/3.900:1 (V/J = heavy duty)
D = 4.125:1 (X = heavy duty)
E = 4.444:1 (Y = heavy duty)
S/8 = 3.444:1 (Z = heavy duty, to August, 1970; Q = heavy duty, from August, 1970)
R = 3.222:1 (U = heavy duty)

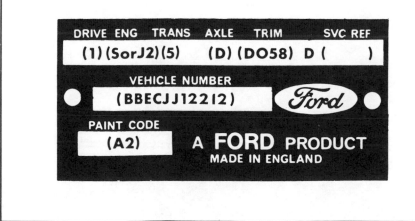

DRIVE	ENG	TRANS	AXLE	TRIM		SVC REF
(1)	(SorJ2)	(5)	(D)	(DO58)	D (	)

VEHICLE NUMBER
(BBECJJ12212)   *Ford*

PAINT CODE
(A2)   A **FORD** PRODUCT
MADE IN ENGLAND

Trim:
Up to August, 1970:
Each car has a trim code number, consisting of a letter, followed by a three figure number, denoting the colours of the seats and floor coverings. The application of the various trim combinations between models was rather complex, so, for clarity and ease of identification, the codes are listed in numerical order, with model designations shown as appropriate.

Trim code No.	Seat colour(s) and seat face material: (P = PVC, C = Cloth)	Floor covering colour	Dates used
Capri De Luxe – except Sweden			
D458	Black, P	Black	Nov.68 – Aug.70
D459	Parchment, P	Black	Nov.68 – Aug.70
D460	Cherry, P	Cherry – dark	Nov.68 – Aug.70
D461	Beechnut, P	Beechnut – dark	Nov.68 – Aug.70
D462	Aqua, P	Aqua – deep	Nov.68 – Aug.70
D463	Blue, P	Blue – deep	Nov.68 – Aug.70
D464	Black, C	Black	Nov.68 – Aug.70
D465	Cherry, C	Cherry – dark	Nov.68 – Aug.70
D466	Beechnut, C	Beechnut – dark	Nov.68 – Aug.70
D467	Aqua, C	Aqua – deep	Nov.68 – Aug.70
D468	Blue, C	Blue – deep	Nov.68 – Aug.70
Capri GT – except Sweden			
D469	Black, P	Black	Nov.68 – Aug.70
D470	Parchment, P	Black	Nov.68 – Aug.70
D471	Cherry, P	Cherry – dark	Nov.68 – Aug.70
D472	Beechnut, P	Beechnut – dark	Nov.68 – Aug.70
D473	Aqua, P	Aqua – deep	Nov.68 – Aug.70
D474	Blue, P	Blue – deep	Nov.68 – Aug.70
D475	Aubergine, P	Aubergine	Nov.68 – Aug.70
D476	Black, C	Black	Nov.68 – Aug.70
D477	Cherry, C	Cherry – dark	Nov.68 – Aug.70
D478	Beechnut, C	Beechnut – dark	Nov.68 – Aug.70
D479	Aqua, C	Aqua – deep	Nov.68 – Aug.70
D480	Blue, C	Blue – deep	Nov.68 – Aug.70
D481	Aubergine, C	Aubergine	Nov.68 – Aug.70
Capri 3000E – except Sweden			
D495	Black, P	Black	Aug.69 – Aug.70
D496	Parchment, P	Black	Aug.69 – Aug.70
D497	Cherry, P	Cherry – dark	Aug.69 – Aug.70
D498	Beechnut, P	Beechnut – dark	Aug.69 – Aug.70
D499	Aqua, P	Aqua – deep	Aug.69 – Aug.70
D500	Blue, P	Blue – deep	Aug.69 – Aug.70
D501	Aubergine, P	Aubergine	Aug.69 – Aug.70
D502	Black, C	Black	Aug.69 – Aug.70
D503	Cherry, C	Cherry	Aug.69 – Aug.70
D504	Beechnut, C	Beechnut	Aug.69 – Aug.70
D505	Aqua, C	Aqua – deep	Aug.69 – Aug.70
D506	Blue, C	Blue – deep	Aug.69 – Aug.70
D507	Aubergine, C	Aubergine	Aug.69 – Aug.70

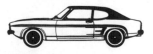

Trim code No.	Seat colour(s) and seat face material: (P = PVC, C = Cloth)	Floor covering colour	Dates used
Capri De Luxe – Sweden only			
D697	Black, P	Black	Aug.69 – Aug.70
D698	Parchment, P	Black	Aug.69 – Aug.70
D699	Cherry, P	Cherry – dark	Aug.69 – Aug.70
D700	Beechnut, P	Beechnut – dark	Aug.69 – Aug.70
D701	Aqua, P	Aqua – deep	Aug.69 – Aug.70
D702	Blue, P	Blue – deep	Aug.69 – Aug.70
D703	Black, C	Black	Aug.69 – Aug.70
D704	Cherry, C	Cherry – dark	Aug.69 – Aug.70
D705	Beechnut, C	Beechnut – dark	Aug.69 – Aug.70
D706	Aqua, C	Aqua – deep	Aug.69 – Aug.70
D707	Blue, C	Blue – deep	Aug.69 – Aug.70
Capri GT Sweden only.			
D708	Black, P	Black	Aug.69 – Aug.70
D709	Parchment, P	Black	Aug.69 – Aug.70
D710	Cherry, P	Cherry – dark	Aug.69 – Aug.70
D711	Beechnut, P	Beechnut – dark	Aug.69 – Aug.70
D712	Aqua, P	Aqua – deep	Aug.69 – Aug.70
D713	Blue, P	Blue – deep	Aug.69 – Aug.70
D714	Aubergine, P	Aubergine	Aug.69 – Aug.70
D715	Black, C	Black	Aug.69 – Aug.70
D716	Cherry, C	Cherry	Aug.69 – Aug.70
D717	Beechnut, C	Beechnut – dark	Aug.69 – Aug.70
D718	Aqua, C	Aqua – deep	Aug.69 – Aug.70
D719	Blue, C	Blue – deep	Aug.69 – Aug.70
D720	Aubergine, C	Aubergine	Aug.69 – Aug.70
Capri 3000E – Sweden only			
D721	Black, P	Black	Aug.69 – Aug.70
D722	Parchment, P	Black	Aug.69 – Aug.70
D723	Cherry, P	Cherry – dark	Aug.69 – Aug.70
D724	Beechnut, P	Beechnut – dark	Aug.69 – Aug.70
D725	Aqua, P	Aqua – deep	Aug.69 – Aug.70
D726	Blue, P	Blue – deep	Aug.69 – Aug.70
D727	Aubergine, P	Aubergine	Aug.69 – Aug.70
D728	Black, C	Black	Aug.69 – Aug.70
D729	Cherry, C	Cherry – dark	Aug.69 – Aug.70
D730	Beechnut, C	Beechnut – dark	Aug.69 – Aug.70
D731	Aqua, C	Aqua – deep	Aug.69 – Aug.70
D732	Blue, C	Blue – deep	Aug.69 – Aug.70
D733	Aubergine, C	Aubergine	Aug.69 – Aug.70

August, 1970 to August, 1972;

Code	Colour	Material
AA	Black	PVC
A1	Black	Cloth
FA	Blue – marquis	PVC
F1	Blue – marquis	Cloth
HA	Ruby	PVC
H1	Ruby	Cloth
JA	Tan	PVC
J1	Tan	Cloth
KA	Parchment	PVC
K1	Parchment	Cloth
MA	Jade	PVC
M1	Jade	Cloth
NA	Olive	PVC
N1	Olive	Cloth
YA	Non-standard	
Y1	Non-standard	

Body (Denoted by letters 'D' or 'G'):
D = De Luxe
G = GT

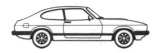

SVC ref:
Denotes date of manufacture, in the case of a vehicle shipped unassembled for assembly in another country.

Vehicle number:
This consists of:
Six letters;
First letter denotes country of origin (or in which assembled);
B = Britain.
D = West Germany
Second letter denotes assembly plant;
Right-hand drive;
B = Halewood.
Left-Hand Drive;
A = Cologne, West Germany
Third letter denotes model type;
E = Capri
Fourth letter denotes body type;
C = Two door coupe
Fifth and sixth letters denote year and month codes, respectively, translated in the following table (applying to all Capris from 1968 to 1986):

F = Beige 67
E = Light Blue/Hellblau
L = Light Green 67/Hellgrun 67
Y = Non-standard

Metallics:
+3 = Silver Fox
+1 = Blue Mink
+6 = Aquatic Jade
+2 = Saluki Bronze
+8 = Light Orchid
+7 = Amber Gold
+5 = Fern Green

August 1970 on (also applies to 'Facelift' models, from September, 1972 on):
B = Ermine White/Pearl White 73
E = Diamond Blue
7 = Light Brown 73
2 = Gunmetal Grey
G = Anchor Blue/Marine Blue 73
J = Sunset
P = Garnet/Burgundy Red 73
S = Tawny +

+3 = Silver Fox
+4 = Glacier
+5 = Fern Green/Light Green 73
+6 = Evergreen/Dark Green 73
+9 = Pacific Blue

Capri I, II, III (September, 1972 on)

The identification plate changed in layout again, from January, 1981, although the information contained on the new plates is similar to that given on earlier cars.
Typ/Type:
GECP = Capri coupe, West Germany
BECP = Capri coupe, Great Britain

Version:
Italian cars only

Ford month and year codes from Vehicle identification plate

Reg. letter (U.K. only)	G	G/H	H/J	J/K	K/L	L/M	M/N	N/P	P/R	R/S	S/T	T/V	V/W	W/X	X/Y	Y/A	A/B	B/C	C/D
Year built:	1968	1969	1970	1971	1972	1973	1974	1975	1976	1977	1978	1979	1980	1981	1982	1983	1984	1985	1986
Month built:																			
January		JJ	KL	LC	MB	NJ	PL	RC	SB	TJ	UL	WC	AB	BJ	CL	DC	EB	FJ	GL
February		JU	KY	LK	MR	NU	PY	RK	SR	TU	UY	WK	AR	BU	CY	DK	ER	FU	GY
March		JM	KS	LD	MA	NM	PS	RD	SA	TM	US	WD	AA	BM	CS	DD	EA	FM	GS
April		JP	KT	LE	MG	NP	PT	RE	SG	TP	UT	WE	AG	BP	CT	DE	EG	FP	GT
May		JB	KJ	LL	MC	NB	PJ	RL	SC	TB	UJ	WL	AC	BB	CJ	DL	EC	FB	GJ
June		JR	KU	LY	MK	NR	PU	RY	SK	TR	UU	WY	AK	BR	CU	DY	EK	FR	GU
July		JA	KM	LS	MD	NA	PM	RS	SD	TA	UM	WS	AD	BA	CM	DS	ED	FA	GM
August		JG	KP	LT	ME	NG	PP	RT	SE	TG	UP	WT	AE	BG	CP	DT	EE	FG	GP
September		JC	KB	LJ	ML	NC	PB	RJ	SL	TC	UB	WJ	AL	BC	CB	DJ	EL	FC	GB
October		JK	KR	LU	MY	NK	PR	RU	SY	TK	UR	WU	AY	BK	CR	DU	EY	FK	GR
November	HS	JD	KA	LM	MS	ND	PA	RM	SS	TD	UA	WM	AS	BD	CA	DM	ES	FD	GA
December	HT	JE	KG	LP	MT	NE	PG	RP	ST	TE	UG	WP	AT	BE	CG	DP	ET	FE	GG

Five figures;
Vehicle identification number, unique to the vehicle

Paint code
November 1968 to August 1970
B = Ermine White
R = Aubergine
G = Anchor Blue
H = 'Rot II 65' (Red)

T = Maize Yellow/Daytona Yellow
D = Light Grey
M = Lime Green/Le Mans Green
N = Flame Red
U = Electric Blue
Y = Non-standard

Metallics:
+1 = Sapphire/Light Blue 73

Fahrgestell/Vehicle No.:
Six letters;
First letter denotes country of origin (or in which assembled);
B = Britain
G = West Germany
Second letter denotes assembly plant;
A = Cologne

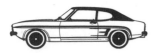

IYC2. ▲ *The identification plate on cars from September, 1972 was written in English and German. The code translations are shown below; they differ in detail from the information already given for Mark I cars to September, 1972.*

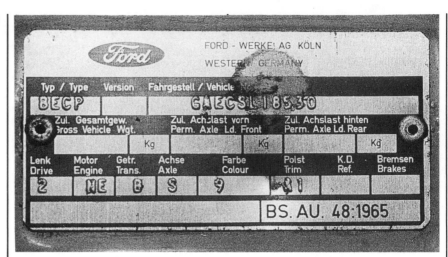

D = Halewood
C = Saarlouis
Third letter denotes model type;
E = Capri
Fourth letter denotes body type;
C = Two door coupe
Fifth and sixth letters denote year and month codes, respectively. Please see translation table included under Capri I (until September, 1972)

Six figures;
Vehicle identification number, unique to the vehicle

Lenk/Drive:
1 = Left-hand drive
2 = Right-hand drive

Motor/Engine:
Denotes engine capacity and type;
J2 = 1300cc OHV
J3 = 1300cc OHV – performance'
LC = 1600cc OHC
LE = 1600cc OHC – performance
NE = 2000
YY = 2300
PR = 2800
HY = 3000

Getr/Trans:
Denotes gearbox type;
B = four-speed manual
F = five-speed manual
D = Automatic

Achse/Axle:
Denotes final drive ratio;
X = 4.125:1
N = 4.111:1
C = 3.889:1
W = 3.778:1
B = 3.750:1
Z = 3.545:1
S = 3.444:1
R = 3.222:1
L = 3.091:1

Farbe/Colour:
Capri I 'Facelift' cars – please see codes included under 'Capri I (until September, 1972)' information.
Capri II/III – codes denote paint colours and year of introduction of colour, plus model year (second digit);
First letter or digit;
A = Black 69
B = Diamond White 73
C = Sahara Beige 74/Oyster Gold 78/Dove Grey 81
D = Carnival Red 75/Regency Green 78/Sienna Brown 82/Glacier Blue 83 with Caspian Blue 83
E = Light Blue 74/Hawaian Blue 78/Forest Green 81 with Crystal Green 81
F = Purple/Oyster Gold 78
G = Marine Blue 72/Royal Blue 75/Tuscan Beige 79/Polar Grey 83/Cardinal Red 82 with Silver
H = Signal Orange 77/Solar Gold 80/Pine Green 83/Crystal Green 81 with Silver
J = Sunset 71/Signal Green 78/Alaska Grey 78/Caribbean Blue 82
K = Laurel Green 76/Jasmine Yellow 82/Silver with Nimbus Grey 84
L = Signal Orange 76/Regency Red 78/Caspian Blue 80/Meadow Green 81/Lacquer Red 85
M = Bitter Green 74/Hawaian Blue 78/Graphite Grey 81 with Silver
N = Sebring Red 73/Saturn

Gold 77/Highland Green 78/Ocean Blue 84/Titan Blue 82 with Silver
P = Signal Green 76/Tropic Green 77/Cardoba Beige 80/Sunburst Red 81
Q = Arizona Gold 75/Fjord Blue 78/Harara Brown 84
R = Venetian Red 77/Cardinal Red 82
S = Roman Bronze 76/Mineral Blue 85/Black 69 with Silver
T = Daytona Yellow 72/Peppermint Red 76 with Silver
U = Platinum 76/Caspian Blue 83 with Silver
V = Phoenix Orange 75 with Silver
X = Midnight Blue 78
Y = Non-standard
Z = Forest Green 81/Silver

1 = Miami Blue 74/Cosmos Blue 79/Tibetan Gold 81/Venus Gold 82/Champagne 83
2 = Aquaris Green 77/Apollo Green 79/Imperial Red 83
3 = Aerosilver 74/Jupiter Red 77/Sirius Red 80/Cobalt Blue 81/Titan Blue 82/Caspian Blue 83/Paris Blue 85
4 = Flame Orange 74/Bermuda Blue 77/Forest Green 81
5 = Onyx Green 74/Jade Green 75/Cosmos Blue 79/Champagne Gold 82/Glacier Blue 83/Mineral Blue 85
6 = Neptune Blue 77/Apollo Green 79/Crystal Green 81
7 = Copper Bronze 73/Jupiter Red 77/Celtic Bronze 82/Nimbus Grey 84

8 = Nevada Beige 77/Jade Green 83

9 = Signal Yellow 77/Graphite Grey 81/Mineral Blue 85 with Strato Silver 76/Signal Amber 78/Signal Orange 79/Champagne Gold 82/Graphite Grey 81 with Silver

Second digit;
4 = 1974
5 = 1975, etc.

German vehicles with a vinyl roof have an additional letter, coded as follows:
A = Vinyl roof – black
C = Vinyl roof – dark brown
D = Vinyl roof – light brown
F = Vinyl roof – silver
K = Vinyl roof – dark brown
L = Vinyl roof – white
S = Sports paint finish
M = A plus S
N = C plus S
P = K plus S
Q = D plus S

Polst/Trim:
Trim codes;

Capri I, August, 1972 on:

Code	Colour	Material
AA	Black	PVC
AI	Black	Cloth
FA	Blue – marquis 71	PVC
FI	Blue – marquis 71	Cloth
HA	Ruby – light 71	PVC
HI	Ruby – light 71	Cloth
KA	Tan – light 73	PVC
KI	Tan – light 73	Cloth
YA	Non-standard	
YI	Non-standard	

Capri II/III:

The code consists of a letter, indicating the colour, followed by a letter or digit, denoting the trim material;

Colours:
A = Black
B = Tan 79
C = Cloud 74
E = Medium Blue 74
F = Blue 79/Navy 83
G = Blue 81
H = Red 79
J = Chocolate 76
K = Light Tan 73/Indian Red 81
L = Saddle Brown 74
M = Green 77
N = Orange 77/Red
P = Chocolate 76/Bitter Chocolate 80
Q = Steel Grey 83
T = Saddle Brown 74/Shark Grey 80
U = Black
W = Light Tan 76
Y = Non standard

Materials
1 = Cloth (L, GL, GT) – Capri II
3 = Cloth (Ghia) – Capri II
E = Vinyl
5 = Sports Trim – Capri II/III
Y = Non Standard
1 = Cloth – Capri III
A = Vinyl – Capri III

Other items:
The 'BS. AU48:1965' simply acknowledges the U.K. safety belt standard.

The remaining sections of the plate are normally found to be blank. They cover axle load, brakes and K.D. reference, and apply to certain export markets only.

⑥ Clubs, specialists and books

When owning – and particularly when restoring – an 'old' car, it is helpful to belong to the 'one make' club or clubs catering for your particular vehicle. Not only then are you brought into contact with other owners of the same type of vehicle, which is enjoyable in itself, but you also gain a great deal of useful information about the car. This includes, of course, background information on the history of the particular model you own, the availability of spares, and so on. Most clubs publish their own newsletters or magazines, which are filled with articles of technical and general interest, and most also arrange get-togethers, rallies etc.

Existing club members are usually only too willing to help with information to enable you to overcome particular problems you may encounter as your restoration project proceeds. In addition you may also have the opportunity of looking closely at other members' cars, to see how they *should* look.

In most clubs there is a certain camaraderie, through sharing a common interest, and you will almost certainly make new friends among the other members. most of whom will be as enthusiastic as you are about your car.

As the cars get older, the availability of spares becomes increasingly important, and the appropriate club for your model is a good place to seek advice on where to get specific parts. Some clubs provide their own spares service, while others normally have an 'information' officer to deal with enquires. You can save a great deal of time and money by approaching the club at the outset for such advice. Just a word of caution here, though – try to restrict your telephone calls to club officials to 'reasonable' hours. Most such officials take on club duties in addition to their normal daily routine activities – like going to work and looking after families – so, with a few exceptions, they probably won't be too pleased to be contacted at midnight about some elusive mechanical part!

If you are interested in finding out more about any of the clubs catering for your particular Capri, please send a large, self-addressed envelope with your enquiry to the club; it helps speed their reply to you, and keeps the club's running costs down as well.

Following the details of the various clubs at present catering for the Capris are details of some of the specialists who may be able to assist in restoring and running your Ford. Of course, there are other suppliers of parts, tools, and so on, around the country. Indeed, one of the advantages of owning a Ford is that there are so many firms who can help with spares and accessories for your car, and it would be impossible to list them all without filling another book!

While on the subject of other books, at the end of this Appendix are details of some of the publications which should help to make owning a Capri a more enjoyable experience.

Clubs

The listings are made here in alphabetical order.

The Ford AVO Owners' Club caters for owners of Mark I Escort Twin Cams, RS1600s, Mexicos and RS2000s as well as the very rare Capri RS2600s and the slightly more numerous RS3100. Although the majority of the members have Escorts, a number own RS Capris; new members with these are always welcome. The club has an enthusiastic membership, all of whom receive the organisation's interesting magazine entitled 'HAVOC'.

If you drive one of the fast RS Capris, write for details to

Dave Hibbin, at 53, Hallsfield Road, Bridgewood, Chatham, Kent, ME5 9RS.

The Capri Owners' Club (Capri Club International) is the largest of the clubs catering for the Capris, and full details are included in a separate section of this Appendix.

The Capri Enthusiasts Register exists for those owners who are primarily interested in attending shows with their Capris, and who also like to take part in day trips, and so on. The members, now around 50 strong,

have cars in standard condition, or 'tastefully modified'. A newsletter is produced each quarter, and the club has a technical adviser.

For further details write to Liz Barnes, who is the Club's secretary, at 46, Manningtree Road, South Ruislip, Middlesex, HA4 0ES.

The Ford Executive Owners' Register deals with the Cortina 1600E and the Escort 1300E, as well as the other Ford 'Executive' models, from the Corsair 2000E to the Zodiac Executive, so there's an interesting range of vehicles in this club. It also, of course, caters for owners of the

luxury Capri 3000E. For details, contact G. Gessey, 3, Shanklin Road, Stonehouse Estate, Coventry.

The Ford RS Owners' Club encompasses all the RS models, including the Mark I and II Escorts, and the 'new' front wheel drive Mark III models, as well as the Capri RS2600 and RS3100, so again, a range of interesting machinery is included. An interesting, well illustrated magazine is just one of the benefits of joining. For full details, write to Jacques Le Clainche, 80, Reepham, Orton Brimbles, Peterborough, Cambs, PE2 0TT.

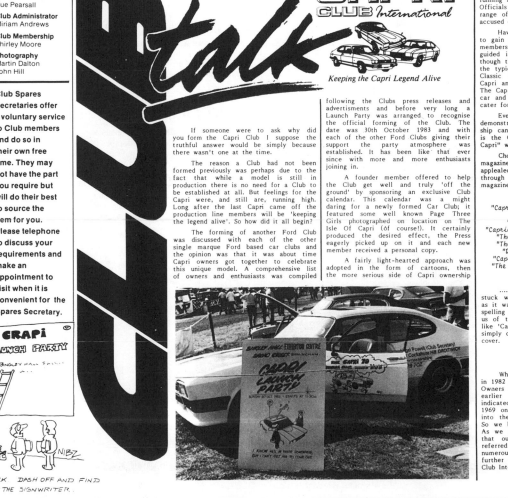

Club Chairman & Magazine Editor
John Hill

Club Secretary & Assistant Editor
Sue Pearsall

Club Administrator
Miriam Andrews

Club Membership
Shirley Moore

Photography
Martin Dalton
John Hill

Club Spares Secretaries offer a voluntary service to Club members and do so in their own free time. They may not have the part you require but will do their best to source the item for you. Please telephone to discuss your requirements and make an appointment to visit when it is convenient for the Spares Secretary.

CRAPI LAUNCH PARTY
BINGLEY HALL...

QUICK DASH OFF AND FIND THE SIGNWRITER.

CAPRI CLUB International
Keeping the Capri Legend Alive

If someone were to ask why did you form the Capri Club I suppose the truthful answer would be simply because there wasn't one at the time.

The reason a Club had not been formed previously was perhaps due to the fact that while a model is still in production there is no need for a Club to be established at all. But feelings for the Capri were, and still are, running high. Long after the last Capri came off the production line members will be 'keeping the legend alive'. So how did it all begin?

The forming of another Ford Club was discussed with each of the other single marque Ford based car clubs and the opinion was that it was about time Capri owners got together to celebrate this unique model. A comprehensive list of owners and enthusiasts was compiled

following the Clubs press releases and advertisments and before very long a Launch Party was arranged to recognise the official forming of the Club. The date was 30th October 1983 and with each of the other Ford Clubs giving their support the party atmosphere was established. It has been like that ever since with more and more enthusiasts joining in.

A founder member offered to help the Club get well and truly 'off the ground' by sponsoring an exclusive Club calendar. This calendar was a might daring for a newly formed Car Club; it featured some well known Page Three Girls photographed on location on The Isle Of Capri (of course!). It certainly produced the desired effect, the Press eagerly picked up on it and each new member received a personal copy.

A fairly light-hearted approach was adopted in the form of cartoons, then the more serious side of Capri ownership

took over - now the scales have balanced with events and magazine containing a little of everything.

Early days saw the Club Secretary running an X-Packed MkII, nowadays Club Officials run and own such a diverse range of Capris that we could never be accused of going in one direction.

Having used every available avenue to gain publicity for the Club it is the members who have built the Club and guided it along its present course. Even though the Capri is undoubtedly a Classic, the typical owner doesn't fall in to the Classic Car Movement, neither is every Capri an out and out customised vehicle. The Capri is in essence an "individualist" car and the Club makes every effort to cater for this attitude.

Events promoted by the Club demonstrate just how diverse the membership can be and 'keep the legend alive' is the Clubs way of saying "I love my Capri" without sounding too twee.

Choosing a title for the Club magazine proved a daunting task, so we appealed for suggestions from the public through a letter published in 'Motor' magazine. Suggestions included :-

"Capricorn" "Re-Cap" "Capreader"
"Capri News & Views"
"The Power and The Glory"
"Capriona" "Capriana" "The Capriot"
"The Capriteer" "The Capriman"
"The Caprigram" "CapriClubMan"
"Divine Motoring Capri Club"
"Capricious" "The Capri Express"
"The Goat" "COC Tales" "Caprice"

.... maybe it was just as well we stuck with the original title, uninspiring as it was, "Capri News". Perhaps the odd spelling mistake by the press convinced us of the danger of playing on a word like 'Capri'. Since 1986 the magazine has simply carried the club title on the front cover.

When the Club was established back in 1982 we were known as "The Capri 70 Owners Club" to differentiate from Ford's earlier Classic Capri Coupe. The '70' indicated the production period from 1969 onward, but as sales continued well into the eighties it became meaningless. So we became 'The Capri Owners Club'. As we entered 1987 it became apparent that our Club is regarded (and often referred to) as 'The Mother Club' of the numerous European Capri clubs, hence a further update on the title to "Capri Club International".

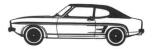

Introduction

THE CARS AND THE MEMBERS

Your Capri and many more like it are treasured by their existing owners and envied by many others. Depending on its engine size and model specification it provides the owner with "frugal, no frills" or "fast and furious" transport. The *Capri Club* therefore caters for all models and ages of the magical Capri marque.

Each car has a personality of its own, whether intentionally built by the Factory or later personalised by Ford agents, specialised firms or owners themselves, in fact no two are the same, many similar but few indentical. Likewise there is no such thing as a 'typical' Club member and it's for this very reason that belonging to the Club becomes addictive. Perhaps colleagues have pointed out that under a Capri's skin there is no technical revolution and the only reason for the models undeniable success story has been the manufacturers policy of 'value and performance for money' — but we know differently don't we? It's the Capris' character which owners fall in love with, you drive the Capri which is everything to you, but not necessarily your neighbours choice of conformity.

Your Capri was a legend in its own time, now through the Club you can help to *"Keep the Capri Legend Alive"*.

CLUB TITLE

Established in 1982 and christened the 'Capri 70 Owners Club' this was abbreviated to Capri Owners Club. Finally it was decided that the official title should be "Capri Club International" it's a classic title and falls in line with the feelings of the numerous European Capri Clubs who refer to us as "the mother Club".

CLUB SCOOPS

The Club has featured on television and radio in addition to many features in the motoring press. You may have heard about the Club at a local level and this would be attributed to the Club Branches. If information about Capris is needed the Club is always on hand to provide the media with Capri news, views and history. It's for this reason that the Club keeps a Show Register to assist the media with the compilation of articles and documentaries.

WHAT THE CLUB CAN OFFER YOU

We can provide Club Members with all their Capri needs; elusive parts through our own Spares Secretaries, discount on production of valid membership cards, technical advice from our own advisers and preferential insurance premiums.

WHAT DO I GET?

Each month you will receive a quality Club magazine packed with useful technical, informative and humourous articles, members stories and special offers. After receiving the first one you will join the thousands of others who look forward to the postman's visit every month.

CLUB ACTIVITIES

If your enthusiasm runs to making contact with like-minded Capri owners you are very welcome to join in the activities of your local Branch. Over twenty Club Branches now hold regular meetings throughout the U.K. You can visit the Club stand at many motoring shows. The Club hosts its own annual National and International Capri gatherings, Winter Capri Convention, Ford Autojumble, and technical seminars for those interested in handling, tuning, bodywork etc. It's all there for you to join in if you wish.

SHOULD I JOIN?

Your Capri doen't have to be in show condition for you to becomes a member of the Club. We welcome as many original cars as we do 'personalised' vehicles, don't wait until your Capri is just right, or just how you want it before you join — you could be enjoying membership and gaining expert advice, experience and discounts through joining today. *Keep the legend alive with CAPRI CLUB International.*

John Hill.

JOHN HILL
Club Chairman

Keep the Capri Legend Alive with

Field House · Redditch · Worcs · B98 0AN

The Capri is back!

The new born Capri — it will be available on the UK market in 1990

Well of course it was inevitable — after an eighteen year success story the name Capri had to reappear very soon, especially as sales remained buoyant even during its 'last' year.

Members will be quick to realise that this new Ford model bears little or no resemblance to our much loved long nosed Capri I, II and III, but surely a new Capri would have to radically different to achieve another success story. Yes, I'll agree that the new 'Capri' does look a little "Japanese" but perhaps by the time we see the first UK models there will be just a hint of its parentage.

However, the story of the re-birth came as no shock to Club H/Q, for on close examination of the very first Club magazine titled 'Capri News' you will see the cover featured the inspiration of this new Capri; it was in fact the 1983 'Barchetta', a styling excersise by Ghia. Later the Clubs own "Design Competition" produced this sketch for a MkIV Capri - which bears an uncanny likeness to the genuine

thing, even though one of the views shows it with the unusual feature of a stowable hardtop. Perhaps our members have more insight than the motoring press!?

This two-seater convertible is to be a 1.6 litre fuel injected model with optional turbocharging, possible four-wheel-drive to follow (a road that Ford have travelled previously with the MkI Rallycross excersise).

Launch date in the UK is planned for March 1990 - pure coincidence that this will be the 21st Birthday of the namesake!

Equipment level even on the base model will include power steering, all round disc brakes, tinted electrically operated windows, electric driving mirrors and of course the obligatory radio and leather-bound steering wheel. Option of five-speed manual or three-speed automatic gearbox.

Although we didn't realise it back in January 1984 we previewed the future Capri.

The turbo version will be fitted with an extra spoiler on the bootlid and will feature two-tone paintwork, alloy roadwheels and foglamps - sounds just like the old days!

Will the new Capri be judged too bizarre looking? We know the idea of a small sports car based on high volume saloon mechanicals has worked well for other manufacturers and has the full support of Ford themselves - only our members will prove if this is the Capri we want.

"The MkIV Capri"
this design sketch was submitted to the Club's 1987 Design Competition.

CAPRI CLUB International

Field House · Redditch · Worcs · B98 0AN

239

POSTBAG POSTBAG

Selection of photographs taken at the many annual events organised and attended by the Club — try one this year for the true flavour of Capri enthusiasm ■

POSTBAG

IF YOU ENJOY READING POSTBAG WHY NOT MAKE A CONTRIBUTION! WRITE TO THE EDITOR WITH YOUR NEWS AND VIEWS, IDEAS, OPINIONS, MOTORING STORIES, HELPFUL TIPS ETC.

DO YOU HAVE A CAPRI PROBLEM YOU CAN'T SOLVE? OUR TECHNICAL ADVISORS WILL DO THEIR BEST TO HELP.

National & International Events

Thinking of selling your Capri, got some parts you want to get rid of - why not advertise them? The Capri Exchange page provides the perfect opportunity to buy and sell Capris and parts and what's more the service is entirely **FREE TO MEMBERS (5.00 per insertion for non-members). We'll get it into the magazine as soon as possible. Please write clearly and remember to include your Membership No. and Telephone Number. (max. 25 words per ad.)**

CAPRI CLUB *International*

Field House · Redditch · Worcs · B98 0AN

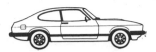

Clubs in the United States

There are a number of clubs catering for the Capris in the U.S.A., including, in alphabetical order:

Associated Capri Clubs. Write to 18011, Ridgewood Avenue, Lansing, IL 60438, U.S.A.

California Capri Club. Write to P.O. Box 871, San Leandro, CA 94577, U.S.A.

Capri Car Club Ltd. Write to Stephen Singletary, P.O. Box 111211, 1101 Ursula, Aurora, Colorado 80011, U.S.A.

Capri Club of Chicago. Write to Wayne Tofel, 7158 W. Armitage, Chicago, IL. 60635, U.S.A.
  The Capri Club of Chicago seems to be particularly active, offering monthly meetings and other events including social get-togethers and touring, for enthusiasts of Capris and other small Fords (Escorts, Fiestas, Mustangs, etc).

Capri 'Hi' Per Club. Write to Steve Bailey, 1044 E. 39th Street, Brooklyn, NY 11210, U.S.A.

Miami Capri Club. Write to Robert Baker, 1760 N.W. 132nd Street, Miami, FL 33167, U.S.A.

Capri clubs elsewhere

Australia:

Capri Car Club. Write to Ken Butcher, P.O. Box 155, Ashburton, Victoria 3147, Australia.

New Zealand:

Ford Capri Owners' Club. Write to C.B. Cotton, P.O. Box 21-268, Christchurch, New Zealand.

West Germany:

There are approximately 70 (!) different Capri owners' clubs in West Germany, the addresses of which would fill a chapter or two on their own. If you are interested in joining a German club, write to John Hill, Chairman of the Capri Owners' Club (in the U.K.), at Field House, Redditch, Worcs., B98 0AN. John has a full list of all the German-based clubs.

Specialists

Anti-theft

Advance Alarms Ltd., (also locks) 30-38, Deptford Bridge, London, SE8. Tel. (01) 692 4688.

Automotive Electronics Ltd., Oxted Mill, Spring Lane, Oxted, Surrey.

Cobra Alarms, Ital Audio Ltd., K and K House, Colonial Way, Watford, Hertfordshire, WD2 4PT. Tel. (0923) 240525.

Cosmic Car Accessories Ltd., Sadler Road, Walsall, West Midlands, WS8 6NA. Tel. (0543) 377001.

Hykee Locks, Security Equipment Installations, Broadstairs, Kent.

Intersport Motor Products, 59, Leicester Road, Oadby, Leicester, LE2 4DF.

Krooklok Dana Ltd., Great Eastern House, Greenbridge Road, Swindon, Wiltshire, SN3 3LB. Tel. (0793) 40151.

Linwood Electronic, Linwood House, Austin Way, Hamstead Industrial Estate, Hamstead, Birmingham, B42 1DU. Tel. (021) 358 2171.

Stellar Components (Sales) Ltd., The Causeway, Maldon, Essex, CM9 7LW. Tel. (0621) 56011.

Stylex Motor Products Ltd., Boby Trading Estate, Bury St. Edmunds, Suffolk, IP33 3PL. Tel. (0284) 701666.

Waso Ltd., Unit 1, Oakwood Estate, Mode Wheel Road, Salford, M5 2DS. Tel (061) 736 0767.

Spares

Affordable Parts are specialist dismantlers of Ford cars, and sell (cleaned) components already removed from the vehicle. They are to be found at Central Garage, Codford, and Green Lane Yard, Codford, Warminster, Wiltshire. Telephone (0985) 50912 (Monday to Saturday, 9am to 5pm), or (0722) 790646, any time.

Automec Equipment and Parts Ltd.,
supply copper brake pipe sets, fully labelled and ready to fit, for all the Capris covered by this book, as well as most other cars. The pipe should last almost indefinitely, and, being made of copper, are easy to bend into position when fitting. Automec also supply silicone and glycol brake fluids, clutch and petrol pipes, and stainless hose clips. They are at Arden House, West Street, Leighton Buzzard, Bedfordshire, LU7 7DD. Tel. (0525) 375775 or 376608.

The Capri Centre offers parts, body panels, service and accessories. Contact Mr. V. Prosser at the Centre, in Cheadle Heath, Cheshire. Tel. (061) 428 6082.

Ford 50 Spares sell parts for the Mark I, II, and III Zephyrs and Zodiacs, primarily, but also keep some spares for the later Fords, from time to time. Therefore an enquiry is always worthwhile. Ken Tingey runs Ford 50 Spares, and the address is 69, Jolliffe Road, Poole, Dorset, BH15 2HA. Tel. (0202) 679258.

Justford Parts Ltd. supply a comprehensive selection of spares for Fords, ranging from Anglias to Sierras. These include mechanical components, trim, bodywork sections and complete panels. Their service is friendly, fast and efficient, and their prices very fair. Martin Frow is the man to contact; the address is 13, Overstone Close, Sutton-in-Ashfield, Nottinghamshire. Tel. (0623) 551782, or 516338 or mobile telephone (0860) 529127.

LMC Panels stock a comprehensive range of body panels for most cars, including the Mark I to III Capris. These include front suspension mounting repair sections, and 'chassis' repair channels, etc. You should be able to obtain LMC panels through retail outlets, but in case of difficulty, contact LMC at Quartermaster Road, West Wilts Trading Estate, Westbury, Wiltshire, BA13 4JT. Tel. (0373) 865088.

The Motor Vehicle Dismantlers' Association, founded in 1943, is the official organisation representing motor vehicle dismantlers, and their excellent booklet 'Spares Market' gives the addresses and telephone numbers of their members around the country. Contact Bob Wyer, 4 , Pant-y-Coed, Llanbethery, Barry,

South Glamorgan, CF6 9AP. Tel. (0446) 710320.

The Newford Parts Centre stocks spares for many Fords, as its name implies, and while they cater mainly for older models, it is always worth inquiring if you need a specific Capri item. Newford are at Abbey Mill, Abbey Village, Nr. Chorley, Lancashire. Tel. (0254) 830343.

Rallye Sport Reproductions provide decals and coachlines no longer available from Ford. Talk to proprietor Chris Day on (0282) 814398.

Remoco are specialist Ford dismantlers, covering models from the 1950s to the present day, with parts 'off the shelf' and ready to fit. Remoco are at Grosvenor Street, Stockport, Cheshire, SK3 8AN (next to Stockport College). Tel. (061) 477 1415.

Speedometers and gauges

Renown Instruments repair or recalibrate speedometers and tachometers, as well as rebuilding all types of vehicle instruments. Renown are at Stonehenge Road, Durrington, Wiltshire, SP4 8BN. Tel. (0980) 53800.

Speedy Cables (London) Ltd., manufacture cables of all descriptions, to patterns, and repair/calibrate speedometers, rev counters, clocks and other gauges. They are at 10–12, Gaskin Lane, Islington, London, N1 2SA. Tel. (01) 226 9228.

Steering rack overhaul

Lione (Merton) Ltd, 101, Hamilton Road, South

Wimbledon, London. Exchange service, and repairs. Tel. (01) 540 9756.

Tuning and modifications

There are many, many firms specialising in tuning and improving Fords, and a number of them advertise in the 'specialist' magazines, for example *Cars and Car Conversions*, *Performance Car*, *The Exchange and Mart* and so on.

It is always worth enquiring at your local motor accessory shop about tuning parts; many can supply these 'off the shelf', and stock a wide range of such components.

Auto Acoustics can supply special rear shelves for Mark II/III Capris to give the best from audio speakers mounted at the rear. The firm are at 22, High Street, Byfleet, Surrey, KT14 7QG. Tel. (093 23) 46373.

Auto Motiv Body Styling supply bodywork kits for Capris. Contact them at Unit 8, Chandlery House, Bridge Wharf, Chertsey, Surrey, KT16 8LG. Tel. (093 28) 69241.

Auto-Power Services supply detailed instructions and kits for converting to V8 Rover power. Their address is South March, Long March Industrial Estate, Daventry, Northants., NN11 4PH. Tel. (03272) 76161.

Belfield Engineering can help with Capri restorations, customising, V8 engine transplants, tubular chassis, steel Cologne arches, and so on. Talk to Andrew Belfield; the address is Pentre Farm, Cefnllys Lane, Llandrindod Wells, Powys, LD1 5PD. Tel. (0597) 3992.

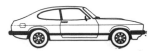

Brooklyn for RS performance components. Brooklyn are at Battens Drive, Redditch, Worcestershire. Tel. (0527) 21212.

Burton Power Products carry out a wide range of tuning, machining and balancing operations on Ford engines. They are at 623, Eastern Avenue, Barkingside, Ilford, Essex, IG2 6PN. Tel. (01) 554 2281.

Cartel Cars and Conversions supply bodywork spoilers and side skirts, in kit form. Cartel are at Monument Road, Woking, Surrey, GU21 5LS. Tel. (04862) 26571/68999.

Ford Rallye Sport Parts offer some tuning components for Capris, although the emphasis today is on the current range of Fords. Ford RS Parts are at Arisdale Avenue, South Ockenden, Essex, RM15 5TJ. Tel. (0708) 858 770.

Richard Grant Motor Accessories Ltd. supply a range of bodywork components to suit the Mark I Capri, and complete kits or individual parts for the Mark II and III models. RGA are at Moor End, Eaton Bray, Nr. Dunstable, Beds., LU6 2JQ. Tel. (0525) 220342.

Holbay Racing Engines provide an extensive range of tuning parts, especially for the overhead camshaft Ford power units. Their address is Betts Avenue, Martlesham Heath, Ipswich, Suffolk, IP5 7RH. Tel. (0473) 623000.

Howe Exhausts specialise in performance exhaust system components of all descriptions. Howe are at Main Road, West Kingsdown, Kent. Tel. (047 485) 2347.

Individual Products Ltd., supply hand made, glass reinforced plastic bodywork styling kits for the Mark II and III

Capris, Their address is 53A, High Street, Reigate, Surrey. Tel. (073 72) 21132/3.

Janspeed Engineering Ltd., is one of the longest established and most respected tuning firms, and they supply performance manifolds, cylinder heads, carburettor kits, and so on. They can supply tuning components for all Capris, from crossflow to overhead cam to V6 varieties. Janspeed are at Castle Road, Salisbury, Wiltshire, SP1 3SQ. Tel. (0722) 21833/4/5/6.

KAT Designs Ltd. specialise in smooth bodywork styling kits and components, plus performance uprating. They are at Hanslope, Buckinghamshire, MK19 7LR. Tel. (0908) 510352.

Oselli Engine Services can recondition and tune all Ford engines, and supply written information specific to Ford tuning. Oselli are at Ferry Hinksey Road, Oxford, OX2 0BY. Tel. (0865) 248100.

A and I Peco Acoustics Ltd. supply high performance exhaust systems and manifolds. Peco's address is Sandford Street, Birkenhead, Merseyside, L41 1AZ. Tel. (051) 647 6041.

Power Engineering offer supercharging conversions for V6 Fords, including the Capri. The address is Unit 9, 5A, Wyvern Road, Uxbridge, Middlesex, UB8 2XN. Tel. (0895) 55699.

Ripspeed sell a wide range of tuning components, of all descriptions, and will sell by mail order. They also supply d-i-y vinyl roof kits. Ripspeed are at 54, Fore Street, Edmonton, North London, N18 2SS. Tel. (01) 803 4355.

Paul A de Rome Coachwork Conversions can carry out a convertible conversion on your Capri. The address for details is 34, Watson Road, Blackpool,

Lancashire. Tel. (0253) 42151/892290.

Roy Retrims can carry out interior re-trimming, or convert your Capri to a soft top. The firm is at Unit 10, Thoresen Auto Centre, New Meadow Road, Redditch, Worcs. Tel. (0527) 501895.

Somar Transtec Ltd., of Gloucestershire, can help with conversion to automatic transmission, and with power steering conversions. Talk to them on (0386) 700127.

Sonica Stainless Steel Exhausts supply high quality stainless systems for all Capris. Sonica are at Unit 14, Blackburn Industrial Estate, Aberdeen, AB5 0TZ. Tel. (0224) 790656.

Specialised Engines deal with rebuilding and tuning all Ford engines, and offer an exchange scheme under which you will gain a larger capacity engine than the one you hand in! The firm are at 15, Curzon Drive, Manorway Industrial Estate, Grays, Essex. Tel. (0375) 378606.

Swaymar Engineering are tuning specialists, and are particularly conversant with the V6 Cologne and Essex engines. They are at Unit 9A, Kingston Road, Commerce Estate, Leatherhead, Surrey, KT22 7LA. Tel. (0372) 379 495.

Turbo Technics Ltd. are specialists in turbocharger conversions. They are at 17, Galowhill Road, Brackmills, Northampton, NN4 0EE. Tel. (0604) 764005.

Vulcan Engineering are specialists in tuning Fords, and can supply ranges of parts to suit all Capri engines, as well as uprated ancillaries. Vulcan are at 185, Uxbridge Road, Hanwell, London. W7 3TH. Tel. (01) 579 3202.

Withers of Winsford stock a range of RS spares. Telephone them on (0606) 594422.

The XR Centre Ltd. can supply limited slip differentials, suspension uprating components and brake improvement parts. These include larger discs with four-cylinder calipers, and rear brake disc conversions. Most of these mods are aimed at the 2.8i/turbocharged models. The XR Centre are at Brooklands Garages, Oyster Lane, Byfleet, Surrey. Tel. (093 23) 52588.

Upholstery/trim suppliers

AutoTrim, Wesley Street, Leicester, LE4 5QC. Tel. (0533) 664112.

Paul Beck Vintage Supplies, High Street, Stalham, Norwich, Norfolk, NR12 9BB. Tel. (0692) 81534.

Coachtrimming Supplies, 111, Flaxley Road, Stechford, Birmingham, B33 9HQ. Tel. (021) 784 5821.

Creech Coachtrimming Centre, 45, Anerley Road, Crystal Palace, London, SE19 2AS. Tel. (01) 659 4135.

Edgware Motor Accessories, 94, High Street, Edgware, Middlesex. Tel. (01) 952 4789 or 9311.

Woolies off Blenheim Way Northfields Industrial Estate, Market Deeping, Peterborough, Cambridgeshire, PE6 8LD. Tel. (0778) 347347.

Wiring materials

Merv Plastics, supply wiring and connectors. They are at 201, Station Road, Beeston, Nottinghamshire, NG9 2AB.

Tools and equipment, etc:

BOC Ltd. supply welding gases including acetylene, argon, and oxygen. BOC are at Great West House, P.O. Box 39, Great West Road, Brentford, Middlesex. TW8 9DQ. Tel. (01) 560 5166.

Draper Tools Ltd. supply a wide range of d-i-y hand tools. These are available from retail outlets, but in case of difficulty Draper are at Hursley Road, Chandlers Ford, Eastleigh, Hampshire, SO5 5YF. Tel. (04215) 66355.

Finnigan's Hammerite paint and Waxoyl anti-rust wax treatment are excellent for d-i-y vehicle rust proofing. Finnigan's Speciality Paints Ltd., a division of Hunting Sales and Marketing Ltd., P.O. Box 67, Cross Green Industrial Estate, Leeds, LS1 1LS. Tel. (0532) 492820.

Murex Welding Products Ltd, supply welding equipment including Portapak gas welding and MIG welding sets. Murex are at Hertford Road, Waltham Cross, Hertfordshire, EN8 7RP.

S.I.P (Industrial Products) Ltd. sell a range of MIG welding machines, including their 'Ideal' range, for the d-i-y car restorer and professional users, and a variety of 'miniature' portable MIG welders. Their machines are solid and reliable. S.I.P. also make arc welders, spray guns and compressors. They are at Gelders Hall Road, Shepshed, Loughborough, Leicestershire, LE12 9NH. Tel. (0509) 503141.

Sykes-Pickavant Ltd. provide a comprehensive range of tools, including those specifically designed for the d-i-y car enthusiast. Their 'Speedline' range in particular contains d-i-y tools ranging from bodywork repair implements to piston ring compressors, brake pipe spanners to ball joint separators. They also have an excellent, separate range of body tools, including many designed specifically for sheet metal work on motor cars. Sykes-Pickavant tools should be readily available through retail outlets, but, in case of difficulty, Sykes-Pickavant are at Warwick Works, Kilnhouse Lane, Lytham St. Annes, Lancashire, FY8 3DU. Tel. (0253) 721291.

The Welding Centre supplies d-i-y welding sets at various prices. They are at 293, Ewell Road, Surbiton, Surrey. Tel. (01) 399 2448/9.

The Welding Centre in Scotland sells d-i-y welding sets of varying degrees of sophistication. The address is 165, Netherauldhouse Road, Newlands, Glasgow. Tel. (041) 649 7536.

DON'T FORGET YOUR FORD DEALER!!
Finally, while specialist suppliers of spares and tools are very helpful when carrying out work on older model Fords, don't overlook or under-estimate the value of talking to the Parts Department of your local Ford dealer. Of course, their main volume business is in spares for current and recent models, and it would perhaps be unreasonable to expect them to maintain stocks indefinitely for earlier cars. However, it is always worth enquiring, and you may be surprised just how much can be obtained from them, for the Capris covered by this book,

The Capri Owners' Club often arrange special offers for their members, on items as diverse as mechanical components and bodywork kits.

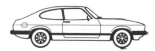

Books

There are numerous publications which are interesting and useful for any Capri owner, and it is impossible to give details of them all here. However, the following list includes some of the books which may be of particular interest:

History and character

CAPRI – The Development and Competition History of Ford's European GT Car (New Edition) by Jeremy Walton, published by Haynes Publishing Group (reference F548).

If you are interested in Capris you should have this book. Written by long-standing Capri enthusiast Jeremy Walton in his own inimitable style, it brings to life the history, character and sporting pedigree of the car, from its beginnings right up to the final 280 model.

Maintenance and restoration

The Car Bodywork Repair Manual by Lindsay Porter, published by Haynes Publishing Group (reference F373).

Handbooks and instruction manuals

Haynes Car Owners Handbook – Ford Capri II – reference 405.

Haynes Owners Workshop Manuals include detailed descriptions, with diagrams and a photographic record, covering maintenance and overhaul of each part of the vehicle. Separate chapters deal with the engine, cooling system, carburation and fuel system, ignition system, clutch, gearbox, propeller shaft,

rear axle, braking system, electrical system, suspension and steering, bodywork and fittings, and supplementary information. As indicated at the start of this book, it is strongly recommended that the appropriate manual for your Capri should be used in conjunction with this book, during restoration work.

Haynes Owners Workshop Manuals cover the following Capris:

Mk I 1300/1600 – reference 029
Mk I 1600 ohc – reference 296
Mk I 2000 (V4)/3000 (V6) – reference 035
Mk II/III 1.3 – reference 338
Mk II/III 1.6/2.0 ohc – reference 283
Mk II/III 3.0 (V6) – reference 375
Mk II/III 2.8i/3.0 V6 – reference 1309

It is also worth noting that *Car Mechanics* magazine published a comprehensive, in-depth, three part special supplement covering 'Cortina and Capri Mechanics', in their January, February and March, 1987 issues.

General interest, tuning and modifications

Capri – Mild to Wild and **Capri International – Mild to Wild** were published in 1985 and 1986 respectively, by AGB Specialist Publications Ltd. Edited by Tony Bostock, the publications cover history, road tests, restoration and power tuning, plus descriptions of Europe's fastest and wildest Capris.

Capri Club International, published by the Capri Owners' Club, is a fascinating and useful semi-hardback compendium of features which have appeared in the club's magazine of the same name. These include articles on the history of the cars, servicing and uprating mechanical components, bodywork touch-up

and modifications, special Capris, and so on.

Ford Power, edited by Tony Bostock, was published in October 1987 by AGB Specialist Publications Ltd., and, as its name implies, covers tuning and modifications to Fords, including, of course, the Capri. Detailed sections cover each engine type, the ignition system, carburation, exhausts, turbocharging, specialist suppliers, and so on and so on. A must if you intend to uprate your Capri.

How to Modify Ford SOHC Engines, by David Vizard, published by Fountain Press Ltd., takes the reader through the various stages of tuning this popular engine, covering all aspects from cylinder head to camshafts, turbocharging to valve gear.

Performance Tuning in Theory and Practice (4 stroke), published by Haynes Publishing Group (reference F275).

Tuning Ford Escorts and Capris, by David Vizard, published by Speedsport Motobooks, deals exclusively with Fords fitted with the cross-flow engine in all its sizes. Information is given on cylinder heads, carburation, manifolding, suspension, brakes, and so on.

Tuning Four Cylinder Fords, by Paul Davies, published by Speedsport Motobooks, covers histories of the various Fords (among them the Capri) and their engines. Details of engine swaps are also given, plus advice on tuning the various engine types, including the V4 unit.

7 British and American technical terms

As this book has been written in England, it uses the appropriate English component names, phrases, and spelling. Some of these differ from those used in America. Normally, these cause no difficulty, but to make sure, a glossary is printed below. In ordering spare parts remember the parts list may use some of these words:

English	American	English	American
Accelerator	Gas pedal	Locks	Latches
Aerial	Antenna	Methylated spirit	Denatured alcohol
Anti-roll bar	Stabiliser or sway bar	Motorway	Freeway, turnpike etc
Big-end bearing	Rod bearing	Number plate	License plate
Bonnet (engine cover)	Hood	Paraffin	Kerosene
Boot (luggage compartment)	Trunk	Petrol	Gasoline (gas)
Bulkhead	Firewall	Petrol tank	Gas tank
Bush	Bushing	'Pinking'	'Pinging'
Cam follower or tappet	Valve lifter or tappet	Prise (force apart)	Pry
Carburettor	Carburetor	Propeller shaft	Driveshaft
Catch	Latch	Quarterlight	Quarter window
Choke/venturi	Barrel	Retread	Recap
Circlip	Snap-ring	Reverse	Back-up
Clearance	Lash	Rocker cover	Valve cover
Crownwheel	Ring gear (of differential)	Saloon	Sedan
Damper	Shock absorber, shock	Seized	Frozen
Disc (brake)	Rotor/disk	Sidelight	Parking light
Distance piece	Spacer	Silencer	Muffler
Drop arm	Pitman arm	Sill panel (beneath doors)	Rocker panel
Drop head coupe	Convertible	Small end, little end	Piston pin or wrist pin
Dynamo	Generator (DC)	Spanner	Wrench
Earth (electrical)	Ground	Split cotter (for valve spring cap)	Lock (for valve spring retainer)
Engineer's blue	Prussian blue	Split pin	Cotter pin
Estate car	Station wagon	Steering arm	Spindle arm
Exhaust manifold	Header	Sump	Oil pan
Fault finding/diagnosis	Troubleshooting	Swarf	Metal chips or debris
Float chamber	Float bowl	Tab washer	Tang or lock
Free-play	Lash	Tappet	Valve lifter
Freewheel	Coast	Thrust bearing	Throw-out bearing
Gearbox	Transmission	Top gear	High
Gearchange	Shift	Torch	Flashlight
Grub screw	Setscrew, Allen screw	Trackrod (of steering)	Tie-rod (or connecting rod)
Gudgeon pin	Piston pin or wrist pin	Trailing shoe (of brake)	Secondary shoe
Halfshaft	Axleshaft	Transmission	Whole drive line
Handbrake	Parking brake	Tyre	Tire
Hood	Soft top	Van	Panel wagon/van
Hot spot	Heat riser	Vice	Vise
Indicator	Turn signal	Wheel nut	Lug nut
Interior light	Dome lamp	Windscreen	Windshield
Layshaft (of gearbox)	Countershaft	Wing/mudguard	Fender
Leading shoe (of brake)	Primary shoe		